NUTRITION AND DIET RESEARCH PROGRESS

GALACTOSE

STRUCTURE AND FUNCTION IN BIOLOGY AND MEDICINE

NUTRITION AND DIET RESEARCH PROGRESS

Additional books in this series can be found on Nova's website under the Series tab.

Additional e-books in this series can be found on Nova's website under the e-book tab.

NUTRITION AND DIET RESEARCH PROGRESS

GALACTOSE

STRUCTURE AND FUNCTION IN BIOLOGY AND MEDICINE

VITOR HUGO POMIN
EDITOR

nova publishers
New York

For permission to use material from this book please contact us:
Telephone 631-231-7269; Fax 631-231-8175
Web Site: http://www.novapublishers.com

Library of Congress Cataloging-in-Publication Data

ISBN: 978-1-63117-928-0

LCCN: 2014938746

Published by Nova Science Publishers, Inc. † New York

CONTENTS

PREFACE

Galactose (from the Greek *galakt* which means milk), a C4 epimer of glucose, is a hexose widely used to build up biologically functional glycoconjugates in living organisms. When combined with glucose through covalent bonds, it makes the widely known lactose, a disaccharide largely found in milk. Besides participating in metabolism, galactose also has multiple clinical roles. This book aims to report most of the science concerning the sugar type, galactose. The content of this book is heavily based on scientific results from renowned research groups of different countries. This contributes to the high-quality of this collection. Novelty and updated content are also features of this publication. The six containing chapters discuss: 1) the structure, dietary sources and clinical significance of galactose; 2) clinical relevance of galactose; 3) diet and implications of galactose in galactosemia; 4) recent advances in the science of galacto-oligosaccharides as prebiotics; 5) the structural configuration of galactose and its role in glycan biosyntheses; and 6) regulation of galactose operon in *Escherichia coli*. This book is recommended to anyone involved or interested in the science of galactose.

Chapter 1 - Galactose, just like its C-4 epimer glucose, is one of the most common aldohexose. Natural galactose is mostly D-family aldose and often found in the forms of galactan and gum, such as the galactan carrageenan and agaran, which are composed of β-D-galactose and 3,6-anhydro-α-D/L-galactose, and larch gum (arabinogalactan), locust bean gum and guar gum (galactomannan) etc, which are made up of galactose, arabinose and mannose. The galactose is rarely existe in free form but in glycoconjugates. In mammal milk, galactose mainly exists in the form of lactose, human milk contains 5.5±8.0% lactose by weight and cow milk 4.5±5.5%. In the IgG, ceruloplasmin, sialyl Lewis a/x, lectins, keratan sulfate and other important biological molecules, galactose is the essential monosaccharide. Foods such as beans, peas, figs, grapes and dairy products remain the most common source of galactose in the diet. The development of infant's brain cells and the nervous system needs an enormous amount of lactose, and galactose can promote the cerebroside lipids and mucopolysaccharides generation. In the intestine, galactose is beneficial for the growth and reproduction of lactobacillus and the vitamin K and B synthesis. Many diseases are associate with galactose, including its metabolism, content and the corresponding antigen, antibody and galectins. Galactosemia is a hereditary disease of galactose metabolic abnormalities, and the cause of the illness is due to the 1-phosphate galactose uridine to acyl transferase defect, which results in the deposition of galactose 1-phosphate and galactitol. The human blood type is determined by the terminal monosaccharide of the blood group antigen. Blood types A and B only differ from blood type O by the presence of an additional monosaccharide, N-acetylgalactosamine for type A and galactose for type B. α-Galactose antigen (Galαl-3Galβl-4GlcNAc-R) on the surface of mammalian cells is the main antigen which causes the hyperacute rejection (HAR) for xenotransplants. Although free D-glactose is often used to make aging models, the galacto-oligosaccharides (Gal-(Gal)n-Glc/Gal, n= 0-6) are though as functional food additive.

Chapter 2 - D-galactose induced memory dysfunction, mito-oxidative damage and apoptosis via activation of PPAR-gamma receptors. D-galactose-induced aging in mice.Terminal galactosylation of transferrin may be a biomarker of healthy ageing. A 6% gallactose drink does not enhance performance time during a self-paced cycling performance trial in highly trained endurance cyclists compared with a formula typically used by endurance athletes but may improve the ability to produce intermediate self-paced efforts. Glucose and galactose regulate intestinal absorption of cholesterol. Galactose malabsorption complicated with rickets and nephrogenic diabetes insipidus has been. Galactose accelerates cataract development. Feeding dogs a diet containing 30% galactose induces experimental galactosemia and results in the formation of diabetes-like microvascular lesions of the retina. The galactose-fed beagle develops diabetes-like microvascular changes that are histologically and clinically similar in appearance to all stages of human diabetic retinopathy. Expression of an endogenous galactose-binding lectin correlates with neoplastic progression in the colon. Identification and upregulation of galactose/N-acetylgalactosamine macrophage lectin in rat cardiac allografts with arteriosclerosis has been demonstrated. Uridine diphosphate galactose-4-epimerase deficiency has been detected by neonatal screening for galactosaemia which has a variety of symptoms.Delayed hypersensitivity reactions to mammalian meat mediated by IgE antibodies to galactose-alpha 1,3-galactose (alpha-gal), an oligosaccharide,has been reported.

Chapter 3 - The goal of this chapter is to update recent developments in the Galactosemia field and offer new perspectives into the as yet unknown. Galactose is an energy-providing nutrient and also a necessary basic substrate for the biosynthesis of many molecules in body, where it forms part of glycolipids and glycoproteins in several tissues. Galactose is found in dairy products, sugar beet, and others gums and mucilage and also in some meats, legumes and fruits, but in lesser amount. It is a monosaccharide which when combined with glucose, through a dehydration process, results in lactose, the milk sugar. In galactose metabolism, the liver plays an essential role. Carbohydrates derived from the diet as disaccharides or polysaccharides are broken down into simpler monosaccharides, which reach the liver via the portal blood system. The primary sugars in newborns and infants come from breakdown of disaccharide lactose in milk; lactose is broken down to glucose and galactose and when it reaches the hepatocytes, galactose is converted to glucose by a series of enzymatic reactions. Galactosemia is a relatively rare inherited enzyme deficiency with variable worldwide incidence. The pathogenic potential of ingested galactose results from a defect in the galactose metabolic pathway, the Leloir pathway, which consists of three enzymes, the galactose specific kinase (Galactokinase/GALK), galactose-1-phosphate uridyltransferase (GALT) and uridine diphosphate galactose - 4´-epimerase (GALE). The most common cause of the failure to convert galactose to glucose results from the deficit of galactose-1-P-uridyltransferase (GALT), the second enzyme of the pivotal Leloir pathway, and is known as classical galactosemia (OMIM 230400), a severe genetic disease of the newborn, an autosomal recessive condition that give an acute toxicity syndrome. In this disease, galactose-1-phosphate accumulates inside hepatocytes and causes rapid liver failure with all the common symptoms associated: nausea, vomiting, hepatomegaly, jaundice, hypoglycemia and cataract. The clinical significance of establishing a diagnosis is clear: galactosemia could be fatal if undiagnosed, however, the treatment, that consists in a severe restriction of dietary lactose/galactose and is considered life-saving, is not fully effective since long term follow-up of patients has shown that they may develop chronic complications, such as retarded mental development, verbal dyspraxia, motor abnormalities and in young women hypergonadotrophic hypogonadism and premature ovarian failure.

Chapter 4 - Prebiotic oligosaccharides have attracted an increasing amount of attention because of their physiological importance and functional effects on human health, as well as their physico-chemical properties, which are of interest for various applications in the food industries. Galacto-oligosaccharides (GOS), one of the major groups of prebiotic oligosaccharides, are formed via the transgalactosylation reaction from lactose. This reaction is catalysed by a number of β-galactosidases (lactases) in addition to their hydrolytic activity. GOS are complex mixtures of different oligosaccharides, and the spectrum of the oligosaccharides making up these mixtures strongly depends on the source of the enzyme used for the biocatalytic reaction as well as on the conversion conditions used in their production. These oligosaccharides are of great interest because of their proven prebiotic (bifidogenic) characteristics. A plethora of GOS is also found in human milk, and these differently substituted oligosaccharides are associated with a number of beneficial effects for the breast-fed infant. This chapter reviews the production, the properties, the biological effects as well as the applications of galacto-oligosaccharides as prebiotics. The chapter also includes emerging trends in the production of novel, galactose-containing hetero-oligosaccharides, which are structurally more closely related to human milk oligosaccharides.

Chapter 5 - Glycosylated D-galactose is widely distributed in nature. Less common, L-galactose was found in snail and plant galactans. At difference with the most abundant monosaccharide, D-glucose, D-galactose may be found in pyranosic and furanosic configurations. In the animal kingdom, free D-galactose is not present but is a common constituent of glycoproteins and glycolipids, always as pyranose. In fact, D-galactose is incorporated into human milk oligosaccharides in larger quantities than glucose. The β-1,4-galactosyltransferase links galactose to glucose to form lactose, the core for human milk oligosaccharides (HMO). Interestingly, the furanose form has been identified in important human pathogens like *Mycobacterium tuberculosis, Aspergillus fumigatus and Trypanosoma cruzi*, the agent of Chagas disease. In both configurations, the β-anomer predominates in the glycans. The absence of galactofuranose (Gal*f*) in mammals and the important role that Gal*f*-containing molecules play in host cell recognition led to the enzymes involved in the Gal*f* metabolic pathways as targets for the development of drugs. Both, Gal*p* and Gal*f* must be activated as the nucleotides UDP-Gal*p* and UDP-Gal*f* for their incorporation into glycans. The nucleotide precursor for L-galactose is GDP-L-galactose, which is formed from GDP-mannose by the action of a 3',5'-epimerase. Also, whereas UDP-Gal*p* may be synthesized from the free monosaccharides galactose or glucose, in the latter case through the action of a UDP-Glc-4-epimerase, UDP-Gal*f* is produced from UDP-Gal*p* by the action of a unique enzyme, UDP-Gal*p* mutase (UGM), which catalyzes its conversion into UDP-Gal*f*. In the last two decades several laboratories have been committed to understand the mechanism of action of UGM and its properties. The achievements in this area are presented in this chapter.

Chapter 6 - The galactose (*gal*) operon of *Eschericha coli* consists of four structural genes, E, T, K, and M, that respectively code for Epimerase, Transferase, Kinase and Mutarotase enzymes, needed for D-galactose metabolism. In addition to galactose being an energy source, galactose metabolites are anabolic substrates. The absence of either the *gal*E or *gal*T gene results in the accumulation of galactose intermediates, leading to multiple metabolic disorders. The *gal* genes are transcribed from two overlapping promoters, *P1* and *P2* that have transcription start points (*tsp*) 5-bp apart. Both promoters are typically regulated by the repressor (GalR) and cyclic adenosine 3':5'-monophosphate (cAMP) receptor protein (CRP). GalR binds at two operators, O_E (external operator) located at position -60.5, and O_I (internal operator) located at +53.5 with respect to the *tsp* of *P1*. The binding of GalR to O_E alone represses *P1* and stimulates *P2*, while binding to O_I blocks transcription from both *P1* and *P2*. The cAMP and CRP acting as a complex (CCC) activates *P1* and represses *P2*. A histone-like protein, HU, binds to position +6.5, is also a key player in *gal* regulation by GalR. In this chapter, we will describe the key components of the regulation of the *gal* operon at the level of transcription.

In: Galactose
Editor: Vitor Hugo Pomin

ISBN: 978-1-63117-928-0

Chapter 1

GALACTOSE: CHEMICAL STRUCTURE, DIETARY SOURCES AND CLINICAL SIGNIFICANCE

Youjing Lv* and Guangli Yu
Key Laboratory of Marine Drugs,
Ministry of Education of China
Shandong Provincial Key Laboratory of Glycoscience and
Glycotechnology, School of Medicine and Pharmacy,
Ocean University of China, Qingdao, China

ABSTRACT

Galactose, just like its C-4 epimer glucose, is one of the most common aldohexose. Natural galactose is mostly a D-family aldose and is often found in the forms of galactan and gum, such as gelatin carrageenan and agaran, which are composed of β-D-galactose and 3,6-anhydro-α-D/L-galactose, and larch gum (arabinogalactan), locust bean gum and guar gum (galactomannan) etc., which are made up of galactose, arabinose and mannose. Galactose rarely exists in free form but in glycoconjugates. In mammal milk, galactose mainly exists in the form of lactose; human milk contains 5.5±8.0% lactose by weight and cow milk contains 4.5±5.5%. In the IgG, ceruloplasmin, sialyl Lewis a/x, lectins, keratan sulfate and other important biological molecules, galactose is the

* lvyoujing1988@163.com

essential monosaccharide. Foods such as beans, peas, figs, grapes and dairy products remain the most common source of galactose in the diet.

The development of an infant's brain cells and nervous system requires an enormous amount of lactose, and galactose can promote the generation of cerebroside lipids and mucopolysaccharides. In the intestine, galactose is beneficial for the growth and reproduction of lactobacillus and for vitamin K and B synthesis.

Many diseases are associated with galactose, including its metabolism, content and the corresponding antigen, antibody and galectins. Galactosemia is a hereditary disease of galactose metabolic abnormalities, and the cause of the illness is due to the 1-phosphate galactose uridine to acyl transferase defect, which results in the deposition of galactose 1-phosphate and galactitol.

The human blood type is determined by the terminal monosaccharide of the blood group antigen. Blood types A and B only differ from blood type O by the presence of an additional monosaccharide, N-acetylgalactosamine for type A and galactose for type B. α-Galactose antigen (Galαl-3Galβl-4GlcNAc-R) on the surface of mammalian cells is the main antigen which causes the hyperacute rejection (HAR) for xenotransplants. Although free D-galactose is often used to make aging models, the galacto-oligosaccharides (Gal-$(Gal)_n$-Glc/Gal, n=0-6) can function as food additives.

INTRODUCTION

Galactose is an energy-providing nutrient and also a necessary basic substrate for the biosynthesis of many macromolecules in the body. Galactose in human or plant organisms are usually bound to other monosaccharides and act as an essential component of glycoconjugates, such as the glycosides, glycolipids and glycoproteins. Galactose significantly influences the structure and function of these complex compounds.

Many diseases are associated with galactose, including its metabolism, content, the corresponding antigen, antibodies and galectins. For example, many of the enzymes of the glycolytic pathway are specific to glucose not galactose. Galactose is metabolized by the enzymes of the Leloir pathway [1], which is named after the Nobel Prize-winning Argentinean biochemist Louis Leloir [2]. During the Leloir pathway, five enzymes are needed to convert the galactose to glucose. Mutations in some of the enzymes will cause the genetic disease galactosemia [3,4]. As for the galactosemia patients, preventing galactose in the diet is crucial. It is necessary to investigate the galactose content of the daily diet, including vegetables, fruits and milk.

Therefore, this chapter outlines the chemistry of galactose monosaccharide, highlighting the dietary sources and the formation of galactose, their biological effects and current applications.

1. Chemical Structure of Galactose

Galactose is one of the most common aldohexose and the C-4 epimer of glucose, and the molecular weight is 180 Da. Natural galactose is mostly D-family aldoses and less L-family. Two of the four isomers (α-D, α-L, β-D and β-L) of galactose are pyranose and another two are furanose configurations. Galactofuranose mostly occurs in bacteria, fungi, protozoa, starfish, sponges and green algae [5].

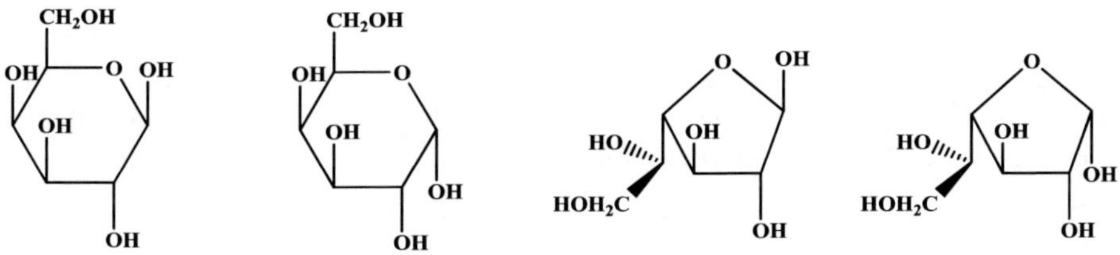

Figure 1. The monosaccharide configurations of galactose (1: β-D-Galactopyranose; 2: α-D-Galactopyranose; 3: β-D-Galactofuranose; 4: α-D-Galactofuranose.

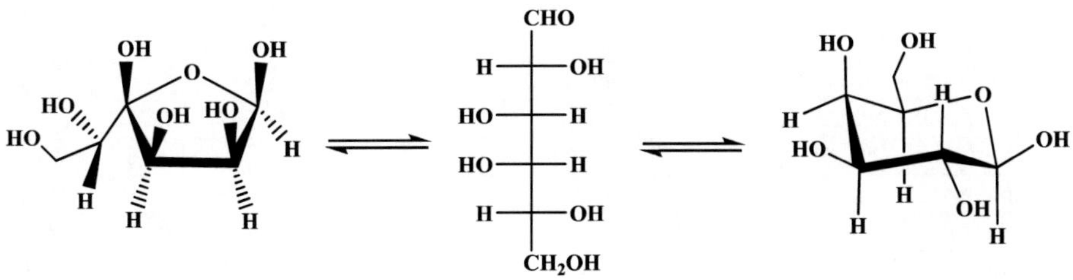

Figure 2. The equilibrium in water solution between Gal$_f$ and Gal$_p$ [6].

2. Dietary Sources of Galactose

For normal people, the ingestion of certain amounts of galactose is beneficial for health. Patients suffering from galactosemia should avoid any intake of galactose. Therefore, it is very important to examine the galactose content of each kind of food. Except for lactose, galactose is found in dairy products, gums, mucilages and edible meats in the form of galactose, galactinol, galactolipids, galactosyl cerebrosides, gangliosides, lactosyl sulfatide, raffinose oligosaccharides, galactans, rhamnogalacturonans, arabinogalactans, galactomannans, carrageenans and agarans.

2.1. Free Galactose

There is a low content of free galactose in fruits and vegetables, mostly ranging from 0.5 to 10.0 mg/100 g fresh weight except in papaya (28.6), persimmon (35.4) and tomato (23.0) [7]. Hyun-Ock Kim [8] selected three soy beverages, and 34 fruits and vegetables to detect the free galactose contents of them. The free galactose contents in the selected plant materials ranged from 2.0±0.1 mg/100 g in red potato to 39.7±1.9 mg/100 g in red pepper. Different varieties, times of the season, and storage of the product affected the free galactose contents of most of the plant materials.

Table 1. The galactose contents in plant materials [9, 10]

Food	Galactose content (mg/100 g)
Fruits	
Dried Figs	4100.0
Grapes, European	400.0
Persimmon, American	35.4
Papaya	28.6
Watermelon	14.7
Apple	8.3
Banana	9.2
Orange, sweet	4.3
Vegetables	
Black-eyed peas	521.0
Green peas, split	493.0
Peas	161.0
Tomato	23.0

Food	Galactose content (mg/100 g)
Pepper, bell	10.2
Potato, sweet	7.7
Nuts, seeds	
Hazelnuts, dried	500
Safflower seed kernels	100
Dairy products	
Milk (human)	5.5-8 % lactose and 350 mg free galactose per 100 mL
Milk (cow)	4.5-5.5 % lactose and 227 mg free galactose per 100 mL
Casein (whole)	134
Cheddar cheese (aged 15 d)	94.5
Beverages	
Coffee, dry	1100 to 150
Watermelon juice	46
Orange juice	19
Apple juice	14
V-8 juice	38
Legumes	
Navy beans	272
Black turtle beans	215
Great northern beans	307
Soybeans	44

2.2. Oligosaccharides Containing Galactose

Lactose, the α-D-galactopyranosyl-(1→4) D-glucose dimer, provides most of the galactose in milk (including human milk), infant formula, and dairy products and is the primary source of galactose in the diet. Human milk contains 5.5-8.0% lactose by weight and cow milk contains 4.5-5.5%. Lactose provides about 40% of the energy for infants, and about 2% in a mixed diet for American adults [11].

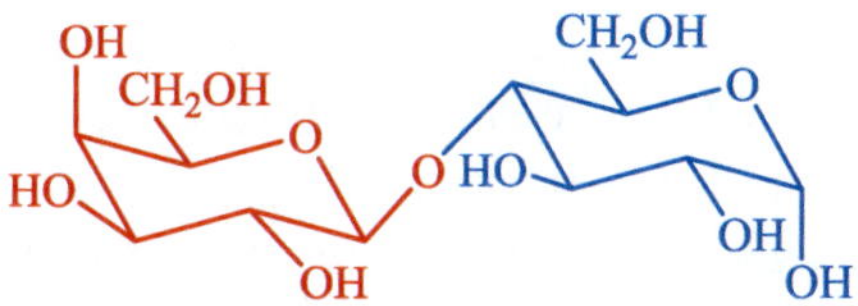

Figure 3. The chemical structure of lactose (In red galactose; in light blue glucose).

The raffinose (Gal α(1→6) Glc α(1→β2) Fru), stachyose (Gal α(1→6) Gal α(1→6) Glc α(1→β2) Fru), and verbascose (Gal α(1→6) Gal α(1→6) Gal α(1→6) Glc α(1→β2) Fru) are also common oligosaccharides with galactose[12]. In these oligosaccharides, one, two or three galactose residues are attached to the α-D-glucose residue in an α(1→6)- linkage.

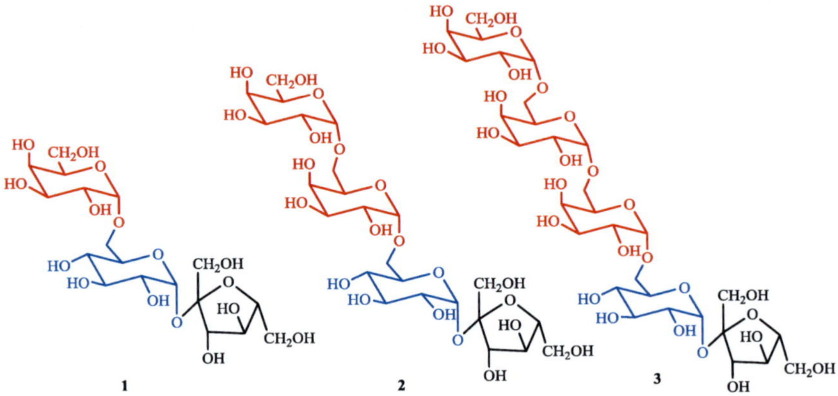

1 2 3

Figure 4. The chemical structure of some oligosaccharides containing galactose (1: raffinose; 2: stachyose; 3: verbascose. In red galactose; in light blue glucose; in black fructose).

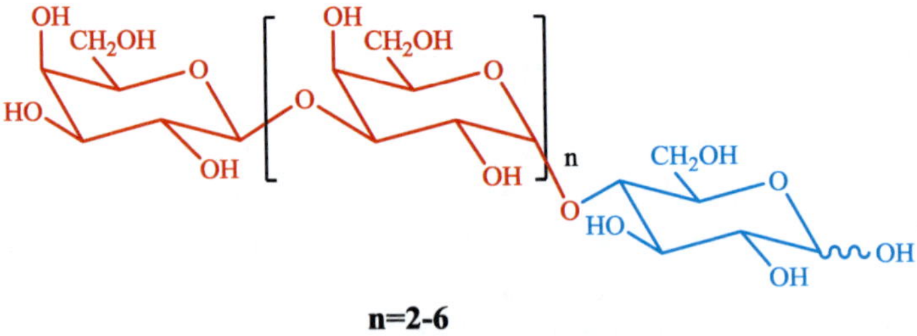

n=2-6

Figure 5. The chemical structure of GOS. (In red galactose; in light blue glucose).

Galacto-oligosaccharides (GOS) are considered non-digestible carbohydrates, which are mainly constituted by galactose units and produced commercially from lactose by β-galactosidase. GOS are chains of galactose units, usually with a single terminal glucose molecule (Gal_n-Glu) [13]. The degree of polymerization of GOS can vary quite markedly, ranging from 2 to 8 [14]. According to the definition of prebiotics raised by Gibson and Roberfroid in 1995 [15], GOS are identified prebiotic. Oligosaccharides resembling GOS occur naturally in human milk and may be one of the factors that protect human infants from gastrointestinal pathogenic bacteria. GOS are widely used as an ingredient in foods.

2.3. Glycolipids Containing Galactose

Apart from lactose, galactose is also distributed in animals in the form of galactosylceramide, cerebroside sulfatide, ganglioside and glyceroglycolipid. Galactose is a structural component of both neutral and acidic cerebrosides and gangliosides. The brain and the myelin sheath of nerves contain particularly large amounts of Gal-linked glycolipids, typically in association with specific glycoproteins. The antigens on the cell surface that determine the ABH and Lewis blood type are also glycosphingolipids [16, 17]. The hydrophobic part of the glycosphingolipids inserts itself into the cell membrane and the polar sugar part exposes itself on the cell surface, which is related to cell recognition and tissue and organ specificity.

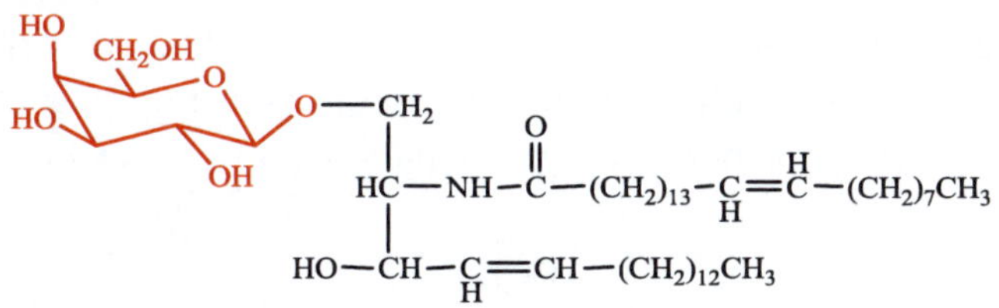

1

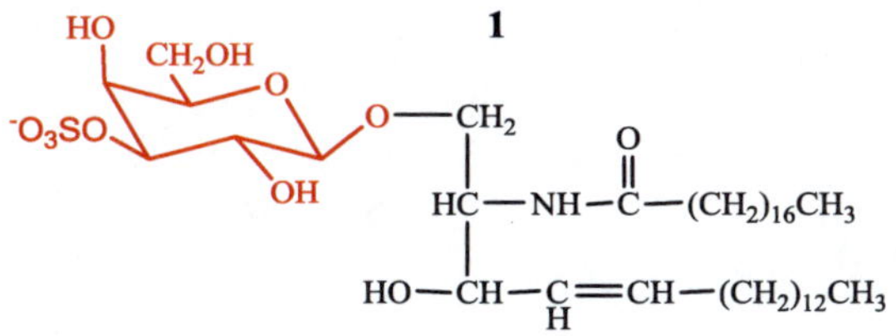

2

Figure 6. The chemical structure of galactosylceramide and cerebroside sulfatide (1: galactosylceramide (Gal β1→1Cer); 2: cerebroside sulfatide (3-OSO_3^--Gal β1→1Cer)).

Sulfatide is widely distributed in the mammal animal organs and is especially abundant in the brain. Gangliosides are the most important glycosphingolipids and have a high content in the nervous system, particularly in the nerve endings. Gangliosides play an important role in the transmission of nerve impulses [18].

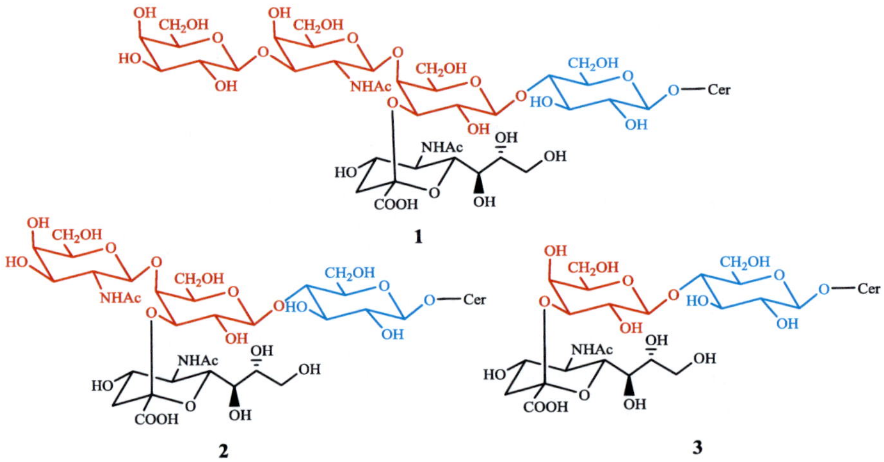

Figure 7. The structure of gangliosides (1: GM1; 2: GM2; 3: GM3. In red galactose and acetylgalactosamine; in light blue glucose; in black sialic acid).

Glyceroglycolipids mainly exist in plants and microorganisms. Chloroplast and microbial membrane contains substantial glyceroglycolipids. In mammals, the distribution of glyceroglycolipids is not so widespread.

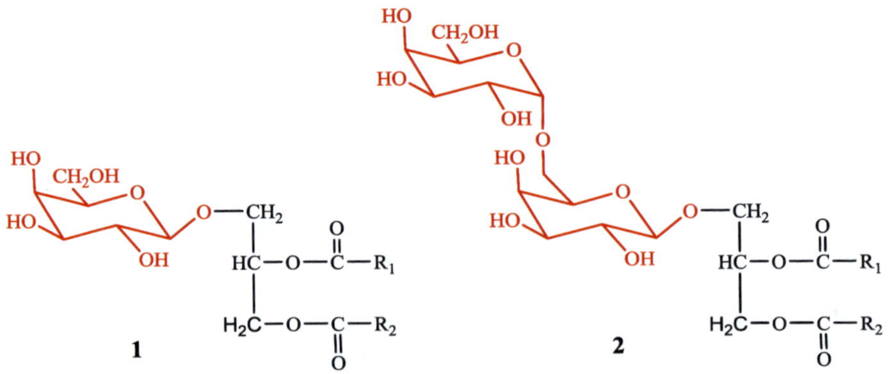

Figure 8. The chemical structure of glyceroglycolipids (1: monogalactosyl diaclyglycerol; 2: digalactosyldiglyceride;).

The development of infant brain cells and the nervous system needs an enormous amount of lactose, and galactose can promote the generation of cerebroside lipids and mucopolysaccharides. In addition, galactose is beneficial for the growth and reproduction of lactobacillus and Vitamin K and B synthesis in the intestine [19, 20].

2.4. Polysaccharides Containing Galactose

The primary cell wall of plants and their various edible parts, on average, make up about 1% of the weight of the plant or fruit and consist of many polysaccharides, some of which contain galactose [11]. Galactose-containing polysaccharides with various glycolytic linkages such as α(1→6), β(1→3), and β(1→4) are ubiquitious in animals and plants. These polysaccharides contain galactans, arabinogalactans (AGs), galactomannans, carrageenans, agran and rhamnogalacturonans (RGs).

Arabinogalactans are essential polymers that exist in the cell walls of plants and are reported to be immunological bioactive substances. Arabinogalactans are divided into two types, arabinogalactan I (AG-I) and arabinogalactan II (AG-II). The AG-I consists of a (1→4)-linked β-D Gal backbone with α-L-Ara units branched at the O-3 or O-6 of Gal residues, while AG-II has a (1→3)-linked β-D Gal backbone with β-1,6-Gal side chains or α-L-Ara residues attached to the O-6 of the Gal backbone [21]. Besides, there are also some reports about a different AG structure, which consist of a (1→6)-linked β-D Gal backbone with β(1→3)-Gal side chains and (1→5)-linked α-L-Ara units branched at the O-3 of Gal residues [22,23].

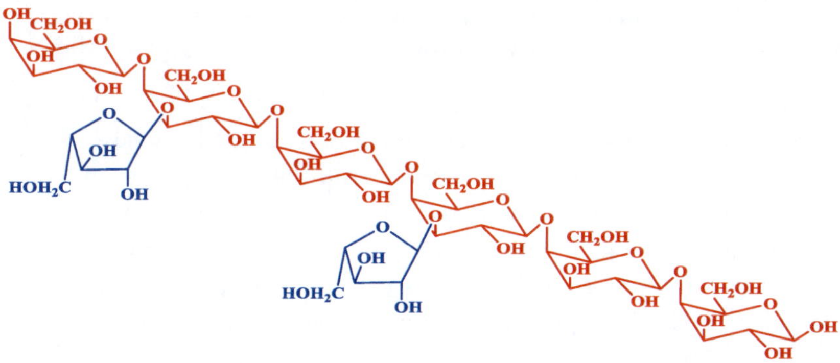

Figure 9. The chemical structure of an AG-I (In red galactose; in blue arabinose).

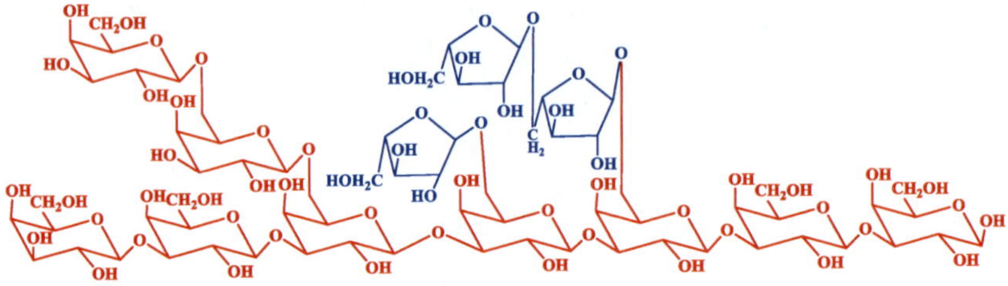

Figure 10. The chemical structure of an AG-II (In red galactose; in blue arabinose).

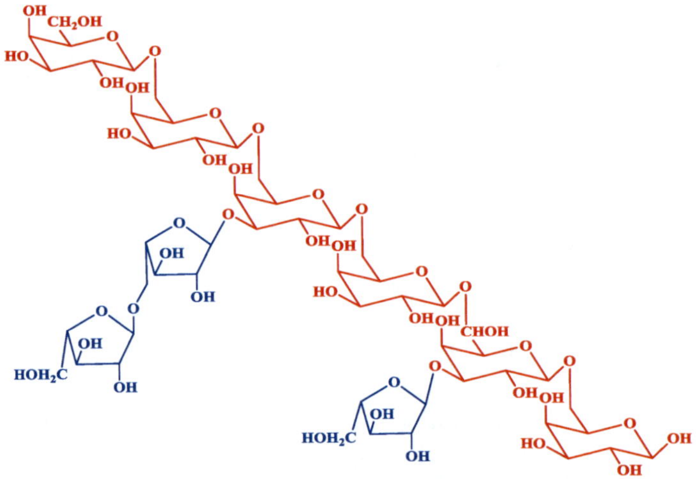

Figure 11. The chemical structure of arabinogalactan with (1→6)-linked β-D Gal backbone and (1→5)-linked α-L-Ara side chains. (In red galactose; in blue arabinose).

Galactomannans are polysaccharides consisting of a mannose backbone with galactose side residues. More specifically, galactomannans have a (1→4)-linked β-D-mannopyranose backbone with branch points from their 6-positions linked to α-D-galactopyranose. The ratio of mannose to galactose ranges from 1 to 4(fenugreek gum 1, guar gum 2, tara gum 3 and locust bean gum 4). Galactomannans are often used as food additives, for example, in ice cream, cream cheese, fruit preparations and salad dressings, to increase the viscosity.

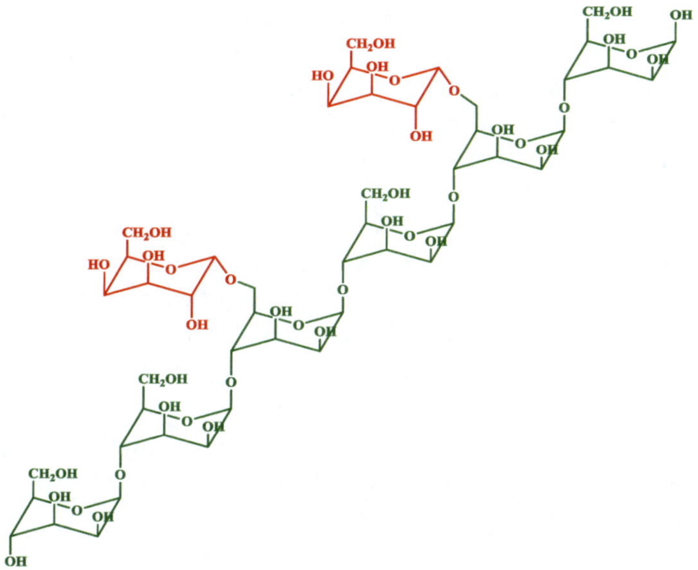

Figure 12. The structure of galactomannan. (In red galactose; in green mannose).

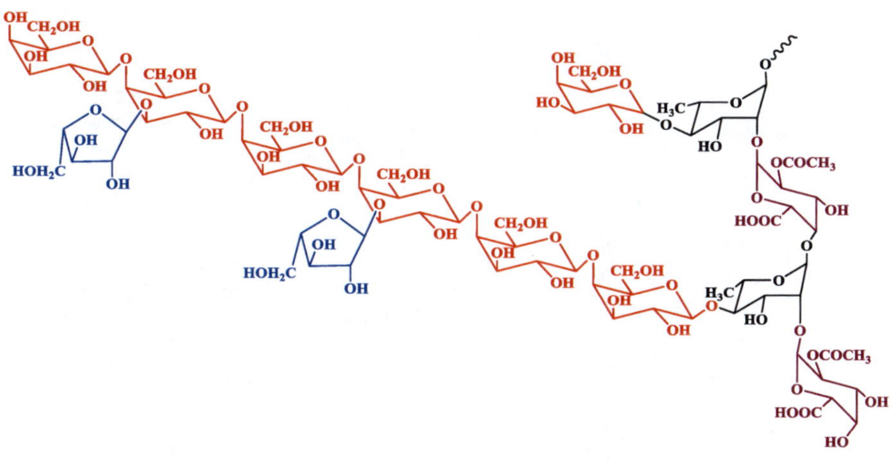

Figure 13. The chemical structure of RG-I. (In red galactose; in blue arabinose; in black rhamnose; in purple 2-O-acetyl-galacturonic acid).

Rhamnogalacturonan is a complex plant cell wall polysaccharide and can be divided to two types, RG-I and RG-II. RG-II is composed of a α-(1→4)-linked homogalacturonan backbone substituted with four side chains and contains rare galactose. RG-I contains a backbone of the repeating disaccharide [α(1→2)-D-GalA-α(1→4)-L-Rha]$_n$, which is partially substituted at the O-4 and/or O-3 positions of α-L rhamnose residue. The structure of side chains are complex and include α-(1→5)-L arabinans, β-(1→4)-D galactans, arabinogalactans-I (AG-I), arabinogalactans-II (AG-II) and possibly galacto-arabinans [24].

Carrageenans consist of linear repeating disaccharide blocks of alternating 3-linked β-D-galactopyranose (β-Gal, unit G) and 4-linked α-D-galactopyranose (α-Gal, unit D), with the D unit often occurring as its 3,6-anhydro form (3,6-AnG, unit A). The classification of carrageenans is based on the presence of a D or an A form of the 4-linked galactose and the differing sulphate contents and substitutions. For example, κ-, ι- and λ-carrageenans have different disaccharide building blocks -[G4S-A]$_n$-, -[G4S-A2S]$_n$-, and -[G2S-D2S6S]$_n$-, respectively [25]. Agaran, a kind of linear polysaccharide composed by 3,6-anhydro-L-galactose (A) and D-galactose (G) units alternately linked by α(1→3) and β(1→4) glycosidic bonds, is mainly extracted from red marine seaweeds, and have been used as food ingredients as a thickener, stabilizer and gelling agent in China for over one thousand years.

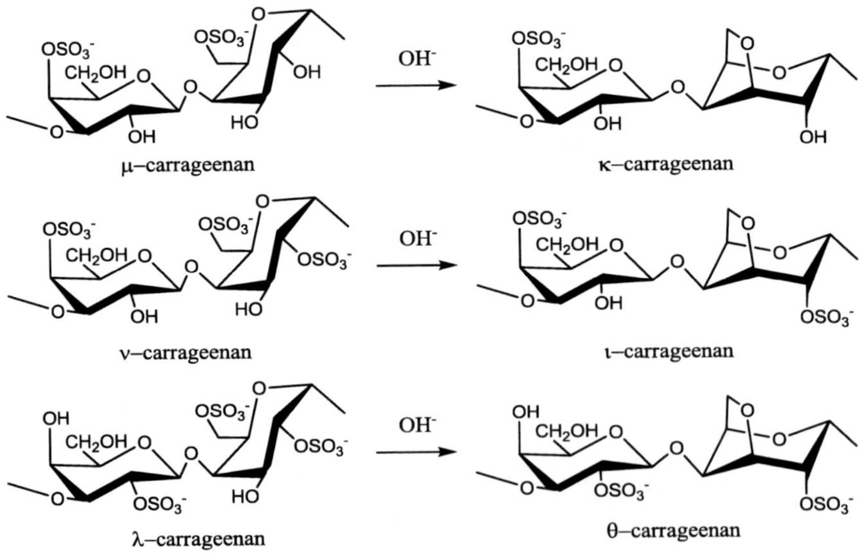

Figure 14. The repeating disaccharide units of different types of carrageenans.

Keratan sulfate (KS) is one of the sulfated glycosaminoglycans and composed of the -3Galβ1→4GlcNAcβ1- repeating disaccharide unit. KS have been found especially in the cornea, cartilage, and bone. KS play important functional roles in cellular recognition of protein ligands, axonal guidance, cell motility, and in embryo implantation. KS are large, highly hydrated molecules, which in joints can act as a cushion to absorb mechanical shock [26].

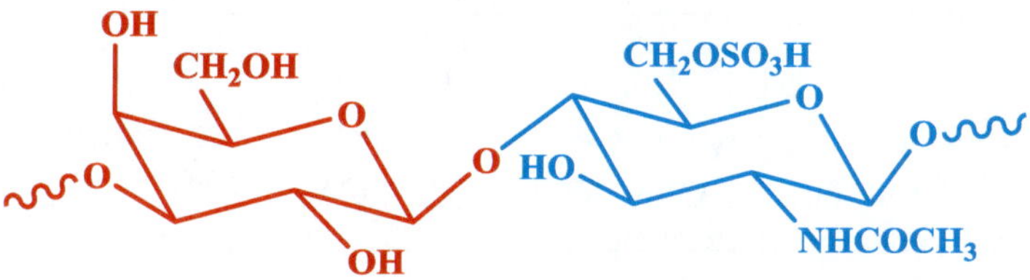

Figure 15. The repeating disaccharide unit of keratan sulfate. (In red galactose; in light blue acetylglucosamine).

2.5. Degrading of Galactose-Containing Saccharides

Polysaccharides and some oligosaccharides cannot be absorbed and utilized directly. The galactose from dietary foods must first be degraded in the body. Galactosidases are the most important tools when converting bound galactose into utilized substances. The α-Galactosidases digest carbohydrates with galactose in α-linkages and are found in human tissues and are probably responsible for the degradation of human galactosylcerebrosides, galactosylsulfatides, and gangliosides [27]. Human intestinal mucosa in vitro did not hydrolyze stachyose, raffinose and melibiose oligosaccharides appreciably and α-Galactosidases can make a perfect supplement [28]. It is notable that α-galactosidase is active in the lysosomes of most cells, but not in the digestive secretions or the luminal side of the human intestine. The β-Galactosidases have been found in many foods including apples and pears, peppers, tomatoes and cocoa beans [11]. Mammalian β-galactosidase activity is localized in the brush border fraction of the mucosal cells of the small intestine. The β-galactosidases in the human intestine digest lactose, but also have heterogeneous activity on compounds with galactose in β-1,4 linkages [29].

Except for the galactosidases, microbes in the intestines may also play an essential role in degrading the compounds containing galactose. Recently,

Hehemann *et al.* reported that *B. uniformis* NP1, a gut bacterium, could grow on agarose plates and use agarose [30]. However, whether *B. uniformis* or any other colonic microbiota are involved in the degradation of agarose are still not fully documented.

3. Clinical Significance of Galactose

Galactose is an integral component of glycoproteins, glycolipids and proteoglycans. These glycoconjugates are significant components of the plasma membranes that surround all animal cells. They form a protective barrier around cells and participate in the contact to surrounding milieu, the extracellular matrix and neighboring cells. In plants, bonded galactose is an important component of various lectins and cell wall components. Lectins have the ability to bind to sugar-containing molecules, but have no enzymatic function [31]. The cell wall polymers support the cell membrane, sense extracellular information and mediate signaling processes. Many diseases are associated with galactose, including its metabolism, content, and the corresponding antigen, antibodies and galectins.

3.1. Lactose Intolerance

Lactose intolerance, also called lactase deficiency and hypolactasia, is the inability to digest lactose. In mammals, the first step of lactose metabolism is digested into galactose and glucose by lactase in the small intestine. The ability to hydrolyze lactose, present during infancy, disappears in many adults who become lactose intolerant. In most cases, the primary symptoms of lactose intolerance are diarrhea, flatulence, abdominal pain, nausea, borborygmi and vomiting. Lactose intolerance can be treated with dietary restriction or enzyme replacement, depending on the amount of lactose consumed and the degree of lactase deficiency [32].

Lactase deficiency may occur for one of three reasons, congenital, secondary or developmental. In rare cases, lactose intolerance is due to the mutation of the gene that is responsible for producing lactase and this type begins shortly after birth. A person born with lactose intolerance cannot eat or drink anything with lactose. Secondary lactase deficiency is due to diseases that destroy the lining of the small intestine. The most common cause is a decrease in the amount of lactase that occurs after childhood and persists into adulthood. Symptoms do not appear immediately after the ingestion of milk but when intake exceeds a certain amount. So most people with lactose intolerance can still drink some milk [33].

3.2. Clinical Significance of GOS

GOS have several health promoting effects, including stimulation of bifidobacteria and lactobacilli growth, improvement of calcium absorption, relief of constipation, support of natural defenses, and inhibition of the development of colon cancer.

Consumption of GOS increases calcium absorption in postmenopausal women by increasing the uptake of calcium by the bones and/or inhibiting bone resorption [34]. The use of GOS (5-15 g/day) may relieve the symptoms of constipation in adults and elderly people. In infants, the supplementation of formula with a mixture of GOS and fructo-oligosaccharides (FOS) can modulate bowel function and stool characters in the same direction as does breast-feeding. Gastrointestinal symptoms may occur as side-effects of oligosaccharides, but 12g GOS per day or less is usually well tolerated [35]. GOS could inhibit adherence of *E. Coli* to tissue culture cells [36], reduce the clinically relevant pathogen germs [37] and the incidence of atopic dermatitis [38].

GOS are mainly used in infant milk formula, follow-on formula, and infant foods [39]. Supplemented infant formulas usually contain 6.0 to 7.2 g/L GOS together with 0.6 to 0.8 g/L fructo-oligosaccharide [40]. Besides, GOS have been used in beverages (fruit juices and other acid drinks), meal replacers, fermented milks, flavored milks, and confectionery products [41].

3.3. Activities of Carrageenan and Agran

Carrageenan is used in many dairy products such as cream cheese, cottage cheese, skimmed milk, and yogurt as well as desserts and sweets such as custards, ice cream, milk shakes, pie fillings and chocolate products [8]. In addition to its use as a food additive, owing to its high negative charges, carrageenan also has diverse biological activities including immunomodulatory, anticoagulant, antithrombotic, antiviral and antitumor effects.

The most active carrageenan, λ-carrageenan, has approximately one-fifteenth the anticoagulant activity of heparin. Among the carrageenan types, λ-carrageenan has approximately twice the activity of unfractionated carrageenan and four times the activity of κ-carrageenan probably due to its higher sulphate content [42]. Carrageenan is a selective inhibitor of several viruses, including herpes simplex virus [43], genital human papillomaviruses [44], human cytomegalovirus, human rhinoviruses, dengue virus [45] and others. Carrageenan has no effect on virus attachment or penetration into host cells, but the synthesis of viral proteins inside the cells was inhibited. Carrageenan has been reported to have anti-HIV activity [46-48], but its strong anticoagulant activity is considered to be an adverse reaction when used as a therapeutic drug for AIDS. In recent years, carrageenan also has been demonstrated to show anti-angiogenesis activity by inhibiting heparanase or blocking the binding of growth factors with their receptors and antimetastatic activity by blocking the interactions between cancer cells and the basement membrane, inhibiting tumor cell proliferation and tumor cell adhesion to various substrates [25, 49, 50].

Recently, there is emerging evidence that agaro-oligosaccharides (AO) can act as a source of soluble fiber that may exert potential prebiotic effects. Hu *et al.* [51] found that the AO could stimulate the growth of bifidobactetia and lactobacilli *in vivo* on mice. Ramnani *et al.* [52] reported that AO with a molecular weight of 64.64 kDa could significantly increase the population of bifidobacteria in the *in vitro* fermentation system inoculated with the human intestinal microbiota. On the other hand, AO has demonstrated a range of health promoting activities such as anti-tumor, anti-inflammatory and anti-oxidant properties.

3.4. Deficiency of Galactosidase

Deficiencies of lysosomal α- and β-galactosidases have recently been described. In Fabry's disease, the α-galactosidase activity in the leukocytes of female carriers of the disease is 15 to 40 percent of the amount present in normal leukocytes while the β-galactosidase activity is normal. As a result, trihexosylceramide in various organs, primarily in the kidneys, is accumulated [53]. Krabbe's disease is a rare, often fatal degenerative disorder. It is caused by the deficiency of galactosylceramidase and impairs the growth and maintenance of myelin, the protective covering around certain nerve cells that ensures the rapid transmission of nerve impulses [54].

3.5. Metabolism Disorders: Galactosemia

The pathways of galactose metabolism, and associated enzyme reactions and corresponding diseases, are shown in Figure 15. Galactose from the diet is mainly converted to Gal-1-P first with the catalysis of galactokinase (GALK, EC 2.7.1.6, McKusick 23020), and then UDP-Gal is produced from Gal-1-P. The UDP-Gal-4-epimerase (GALE, EC 5.1.3.2, McKusick 23035) epimerizes UDP-Gal to UDP-Glc, which will be converted to Glc-1-P and afterwards to Glc-6-P in the liver [1, 3]. The metabolism process involves three major enzymes, GALK, Gal-1-P uridyltransferase (GALT, EC 2.7.7.10, McKusick 23040), and GALE. Any kind of enzyme deficiency will cause galactosemia. The most common type galactosemia is called classical galactosemia, which is caused by the deficiency of GALT.

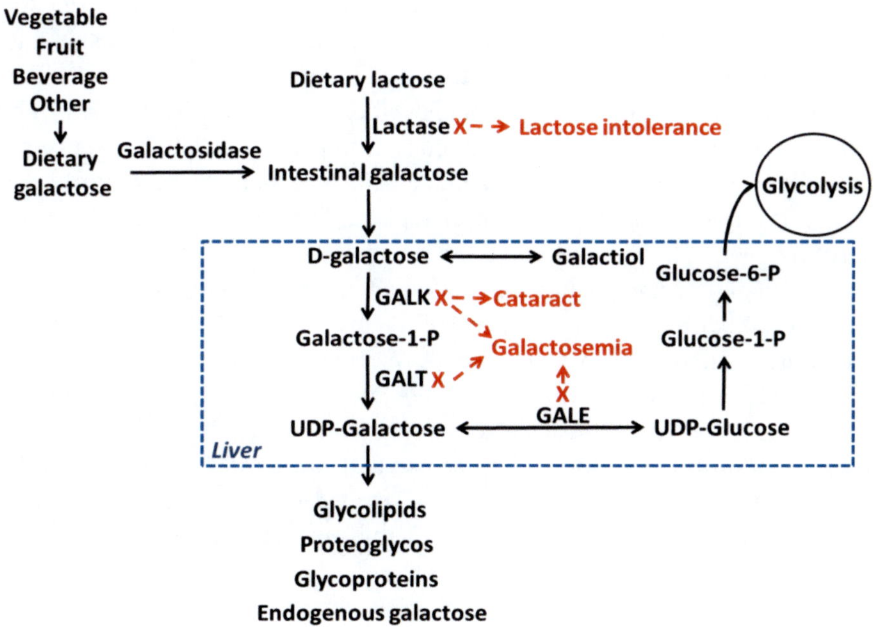

Figure 16. The metabolism of galactose in human body (GALE: uridine diphosphate-4-galactose epimerase; GALT: galactose-1-phosphate uridyltransferase; GALK: galactokinase).

The signs and symptoms of classical galactosemia typically appear within the first few days of life. Children with classical galactosemia may present with feeding problems, jaundice, vomiting, lethargy, edema, ascites, hepatomegaly and sometimes diarrhea. If milk feeding continues, the disease is usually rapidly fatal. The symptom of galactosemia includes cataracts, gynecologic failure, speech and language delays, neurological impairment, and growth inhibition in infants. Septicemia due to *E. coli* infection is a major cause of morbidity/mortality in infants with untreated galactosemia [55, 56]

In galactosemia, the accumulated galactose is galactitol, Gal-1-P and galactonic acid. The Gal-1-P has cell toxicity and could inhibit virus enzymes that participate in the carbohydrate metabolism, such as phosphoglucomutase, glucose-6-phosphatase and glucose-6-phosphate dehydrogenase. Especially, phosphoglucomutase activity is reduced by high Gal-1-P content and the conversion from Glc-1-P to Glc-6-P is inhibited. As a result, the process of glycogen decomposition is blocked. High Gal-1-P concentration also inhibits the gluconeogenesis process of glucose and leads to the hypoglycemia symptom in clinic. Excessive galactose and Gal-1-P accumulate in the aqueous humor and crystal. In classical galactosaemia, Gal-1-P accumulates within cells and there is damage to the brain, liver and kidney. Intracellular Gal-1-P is the toxic agent causing most of the changes in classical galactosaemia [57]. In the lens of the eye, excess galactose is reduced to galactitol. The human being has a limited capacity to further metabolize galactitol and when the amount of galactitol is higher than the capacity, it gives rise to crystal fiber edema, opacity and eventually to cataracts [58, 59].

Early diagnosis and dietary restriction of galactose will work out. It is efficient to take a blood test right after the baby is born. Different screening methods are carried out. In some places, the newborn will be screened for galactosemia by testing the activity of GALT in blood samples and others measure the amount of galactose in the blood sample. Babies with galactosemia have a high level of galactose and low GALT activity [55]. To treat the galactosemia, the baby should have a galactose-free diet throughout its entire lifetime and fortunately, treated babies usually live a fairly healthy, normal life.

The predominant feature of GALK deficiency is bilateral cataracts and very rarely with the complication Pseudotumour cerebri [60]. Galactokinase deficient people have no aversion to milk and experience no discomfort from drinking it. They are asymptomatic with the exception of nuclear cataracts, which appear in infancy. If milk intake is high, they excrete substantial amounts not only of galactose, but also of galactitol. After an oral galactose load, blood galactose rises excessively [57].

GALK deficiency was first described in 1965 in a blind gypsy ('H.K.') who, as a 9-year-old boy, had recurrent cataracts [61]. In H.K. galactose does not stimulate insulin release [62]. The cultured skin fibroblasts of H.K. had no GALK activity. Galactokinase-deficiency could be discovered early if newborns are tested for elevated blood galactose. Galactokinase-deficient newborns will not develop cataracts if fed a galactose-exclusion diet.

GALE deficiency is usually not associated with clinical disease. Up to this date, epimerase deficiency should not be considered a clinical entity although it is perhaps a nuisance to the newborn screening laboratory.

3.6. Human Blood Type

The human blood type is determined by the terminal monosaccharide of the blood group antigen. Blood types A and B only differ from blood type O by the presence of an additional monosaccharide, N-acetylgalactosamine (GalNAc) for type A and galactose (Gal) for type B.

Type O blood cells have neither A nor B antigens, so they may be safely transfused into anyone. But type A, B and AB blood do not. Type O blood is usually used in all emergency situations where there is no time to determine the patient's own group. Scientists have discovered two enzymes that can efficiently convert blood groups A, B and AB into O group, which can be given to anyone but is always in short supply. One of the enzymes is from a gut bacterium called *Bacteroides fragilis* and removes the B antigen. The other is from *Elizabethkingia meningosepticum* and removes the A antigen. Both of the two purified enzymes are highly efficient [63].

3.7. Antitumor Activity of Galactose

It has been determined that the growth of Ehrlich ascitic tumor cells is inhibited by D-galactose but not by D-glucose. A clinically impressive effect of galactose has been demonstrated by its pre-, intra-, and postoperative infusion in the operative removal of colon carcinomas. Patients who receive this treatment experience far fewer liver metastases than do those who receive no galactose [64]. More recently, there have been indications that arabinogalactan can stimulate natural killer cell cytotoxicity, enhance function of the immune system, and inhibit the metastasis of tumor cells to the liver [65]. A preinjection and regular injections of D-galactose or arabinogalactan prevent settling in the liver, but does not influence the homing to the lung. Inhibition studies with D-galactose and various glycoconjugates exhibit terminal D-galactose residues established that cell contacts between hepatocytes and tumor cells involve lectin-carbohydrate interactions [66].

3.8. Galactose-Induced Aging Model

The Galactose-induced aging model has been gradually accepted as a model for study on aging. Compared to other aging models, such as the ozone-induced aging model, the thymus-removed model and the natural aging model, the D-Galactose-induced aging model has a low cost and fast turnaround [67].

Excessive galactose supply causes metabolic disorders, changes the activity of oxidation in various organs, and generates various oxidation products. As a result, cells and organs are damaged, and multi-system dysfunction appears. The aging model induced by D-galactose shows several symptoms, including immune function damage, gene expression and regulation dysfunction, a decrease in cell growth and reproduction ability, cell degenerative disease, memory consolidation and reproduction disorders, and a shortening of life expectancy [68].

REFERENCES

[1] P. A. Frey, *FASEB J.* 10, 461. (1996).
[2] E. Cabib, *Science,* 6, 608. (1970).
[3] D. J. Timson, Dynamic Biochem, Pro Biotech Mol Biology, 1, 63. (2007).
[4] D. J. Timson, *IUBMB Life*, 58, 21. (2006).
[5] P. Peltier, R. Euzen, R. Daniellou, N. C. Caroline, V. Ferrières, *Carbohydr Res,* 343, 1897. (2008).
[6] B. Tefsen, A .F. J. Ram, I. V. Die, F.H. Routier, *Glycobiology,* 22, 456. (2012).
[7] K. C. Gross, P. B. Acosta, *J Inherit Metab Dis,* 14, 253. (1991).
[8] H. O. Kim, C. Hartcntt, C. Scaman, J Agri Food Chem, 55, 8133. (2007).
[9] G. Liu, G. E. Hale, C. L. Hughes, *Reprod Toxicol,* 14, 377. (2000).
[10] P. A. Portnoi, A. MacDonald, *J Hum Nutr Diet,* 22, 400. (2009).
[11] P. B. Acosta, K. C. Gross, *Eur Journal Pediatr,* 154, S87. (1995).

[12] M. Tanaka, D. Thananunkul, T. C. Lee, C. O. Chichester, *J Food Sci,* 40, 1087. (1975).

[13] G. T. Macfarlane, H. Steed, S. Macfarlane, *J Appl Microbio,* 104, 305. (2008).

[14] E. V. Hoffen, B. Ruiter, J. Faberv, L. Mrabet, E. F. Knol, B. Stahol, S. Arslanoglu, G. Moro, G. Boehm, J. Garssen, *Allergy,* 64, 484. (2009).

[15] G. R. Gibson, M. B. Roberfroid, *J Nutr,* 125, 1401. (1995).

[16] L. Rydberg, J. Holgersson, B. E. Samuelsson, M. E. Breimer, *Biochimie,* 83, 565 (1999).

[17] S. Marionneau, A. Cailleau-Thomas, J. Rocher, B. L. Moullac-Vaidye, N. Ruvoën, M. Clément, J. L. Pendu, *Biochimie,* 83, 565. (2001).

[18] K. Y. Robert, Y. T. Tsai, T. Ariga, *Neurochem Res,* 37, 1230. (2012).

[19] R. Bentley, R. Meganathan, *Microbiol Rev,* 46, 241. (1982).

[20] J. S. Dinning, B. K. Allen, R. S. Young, P. L. Day, *J Bio Chem,* 233, 674. (1958).

[21] N. X. Y. Ling, J. Lee, M. Ellis, M. L. Liao, S. L. Mau, D. Guest, P. H. Jansssen, P. Kovac, A. Bacic, F. A. Pettolino, *Carbohyd Res,* 352, 70. (2012).

[22] F. Liang, C. Hu, Z. He, Y. Pan, *Carbohyd Res,* Available online 14 September 2013. (2013).

[23] A. J. B. Oliveira, L. Cordeiro, R. A. C. Gonçalves, L. F. Ceole, U. N. Tania, M. Lacomoni, *Carbohyd Res,* 94, 179. (2013).

[24] J. Obro, J. Harholt, H. V. Sheller, C. Orfila, *Phytochemistry,* 65, 1429. (2004).

[25] G. Jiao, G. Yu, J. Zhang, H. S. Ewart, *Marine Drugs,* 9, 196. (2011).

[26] J. L. Funderburgh, *Glycobiology,* 10, 951. (2000).

[27] J. B. Pridham, P. M .Dey, *Plant carbohydrate biochemistry*, Academic Press, New York, (1974).

[28] R. Gitzelmann, S. Auricchio, *Pediatrics,* 36, 231. (1965).

[29] N. G. Asp, *Biochem J,* 191, 229. (1971).

[30] J. H. Hehemann, A. G. Kelly, N. A. Pudlo, E. C. Martens, A. B. Boraston, *P Natl Acad Sci USA,* 109, 19786. (2012).

[31] R. Mosetter. Galactose.org at http://www.galactose.org/;

[32] M. B. Heyman, *Pediatrics,* 118, 1279. (2006).

[33] J. W. Marks, B. Anand, Medicine Net.com. Lactose Intolerance (Lactase Deficiency). at http://www.medicinenet.com/lactose_intolerance/article.htm;

[34] O. Chonan, K. Matsumoto, M. Watanuki, *Biosci Biotech Bioch,* 59, 236. (1995).

[35] L. Niittynen, K. Kajander, R. Korpela, *Scand J Food Nutr,* 51, 62. (2007).

[36] K. Shoaf, G. L. Mulvey, G. D. Armstrong and R. W. Hutkins, *Infection Immunity,* 74, 6920. (2006).

[37] J. Knol &, G. Boehm, M. Lidestri, F. Negretti, J. Jelinek, M. Agosti, B. Stahl, A. Marini and F. Mosca, *Acta Paediatri,* 94, 31. (2005).

[38] G. Moro, S. Arslanoglu, B. Stahl, J. Jelinek, U. Wahn and G. Boehm, *Arch Dis child,* 91, 814. (2006).

[39] M. J. Playne, R. G. Crittenden, Advanced Dairy Chemistry, Volume 3: Lactose, Water, Salts and Minor Constituents, Springer Science, New York (2009).

[40] R. A. Rastall, *Prebiotics: Development and Application*, John Wiley & Sons Ltd., Chichester (2006).

[41] D. P. M.Torres, M. P. F.Goncalves, J. A. Teixeira and L. R. Rodiagues, *Compr Rev Food Sci,* 9, 438. (2010).

[42] M. Shanmugam, K. H.Mody, *Curr Sci,* 79, 1672. (2000).

[43] K. Chattopadhyay. T. Ghosh, C. A. Pujol, M. J. Carlucci, E. B. Damonte, B. Ray, *Int J Bio Macromol,* 43, 346. (2008).

[44] C. B. Buck, C. D. Thompson, J. N. Roberts, M. Muller, D. R. Lowy, J. T. Schiller, *PLoS Pathogens,* 2, e69. (2006).

[45] L. B. Talarico, C. A. Pujol, R. G. M. Zibetti, P.C.S. Faría, M.D. Noseda, M.E.R. Duarte, E.B. Damonte, *Antiviral. Research,* 66, 103. (2005).

[46] T. Yamada, A. Ogamo, T. Saito, J. Watanabe, H. Uchiyama, Y. Nakagawa, *Carbohyd Polym,* 32, 51. (1997).

[47] D. J. Schaeffer, V. S. Krylov, *Ecoto Environ Safe,* 45, 208. (2000).

[48] I. Wijesekara, R. Pangestuti, S. K. Kim, *Carbohyd Poly,* 84, 14. (2011).

[49] C. R. Parish, D. R. Coombe, K. B. Jakobsen, F. A. Bennett, P. A.Underwood, *Int J Cancer,* 40, 511. (1987).

[50] G. Zhou, Y. Sun, H. Xin, Y. Zhang, Z. Li, Z. Xu, *Pharmacol Res,* 50, 47. (2004).

[51] B. Hu, Q. Gong, Y. Wang, Y. Ma, J. Li, W. Yu, *Anaerobe,* 12, 260. (2006).

[52] P. Ramnani, R. Chitarrari, K. Tuohy, J. Grant, S. Hotchkiss, K. Philp, R. Campbell, C. Gill, I. Rowland, *Anaerobe,* 18, 1. (2012).

[53] J. A. Kint, *Sci,* 167, 1268. (1970).

[54] L. Svennerholm, M. T. Vanier, J. E. Mansson, *J Lipid Res,* 21, 53. (1980).

[55] G. T. Berry, *Mol Genet Metab,* 106, 7. (2012).

[56] J. C. Petricciani, M. K. Binder, C. R. Merril, M. R. Geiter, *Sci,* 175, 1368. (1972).

[57] R. Gitzelmann, R. G. Hansen, *Inherited Disorders of Carbohydrate Metabolism*, Springer Netherlands, Dordrecht (1980).

[58] J. B. Holton, *J Inherit Metab Dis,* 13, 476. (1990).

[59] S. Segal, S. Rogers, *J Inherit Metab Dis,* 13, 487. (1990).

[60] R. R. Huttenlocher, R. E. Hillman, Y. E. Hsia, *J Pediatr,* 76, 902. (1970).

[61] R. Gitzelmann, *Pediatri Res*, 1, 14. (1967).

[62] R. Gitzelmann, R. Illig, *Diabetologia,* 5, 143. (1969).

[63] Q. P. Liu, G. Sulzenbacher, H. Yuan, E. P. Bennett, G. Pietz, K. Saunders, J. Spence, E. Nudelman, S. B. Levery, T. White, J. M. Neveu, W. S. Lane, Y. Bourne, M. L. Olsson, B. Henrissat, H. Clausen, *Nat Biotechnol,* 25, 454. (2007).

[64] J. Kosik, J. Gil, S. Szmigielski, J. Beuth, G. Pulyerer, *Anticancer Res,* 17,1411. (1997).

[65] G. S. Kelly, Alternative Medicine Rev: J Clin Ther, 4, 96. (1999).

[66] J. Beuth, H. L. Ko, K. Oette, G. Pulverer, K. Roszkowski, G. Uhlenbruck, *J Cancer Res Clin,* 113, 51. (1987).

[67] X. Song, M. Bao, D. Li, Y. Li, *Mech Ageing Dev,* 108, 239. (1999).

[68] J. Lu , D. Wu, Y. Zheng, B. Hu, Z. Zhang, *Brain Pathol,* 20, 598. (2005).

In: Galactose
Editor: Vitor Hugo Pomin
ISBN: 978-1-63117-928-0

Chapter 2

Clinical Relevance of Galactose

Tzi Bun Ng*[*] *and Charlene Cheuk Wing Ng
School of Biomedical Sciences,Faculty of Medicine, The Chinese University of Hong Kong, New Territories, Hong Kong, China

Abstract

D-galactose elicited memory dysfunction, brought about mito-oxidative damage and triggered apoptosis via activation of PPAR-gamma receptors and induced aging in mice. Terminal galactosylation of transferrin due to loss of terminal N-acetylneuraminic acid residues, which leads to a more acid pI, may be a biomarker of healthy ageing. Glucose and galactose regulate intestinal absorption of cholesterol. Galactose malabsorption complicated with rickets and nephrogenic diabetes insipidus has been reported. Galactose accelerates cataract development. Feeding dogs with a diet containing 30% galactose induces experimental galactosemia and results in the formation of diabetes-like microvascular lesions in the retina. Galactose-fed beagles develop diabetes-like microvascular changes that are histologically and clinically similar in appearance to all stages of human diabetic retinopathy. Expression of an endogenous galactose-binding lectin correlates with neoplastic progression in the colon. Identification and upregulation of galactose/N-acetylgalactosamine macrophage lectin in rat cardiac allografts with arteriosclerosis has been demonstrated. Uridine

[*] Corresponding author: Email: b021770@mailserv.cuhk.edu.hk, fax: 852 26035123, phone: 852 39436872.

diphosphate galactose-4-epimerase deficiency has been detected by neonatal screening for galactosaemia which has a variety of symptoms. Delayed hypersensitivity reactions to mammalian meat mediated by IgE antibodies to galactose-alpha 1,3-galactose (alpha-gal), an oligosaccharide, has been reported.

Keywords: Galactose, clinical significance

INTRODUCTION

The sugar galactose is present in lactose, polysaccharides, glycoproteins, and glycolipids. This indicates its importance. However, it has some untoward effects. For instance, galactose feeding is used experimentally to produce an animal model of senescence. When galactose accumulates as a result of deficiency of the enzymes that catalyze the metabolism of the sugar, it brings about pathological consequences. The purpose of this article is to examine the various aspects of galactose metabolism that has an influence on health.

D-Galactose-Induced Oxidative Damage

The administration of the glutathione transferase-small ubiquitin-related modifier-metallothionein (GST-SUMO-MT) fusion protein to mice treated with D-galactose improved the learning and memory capacity of the animals. It inhibited D-galactose-induced elevation of malondialdehyde and nitric oxide levels. Histopathological alterations and reduced superoxide dismutase activity in the brain and liver were prevented by GST-SUMO-MT. GST-SUMO-MT protected various tissues against oxidative injury brought about by D-galactose (Huang et al., 2009).

D-galactose brought about a rise in the lipid peroxide level in the brain, blood, and liver, an elevation of brain monoamine oxidase-B activity, a decline in glutathione peroxidase activity in blood and liver, and a fall in the activity of superoxide dismutase in liver and erythrocytes. Oral administration of procyanidin and vitamin E counteracted the oxidative stress induced by D-galactose (Shu et al., 2002)

Galactose and Mitochondrial Apoptotic Pathway and Mito-Oxidative Damage

D-galactose administration (100 mg/kg for 1.5 months) to rats caused changes in behavior, biochemical parameters, mitochondrial enzymes and activation of acetylcholineesterase and caspase-3. Piogliatzone (a PPAR-gamma agonist) administration (10 and 30 mg/kg daily) alleviated the aforementioned changes. BADGE (a PPAR-gamma antagonist) antagonized the action of pioglitazone in the D-galactose induced aging mice. Thus pioglitzone protects against memory deterioration, oxidative damage and apoptosis induced by D-galactose via activating the PPAR-gamma receptors. These findings suggest that pioglitazone might be helpful for the prevention or alleviation of aging (Prakash and Kumar 2013).

D-Galactose-Induced Aging in Rats

Age-related renal insufficiency has important implications due to impaired redox homeostasis. D-galactose administration (60 mg/kg/day for 1.5 months) was employed to induce aging in 20-week-old rats. Consequently the concentrations of 8-hydroxy-2'deoxyguanosine, lipid hydroperoxides, malondialdehyde, and protein carbonyl groups were elevated, whereas concentrations of total thiol groups and protein thiol groups were depressed. In both D-galactose induced aging and young control rats, the concentrations of non-protein thiol groups and protein-bound sialic acid concentrations were essentially similar. In naturally aging rats, malondialdehyde and protein carbonyl groups were elevated while concentrations of total thiol groups, protein thiol groups and non-protein thiol groups were depressed compared to young controls. The concentrations of 8-hydroxy-2'deoxyguanosine and protein-bound sialic acid did not differ between the naturally aging group and the young control group. Both D-galactose induced aging rats and the naturally aged rats exhibited impaired redox homeostasis (Aydın et al., 2012).

D-galactose (intraperitoneal injections, 150mg/kg/day) administered to rats for four months resulted in elevated activities of aspartate transaminase and ã –glutamyl transferase in plasma and â-galactosidase protein expression levels. A swimming exercise program of three-month duration inhibited senescence markers and hepatic inflammatory mediators including p21, p53, and downregulated interleukin-6 protein levels (Huang et al., 2013).

The Changes of Spleen B Cells of D-Galactose-Induced Aging Mice

D-galactose administration (100 ng/L, 0.25 mL/20 g, once daily for 42 days) into the back necks of mice upregulated splenocyte expression of CD20, CD40, CD45RA, CD86 and CD196 and downregulated serum concentrations of interleukin-4. The reduced expression of interleukin-4 in serum brought about dysfunction of the immune system (Huang et al., 2012)

Terminal Galactosylation of Transferrin May be a Biomarker of Healthy Aging

Terminal galactosylation of transferrin in older men due to loss of terminal N-acetylneuraminic acid residues, which leads to a more acid pI, may serve as a biomarker of healthy aging and is now under investigation in the MARK-AGE study (Dunston et al., 2012).

Galactose-á-1,3-Galactose-Induced Allergy

IgE antibodies to galactose-alpha-1,3-galactose (alpha-gal), an oligosaccharide often found in nonprimate mammalian proteins, can bring about serious and sometimes life-threatening reactions. The allergic patients may manifest anaphylaxis, angioedema, or urticaria several hours after consuming beef, lamb or pork. A form of delayed anaphylaxis to red meat, related to serum IgE antibodies to alpha-gal, has been reported. The majority of the patients had shown tolerance to meat in preceding years. In three subjects there was a surge in the alpha-gal IgE titer following tick bites. A strong correlation existed between tick bite history and alpha-gal IgE levels. A good correlation existed between alpha-gal IgE antibodies and IgE antibodies to proteins of the tick *Amblyomma americanum*. IgE antibodies are common in locations in which *A americanum* prevails. Hence tick bites are a cause of alpha-gal IgE antibodies (Commins et al., 2009, 2010, 2011, 2012, 2013) These cases had a history of tick bites within the past year, which caused itchiness (Kennedy et al.,2013; Platts-Mills and Commins, 2013; Berg et al., 2014).

The majority of patients with a red meat allergy were allergic to gelatin. The detection of á-Gal in gelatin and correlation between the results of á-Gal and gelatin testing suggest that á-Gal IgE might be the target of reactivity to gelatin. The pathogenic relationship between tick bites and allergy to red meat, á-Gal, and gelatin (with or without clinical reactivity) awaits elucidation (Mullins et al., 2012).

Galactose and Eyes

Galactose restriction in the diet is recommended for patients with galactokinase deficiency, a disease characterized by autosomal recessive inheritance. A case in which cataracts and associated bilateral macular deposits were found in a white male with heterozygous galactokinase deficiency and excessive intake of dairy products has been reported (Hodes et al., 1985).

Administration of a normal diet to dogs for 14 or 7 months subsequent to galactose feeding for either 24 months or 31 months failed to mitigate corneal endothelial changes (Neuenschwander et al., 1995).

Male dogs (nine months of age) fed a 30% galactose diet developed retinopathy. Control dogs not treated with galactose did not exhibit similar changes after 84 months (Kador et al., 1995). The retinal microangiopathy was inhibited by the aldose reductase inhibitor sorbinil (0.05% wt/wt) (Robison et al., 1995).Cataracts due to feeding with galactose in dogs (nine months of age) have been reported (Lackner et al., 1997).

ARI-50925, a potent new aldose reductase inhibitor, attenuated retinal capillary basement membrane thickening in rats fed a 50% D-galactose diet compared with rats fed the same diet but not treated with the inhibitor. The reduced thickening was not conspicuous until 16 to 20 months following treatment with the inhibitor. Hence intervention should be initiated soon after onset of diabetes, and follow-up should be employed to assess the effectiveness (Robison et al., 1998).

Chronic administration of galactose to rats brought about a breakdown of the blood-aqueous barrier because of alterations in the iris vessel comprising focal straightening, constriction, dilation, increased permeability, ischemia and new vessel proliferation. These changes could be inhibited by aldose reductase inhibitors, signifying a relationship between the sorbitol pathway and changes in the iris vessels (Caspers-Velu et al., 1999).

In 12-month-old rats, a rise in the lens content of galactitol, lipid peroxide and water and serum concentration of total cholesterol, and a decline in reduced glutathione and protein content of the lens occurred after several months of feeding with a 25% galactose diet. In the galactosemic aged rats, osmotic stress and oxidative damage led to cataract formation and progression (Ohta et al., 1999). Chronic galactose administration ensued in a diversity of neutrophil dysfunctions which might lead to the development of retinal microangiopathy associated with diabetes and galactosemia (Ohta et al., 1999).

Galactose-treated dogs manifested changes in retinal capillaries resembling diabetic retinopathy. Pericyte degeneration appeared initially, escorted by microaneurysms, hemorrhages, and some areas of acellularity. The selective degeneration of retinal capillary pericytes in galactose-fed dogs was associated with heightened activity of aldose reductase in these cells (Murata et al., 2002). Restoration of normoglycemia, discontinuation of dietary galactose, and administration of the aldose reductase inhibitor M79175 (2-methyl-6-fluoro-spiro-chroman-4-5'- imidazolidine-2',4'-dione) might retard the onset and deterioration of retinal damage in galactose-fed dogs (Cusick et al., 2003). Termination of dietary galactose administration at the early stages of retinopathy retarded the progression of retinal lesions (Kador et al., 2002).Ohta et al. (2000) reported that vitamin E was capable of preventing progression of galactose-induced cataractogenesis in rats.

Neovascularization in the galactose-fed dog is a slowly progressing event, analogous to clinical diabetic retinopathy. Combretastatin A-4, a vascular targeting agent that quickly disrupts blood flow in new vessels, did not affect neovascularization. Hence chronic treatment may be necessary (Kador et al., 2007).

Galactose Metabolism and Ovarian Toxicity

The galactose metabolites Gal-1-P, galactitol, and UDPgal all play a role in ovarian toxicity. The mechanisms comprise interference with ovarian apoptosis and gonadotrophin signaling. Hormones and antioxidants may have therapeutic value (Liu et al., 2000).

Duarte Galactose-1-Phosphate Uridyl Transferase Genotypes Are Not Associated with Ovarian Cancer Risk

Duarte1 (D1) genotype individuals have a missense mutation (N314D) associated with normal galactose-1-phosphate uridyl transferase (GALT) activity unless it occurs together with an associated 4-bp deletion leading to reduced GALT activity (Duarte2 or D2).D1 and D2 genotypes are not involved in the relationship between galactose intake and possible ovarian dysfunction (Merritt et al., 2012).

N314D Polymorphism of Galactose-1-Phosphate Uridyl Transferase Does Not Modify the Risk of Ovarian Cancer

Published data refute the hypothesis that aspects of lactose and galactose consumption and metabolism have a bearing on the etiology of ovarian cancer (Herrinton et al., 1995).GALT N314D allele does not predispose to epithelial ovarian cancer (Fung et al., 2003). .

Fucosylation and Gastrointestinal Cancer

Fucose (6-deoxy-L-galactose) is found on glycoproteins and glycolipids. Striking alterations in the expression of fucosylated oligosaccharides occur in cancer and inflammation. Monoclonal antibodies and lectins capable of recognizing fucosylated oligosaccharides associated with cancer have been employed clinically as tumor markers (Moriwaki and Miyoshi 2010).

Unusual Accumulation of Sulfated Glycosphingolipids in Colon Cancer Cells

In the investigation of Shida et al. (2009), colon cancer cells from two patients displayed large amounts of unusual glycosphingolipids containing sulfated oligosaccharides not encountered in colorectal cancer cells or normal colorectal epithelial cells from other patients. The colon cancer cells from one of the patients exhibited oligosaccharides sulfated at the C6 position of subterminal GlcNAc and at C3 positions of terminal galactose with or without sialylation or fucosylation. The colon cancer cells from the other patient demonstrated two types of sulfated oligosaccharides.

Galactose Oxidase-Schiff Reaction in the Detection of Carcinoma and Precancerous Lesions of Large Intestine

The positive rates, specificity, sensitivity and positive predictive value of the galactose oxidase-Schiff reaction for detection of carcinoma and precancerous lesions of the large intestine exceeded 80%, 98% 86%, and 90%, respectively. The reaction can be used for screening purposes (Qin et al., 1997).

Galactose Specific Lectin-Epithelial Interactions in the Human Colon

An increased concentration of the human galactose-binding lectin, galectin-3, is found in the serum samples of patients with metastatic cancer and binds Thomsen-Friedenreich antigen on cancer cell surface, causing clustering of mucin 1 and revealing underlying adhesion molecules which facilitate adhesion to the endothelium. This is an important mechanism in cancer metastasis and represents a valid therapeutic target (Rhodes et al., 2008).

Alpha-Galactosyl Epitope on Human Tumor Cells

Developing methods for the *in vitro* synthesis of the carbohydrate Galalpha1-3Galbeta1-4GlcNAc-R (referred to as alpha-galactosyl epitope) on human tumour cells may be exploitable in cancer immunotherapy. Tumor vaccines carrying the epitope would be opsonized *in vivo* by the natural anti-Gal antibody present at high levels in humans, which specifically interact with alpha-galactosyl epitopes. Anti-Gal binding to alpha-galactosyl epitopes on membranes of tumor cells facilitates uptake of the cell membranes by antigen-presenting cells like macrophages, by adhesion of the Fc portion of anti-Gal to Fc receptors on these cells. This, in turn, may promote the processing and presentation of tumor-associated antigens by antigen-presenting cells, and may elicit an immune response against tumor cells bearing these antigens (Galili and Anaraki, 1995).

Possible Significance of Receptors for Galactose-Specific Peanut Agglutinin in Childhood Acute Lymphoblastic Leukemia

The presence of a considerable number (>15%) of lymphocyte receptors for peanut agglutinin was identified on leukemic cells from T-cell acute lymphoblastic leukemia, and on normal fetal thymic lymphocytes, but not on normal human peripheral blood lymphocytes.

Galactose inhibited the binding of peanut agglutinin to leukemic lymphoblasts and thymic lymphocytes. When the different immunologic subgroups of acute lymphoblastic leukemia were pooled, eight out of the thirteen patients with >15% peanut agglutinin-positive lymphoblasts had experienced relapse.

On the other hand, none of the patients with <15% peanut agglutinin-positive cells was afflicted with recurrent disease. Hence analysis of peanut agglutinin receptors on acute lymphoblastic leukemia lymphoblasts may be a useful clinical and immunologic prognostic indicator (Levin et al., 1980).

Characterization of Galactose-Binding Proteins in Equine Testis and Spermatozoa

Carbohydrate-binding proteins are involved in diverse sperm functions including interactions with the oviduct and zona pellucida. Galactose binding proteins which are testis- and sperm-specific are present in the horse. Their physiological roles await elucidation (Sabeur and Ball, 2007).

Glucose and Galactose Regulate Intestinal Absorption of Cholesterol

Galactose or glucose, by interacting with SGLT1, brings about activation of a protein kinase C pathway that regulates the activity of hSR-BI, an intestinal cholesterol transporter (Play et al., 2003).

Glucose-Galactose Malabsorption Complicated with Rickets and Nephrogenic Diabetes Insipidus

Al-Lawati and Vargees (2008) reported the first case of congenital glucose galactose malabsorption in the Arab world: a two-year-old girl who presented with chronic osmotic diarrhea and hypernatraemic dehydration. Pesce and Bodourian (1982) correlated the clinical manifestations of transferase-deficient galactosemia with the plasma levels of galactose and erythrocyte galactose-1-phosphate in six galactosemic patients during dietary treatment, in a child prior to treatment, and in 12 individuals with subnormal erythrocyte hexose-1-phosphate uridylyltransferase activity. All treated patients were asymptomatic with normal galactose and either normal or high galactose-1-phosphate concentrations. Three of them were clinically normal as neonates while consuming foods with galactose and may resemble the asymptomatic Negro galactosemia. The clinical symptoms of galactosemia in untreated patients included excessive urinary concentrations of galactose, galactose-1-phosphate, protein and reducing substances, elevated plasma bilirubin and alkaline phosphatase, but normal plasma concentrations of glucose, gamma-glutamyltransferase, alanine aminotransferase, and aspartate aminotransferase. Clinical improvement in this patient accompanied the fall in erythrocyte galactose-1-phosphate. Patients with low hexose-1-phosphate uridylyltransferase activity were asymptomatic and exhibited normal galactose and galactose-1-phosphate concentrations (Pesce and Bodourian, 1982).

Newborn Screening for Galactosemia

Galactose-1-phosphate uridylyl transferase activity in blood specimens was used for routine neonatal screening for galactosemia and other inborn errors of metabolism (Hammersen and Levy 1977).

Two Familial Cases of High Blood Galactose of Unknown Aetiology

Brunetti-Pierri et al., (2006) reported two newborn male siblings on a breast milk diet presenting with an elevated blood galactose level, a normal blood galactose 1-phosphate level and urinary galactitol excretion.

The symptoms could be alleviated by administration of a diet devoid of lactose. The levels of metabolites were restored to normal. Reintroduction of galactose in the diet resulted in an accumulation of metabolites. Possible causes of galactosaemia comprise: (1) abnormal activities of the enzymes regulating galactose metabolism including galactokinase, galactose-1-phosphate uridyltransferase, and uridine diphosphate galactose 4'-epimerase, (2) tyrosinaemia, (3) Fanconi-Bickel syndrome, and (4) portosystemic shunting. Each possibility was excluded with appropriate tests. The two familial cases may represent a new autosomal or X-linked recessive disease of galactose metabolism, possibly due to a novel defect in the membrane galactose.

Biochemical and Molecular Characterization of Galactose-1-Phosphate Uridyltransferase (GALT) Gene from Indian Galactosemia Patients: Identification of 10 Novel Mutations and their Structural and Functional Implications

Classical galactosemia is an autosomal recessive disorder of galactose metabolism, characterized by a severe reduction or absence of galactose-1-phosphate uridyl transferase (GALT). The characterization of underlying GALT gene lesions was conducted in fifty-five unrelated galactosemic patients in India. There were sixteen distinct GALT mutations, ten of which had not been reported. N314D was the most common mutation with a frequency of 40% followed by Q188R at 2.7%. The novel GALT gene mutations included six missense mutations (K285R, P166A, Q103R, R333L; S181F, Y89H), one nonsense mutation (S307X) and three silent mutations (Q103Q, K210K and H319H).

The functional importance of the novel GALT missense mutations was studied using SNPs & GO and SIFT tools. Modeling investigations deploying 3D models of mutant and wild type GALT proteins revealed mutations to exert their actions at the molecular level by altering H-bonds, salt bridges, secondary structure or surface features. The investigation revealed the heterogeneity of classical galactosemia in the Indian population and also underscored the significance of GALT gene analysis in the diagnosis of galactosemia. It also disclosed that the Indian GALT mutational profile shows differences from other populations examined (Singh et al., 2012).

Uridine Diphosphate Galactose-4-Epimerase Deficiency and Epimerase-Deficiency Galactosemia

The erythrocyte levels of galactose-1-phosphate and uridine diphosphate galactose have been examined in connection with dietary galactose in a case of uridine diphosphate galactose-4-epimerase deficiency (McKusick 23035). Uridine diphosphate galactose built up in concentration quickly following intake of very small amounts of galactose but the galactose-1-phosphate level rose in proportion with galactose consumption (Henderson et al., 1983).

An infant was diagnosed with uridine diphosphate galactose-4-epimerase deficiency during screening of the neonates for galactosemia in Queensland, Australia. No case of epimerase deficiency has been reported previously in Australia and the incidence in the population was not known. This enzyme deficiency is often benign although two cases with a galactosaemia-like syndrome have been reported. This infant showed normal intellectual and physical development, in spite of extremely high levels of erythrocyte galactose-1-phosphate (Bowling et al., 1986).

Epimerase-deficiency galactosemia results from the impairment of UDP-galactose 4'-epimerase (GALE) (Openo et al., 2005).

Living Situation, Occupation and Health-Related Quality of Life in Adult Patients with Classic Galactosemia

Approximately two-thirds of the German galactosemic patients with galactose-1-phosphate uridyltransferase deficiency were single, and most of them stayed with their parents. They did not attain education up to school leaving certificate level, and about one-third of the patients had never commenced or never completed an apprenticeship. Getting along with galactosemia was commented on favorably as 'very good' or 'good' although following the diet was regarded as a burden. Social well-being and social functioning were regarded as inferior in comparison with phenlketonuric patients. Patients with galactosemia require a multi-professional team to pay attention to the physical, biochemical and social aspects of the disease (Hoffmann et al., 2012).

Free Galactose Content in Selected Fresh Fruits and Vegetables and Soy Beverages

Free galactose content in plant materials varied from 2 mg/100 g in red potato to 40 mg/100 g in red pepper. The season, variety, and storage of the product had an impact on the free galactose content in the bulk of plant materials. Free galactose level in Roma tomatoes increased linearly over time, and increased with storage at 4 in tomatoes. Soy beverages derived from soy protein isolate had a lower free galactose content than samples manufactured from whole soybeans. Data on the free galactose content in vegetables and fruits enable galactosemic subjects to make more informed dietary choices (Kim et al., 2007).

Galactose Content of Processed Fruits

The free galactose content of processed fruits was reduced when blanching, canning, drying, freezing, microwaving, and a combination of blanching and freezing were employed (Hartnett et al., 2007).

The Effect of Diet on Paraoxonase 1/Arylesterase Activity in Patients with Disorders of Galactose Metabolism

A high galactose-1-phosphate level and a low total antioxidant status may bring about a decrease in paraoxonase 1/arylesterase activity. Galactosemic patients on a diet restricted in galactose may require a diet with high antiatherogenic ability (Schulpis et al., 200).

Galactose Enhances Oxidative Metabolism and Reveals Mitochondrial Dysfunction in Human Primary Muscle Cells

The oxygen consumption rate in human primary myotubes from non-diabetic obese subjects, but not that in post-diabetic myotubes, was enhanced by galactose. The lack of an increase in oxygen consumption rate in post-diabetic myotubes differentiated in galactose was associated with an unmodified cytochrome C oxidase activity or AMPK phosphorylation. The mechanisms of mitochondrial dysfunction in cells from post-diabetic patients await elucidation (Aguer et al., 2012).

Identification and Upregulation of Galactose/N-Acetylgalactosamine Macrophage Lectin in Rat Cardiac Allografts with Arteriosclerosis

When differential mRNA display was employed to reveal potential mediators associated with chronic rejection, a cDNA fragment inducible in F344 rat cardiac allografts with arteriosclerosis but not in Lewis syngrafts was identified. The full-length cDNA isolated from a rat cardiac allograft cDNA library that exhibited almost complete identity to galactose/N-acetylgalactosamine macrophage lectin, a cell-surface receptor, hybridized with total RNA from eight cardiac allografts but not with host hearts, syngrafts, or other organs. There was a allograft-specific rise in transcript level determined by reverse transcriptase PCR on days 7, 14, 28, and 75 in comparison with paired F344 host hearts, day-0 hearts, and syngrafts. Transcript levels in cardiac allografts were elevated compared with those in paired host spleens (a major source of inflammatory cells), indicating the localized nature of induction of the lectin. By *in situ* hybridization and immunostaining, the lectin expression was found to be localized to a subset of inflammatory cells in cardiac allografts. The data associated the macrophage lectin with the chronic rejection process, as a possible mediator of macrophage infiltration (Russell et al., 1994).

Clinical Xenotransplantation

Clinical xenotransplantation is not feasible because humans produce antibodies that recognize antigens on the surface of pig cells. Galα-1,3-Gal (Gal) and N-glycolylneuraminic acid (Neu5Gc) are two xenoantigens. Homozygous disruption of the α1, 3-galactosyltransferase (GGTA1) and the cytidine monophosphate-N-acetylneuraminic acid hydroxylase (CMAH) genes in liver-derived female pig cells was achieved using zinc-finger nucleases. Somatic cell nuclear transfer was employed to produce healthy cloned piglets from the genetically modified hepatocytes. Antibody-binding and antibody-mediated complement-dependent cytotoxicity assays were utilized to investigate the immunoreactivity of pig cells lacking in Neu5Gc and Gal. This approach facilitated rapid production of a pig strain deficient in multiple genes without extensive breeding protocols. Immune recognition studies showed that pigs lacking both CMAH and GGTA1 gene activities exhibited a reduced humoral barrier to xenotransplantation, further than pigs lacking only GGTA1. This technology will accelerate the development of pigs for xenotransplantation research (Lutz et al., 2013).

Conclusion

Galactose exerts a number of effects with an adverse impact on health. It accelerates aging, causes retinopathy and cataracts, and is toxic to the ovary. The toxic effects of galactose are apparent in the various clinical manifestations of galactosemia.

References

Aguer, C; Gambarotta, D; Mailloux, RJ; Moffat, C; Dent, R; McPherson, R; Harper, ME. Galactose enhances oxidative metabolism and reveals mitochondrial dysfunction in human primary muscle cells. *PLoS One*. 2011, 6(12), e28536.

Al-Lawati, T; Vargees, T. Glucose galactose malabsorption complicated with rickets and nephrogenic diabetes insipidus. *Oman Med J*., 2008, 23(3), 197-8.

Aydın, S; Yanar, K; Atukeren, P; Dalo, E; Sitar, ME; Uslu, E; Caf, N; Cakatay U. Comparison of oxidative stress biomarkers in renal tissues of D-galactose induced, naturally aged and young rats. *Biogerontology*. 2012, 13(3), 251-60.

Bowling, FG; Fraser, DK; Clague, AE; Hayes, A; Morris, DJ. A case of uridine diphosphate galactose-4-epimerase deficiency detected by neonatal screening for galactosaemia. *Med J Aust*. 1986, 44(3), 150-1.

Brunetti-Pierri, N; Opekun, AR; Craigen, WJ. Two familial cases of high blood galactose of unknown aetiology. *J Inherit Metab Dis*. 2006, 29(6), 762.

Caspers-Velu, LE; Wadhwani, KC; Rapoport, SI; Kador, PF. Iris vasculopathy in galactose-fed rats. *Exp Eye Res*. 1999, 68(2), 211-21.

Commins, SP; Platts-Mills, TA. Allergenicity of carbohydrates and their role in anaphylactic events. *Curr Allergy Asthma Rep*. 2010, 10(1), 29-33.

Commins, SP; Platts-Mills, TA. Delayed anaphylaxis to red meat in patients with IgE specific for galactose alpha-1,3-galactose (alpha-gal). *Curr Allergy Asthma Rep*. 2013, 13(1), 72-7.

Commins, SP; Satinover, SM; Hosen, J; Mozena, J; Borish, L; Lewis, BD; Woodfolk, JA; Platts-Mills, TA. Delayed anaphylaxis, angioedema, or urticaria after consumption of red meat in patients with IgE antibodies specific for galactose-alpha-1,3-galactose. *J Allergy Clin Immunol*. 2009, 123(2), 426-33.

Berg, EA; Platts-Mills, TA; Commins, SP. Drug allergens and food-the cetuximab and galactose-α-1,3-galactose story. *Ann Allergy Asthma Immunol*. 2014, 112(2), 97-101.

Platts-Mills, TA; Commins, SP. Emerging antigens involved in allergic responses. *Curr Opin Imunol*. 2013, 25(6), 769-74.

Commins, SP; Platts-Mills, TA. Tick bites and red meat allergy. *Curr Opin Allergy Clin Immunol*. 2013, 13(4), 354-9.

Commins, SP; Kelly, LA; Rönmark, E; James, HR; Pochan, SL; Peters, EJ; Lundbäck, B; Nganga, LW; Cooper, PJ; Hoskins, JM; Eapen, SS; Matos, LA; McBride, DC; Heymann, PW; Woodfolk, JA; Perzanowski, MS; Platts-Mills, TA. Galactose-α-1, 3-galactose-specific IgE is associated with anhylaxis but not asthma. *Am J Respir Crit Care Med*. 2012, 185(7), 723-30.

Commins, SP; James, HR; Kelly, LA; Pochan, SL; Workman, LJ; Perzanowski, MS; Kocan, KM; Fahy, JV; Nganga, LW; Ronmark, E; Cooper, PJ; Platts-Mills, TA. The relevance of tick bites to the production of IgE antibodies to the mammalian oligosaccharide galactose-α-1,3-galactose. *J Allergy Clin Immunol*. 2011, 127(5), 1286-93.

Cusick, M; Chew, EY; Ferris, F, 3rd; Cox, TA; Chan, CC; Kador, PF. Effects of aldose reductase inhibitors and galactose withdrawal on fluorescein angiographic lesions in galactose-fed dogs. *Arch Ophthalmol*. 2003, 121(12), 1745-51

Dixit, H; Rao, L; Padmalatha, V; Raseswari, T; Kapu, AK; Panda, B; Murthy, K; Tosh, D; Nallari, P; Deenadayal, M; Gupta, N; Chakrabarthy, B; Singh, L. Genes governing premature ovarian failure. *Reprod Biomed Online*. 2010, 20(6), 724-40.

Dunston, CR; Choudhury, K; Griffiths, HR. Terminal galactose residues onmtransferrin are increased in midlife adults compared to young adults. *Proteomics*. 2012, 12(21), 3147-53.

Fung, WL; Risch, H; McLaughlin, J; Rosen, B; Cole, D; Vesprini, D; Narod SA. The N314D polymorphism of galactose-1-phosphate uridyl transferase does not modify the risk of ovarian cancer. *Cancer Epidemiol Biomarkers Prev*. 2003,12(7), 678-80.

Galili, U; Anaraki, F. alpha-galactosyl (Galalpha1-3Galbeta1-4GlcNAc-R) epitopes on human cells: synthesis of the epitope on human red cells by recombinant primate alpha1, 3galactosyltransferase expressed in *E.coli*.Glycobiology. 1995, 5(8), 775-

Hammersen, G; Levy, HL. Starch gel electrophoresis for galactose-1-phosphate uridylyl-transferase applied to dried filter paper blood specimens. *Clin Chim Acta*. 1977, 77(3), 295-9.

Hartnett, C; Kim, HO; Scaman, CH. Effect of processing on galactose in selected fruits. *Can J Diet Pract Res*. 2007, 68(1), 46-50.

Henderson, MJ; Holton, JB; MacFaul, R. Further observations in a case of uridine diphosphate galactose-4-epimerase deficiency with a severe clinical presentation. *J Inherit Metab Dis*. 1983, 6(1), 17-20.

Herrinton, LJ; Weiss, NS; Beresford, SA; Stanford, JL; Wolfla, DM; Feng, Z; Scott, CR. Lactose and galactose intake and metabolism in relation to the risk of epithelial ovarian cancer. *Am J Epidemiol*. 1995, 141(5), 407-16.

Hodes, BL; Schietroma, JM; Lane, SS; Sadeghi, J; Cunningham, D; Stambolian, D. Macular deposits in galactokinase deficiency. *Metab Pediatr Syst Ophthalmol*. 1985, 8(2-3), 39-42.

Hoffmann, B; Dragano, N; Schweitzer-Krantz, S. Living situation, occupation and health-related quality of life in adult patients with classic galactosemia. *J Inherit Metab Dis*. 2012, 35(6), 1051-8.

Huang, CC; Chiang, WD; Huang, WC; Huang, CY; Hsu, MC; Lin, WT. Hepatoprotective effects of swimming exercise against D-galactose-induced senescence rat model. *Evid Based Complement Alternat Med*. 2013, 2013, 275431.

Huang, SN; Zhu, HT; Zhang, YJ; Xue, XQ; Qiu, YH. The changes of spleen B cells of D-galactose-induced aging mice. *Xi Bao Yu Fen Zi Mian Yi Xue Za Zhi*. 2012, 28(2), 133-6.

Kennedy, JL; Stallings, AP; Platts-Mills, TA; Oliveira, WM; Workman, L; James, HR; Tripathi, A; Lane, CJ; Matos, L; Heymann, PW; Commins, SP. Galactose-α-1,3-galactose and delayed anaphylaxis, angioedema, and urticaria in children. *Pediatrics*. 2013, 131(5), e1545-52.

Huang, Y; Su, Z; Li, Y; Zhang, Q; Cui, L; Su, Y; Ding, C; Zhang, M; Feng, C; Tan, Y; Feng, W; Li, X; Cai, L. Expression and purification of glutathione transferase-small ubiquitin-related modifier-metallothionein fusion protein and its neuronal and hepatic protection against D-galactose- induced oxidative damage in mouse model. *J Pharmacol Exp Ther*. 2009, 329(2), 469-78.

Imokawa, M; Okabe, H; Ochi, Y; Kajita, Y. Clinical significance of mucin-like high molecular weight glycoprotein originated from lung cancer as tumor marker. *Clin Chim Acta*. 1989, 180(1), 45-58.

Kador, PF; Blessing, K; Randazzo, J; Makita, J; Wyman, M. Evaluation of the vascular targeting agent combretastatin a-4 prodrug on retinal neovascularization in the galactose-fed dog. *J Ocul Pharmacol Ther*. 2007, 23(2), 132-42.

Kador, PF; Takahashi, Y; Wyman, M; Ferris, F 3rd. Diabeteslike proliferative retinal changes in galactose-fed dogs. *Arch Ophthalmol*. 1995, 113(3), 352-4.

Kador, PF; Takahashi, Y; Akagi, Y; Blessing, K; Randazzo, J; Wyman, M. Age-dependent retinal capillary pericyte degeneration in galactose-fed dogs. *J Ocul Pharmacol Ther*. 2007, 23(1), 63-9.

Kador, PF; Takahashi, Y; Akagi, Y; Neuenschwander, H; Greentree, W; Lackner, P; Blessing, K; Wyman, M. Effect of galactose diet removal on the progression of retinal vessel changes in galactose-fed dogs. *Invest Ophthalmol Vis Sci*. 2002, 43(6), 1916-21.

Lutz, AJ; Li, P; Estrada, JL; Sidner, RA; Chihara, RK; Downey, SM; Burlak, C; Wang, ZY; Reyes, LM; Ivary, B; Yin, F; Blankenship, RL; Paris, LL; Tector, AJ. Double knockout pigs deficient in N-glycolylneuraminic acid and galactose α-1,3-galactose reduce the humoral barrier to xenotransplantation. *Xenotransplantation*. 2013, 20(1), 27-35.

Kim, HO; Hartnett, C; Scaman, CH. Free galactose content in selected fresh fruits and vegetables and soy beverages. *J Agric Food Chem*. 2007, 55(20), 8133-7.

Köttgen, E; Bauer, C; Reutter, W; Gerok, W. Glycoproteins: their biological and clinical significance. Klin Wochenschr. 1979, 57(4), 151-9.

Lackner, PA; Rodriguez, L; Sato, S; Lizak, MJ; Wyman, M; Kador, PF. Age-dependent lens changes in galactose-fed dogs. *Exp Eye Res*. 1997, 64(3), 431-6.

Robison, WG Jr; Jacot, JL; Glover, JP; Basso, MD; Hohman, TC. Diabetic-like retinopathy: early and late intervention therapies in galactose-fed rats. Invest Ophthalmol Vis Sci. 1998, 39 (10), 1933-41.

Levin, S; Russell, EC; Blanchard, D; McWilliams, NB; Maurer, HM; Mohanakumar, T. Receptors for peanut agglutinin (*Arachus hypogea*) in childhood acute lymphoblastic leukemia: possible clinical significance. Blood. 1980, 55(1), 37-9.

Liu, G; Hale, GE; Hughes, CL. Galactose metabolism and ovarian toxicity. *Reprod Toxicol.* 2000, 14(5), 377-84.

Liu, HM; Takagaki, K; Schmid, K. *In vitro* nerve-growth-promoting activity of human plasma alpha 1-acid glycoprotein. *J Neurosci Res.* 1988, 20(1), 64-72.

Lutz, AJ; Li, P; Estrada, JL; Sidner, RA; Chihara, RK; Downey, SM; Burlak, C; Wang, ZY; Reyes, LM; Ivary, B; Yin, F; Blankenship, RL; Paris, LL; Tector AJ. Double knockout pigs deficient in N-glycolylneuraminic acid and Galactose α-1,3-Galactose reduce the humoral barrier to xenotransplantation. *Xenotransplantation.* 2013, 20(1), 27-35.

Merritt, MA; Kotsopoulos, J; Cramer, DW; Hankinson, SE; Terry, KL; Tworoger, SS. Duarte galactose-1-phosphate uridyl transferase genotypes are not associated with ovarian cancer risk. *Fertil Steril.* 2012, 98(3), 687-91.

Moriwaki, K; Miyoshi, E. Fucosylation and gastrointestinal cancer. *World J Hepatol.* 2010, 2(4), 151-61.

Mullins, RJ; James, H; Platts-Mills, TA; Commins S. Relationship between red meat allergy and sensitization to gelatin and galactose-α-1,3-galactose. *J Allergy Clin Immunol.* 2012, 129(5), 1334-1342.

Murata, M; Ohta, N; Fujisawa, S; Tsai, JY; Sato, S; Akagi, Y; Takahashi, Y; Neuenschwander, H; Kador, PF. Selective pericyte degeneration in the retinal capillaries of galactose-fed dogs results from apoptosis linked to aldose reductase-catalyzed galactitol accumulation. *J Diabetes Complications.* 2002, 16(5), 363-70.

Neuenschwander, H; Julia, C; Wyman, M; Kador, PF. Endothelial changes in galactose-fed dogs. *Curr Eye Res.* 1995, 14(4), 319-22.

Okayasu, T; Nagano, S; Takada, K; Tomita, M; Arashima, S; Matsumoto, S. Cytotoxicity of galactose, tyrosine and methionine in cultured suckling rat hepatocytes: relation to liver immaturity. *Acta Paediatr Scand.* 1989, 78(6), 930-4.

Ohta, Y; Yamasaki, T; Niwa, T; Majima, Y. Preventive effect of vitamin E-containing liposome instillation on cataract progression in 12-month-old rats fed a 25% galactose diet. *J Ocul Pharmacol Ther.* 2000, 16(4), 323-35.

Ohta, N; Tsai, JY; Secchi, EF; Kador, PF; Sato, S. Neutrophils in galactose-fed dogs: suppressed apoptosis and increased adhesion to retinal capillary endothelial cells. *J Diabetes Complications.* 1999, 13(3), 151-8.

Openo, KK; Schulz, JM; Vargas, CA; Orton, CS; Epstein, MP; Schnur, RE; Scaglia, F; Berry, GT; Gottesman, GS; Ficicioglu, C; Slonim, AE; Schroer, RJ; Yu, C; Rangel, VE; Keenan, J; Lamance, K; Fridovich-Keil JL. Epimerase-deficiency galactosemia is not a binary condition. *Am J Hum Genet*. 2006, 78(1), 89-102.

Pesce, MA; Bodourian, SH. Clinical significance of plasma galactose and erythrocyte galactose-1-phosphate measurements in transferase-deficient galactosemia and in individuals with below-normal transferase activity. *Clin Chem*. 1982, 28(2), 301-5.

Play, B; Salvini, S; Haikal, Z; Charbonnier, M; Harbis, A; Roussel, M; Lairon, D; Jourdheuil-Rahmani, D. Glucose and galactose regulate intestinal absorption of cholesterol. *Biochem Biophys Res Commun*. 2003, 310(2), 446-51.

Prakash, A; Kumar, A. Pioglitazone alleviates mitochondrial apoptotic pathway and mito-oxidative damage in the D-galactose-induced mouse model. *Clin Exp Pharmacol Physiol*. 2013 Jun 25. [Epub ahead ofprint].8(1), 89-102.

Qin, J; Zhang, Q; Fang, X. Clinical significance of galactose oxidase-Schiff reaction in the detection of carcinoma and precancerous lesions of large intestine. *Zhonghua Zhong Liu Za Zhi*. 1997, 19(2), 157-9.

Rhodes, JM; Campbell, BJ; Yu, LG. Lectin-epithelial interactions in the human colon. Biochem Soc Trans. 2008, 36(Pt 6), 1482-6.

Robison, WG, Jr; Laver, NM; Jacot, JL; Glover, JP. Sorbinil prevention of diabetic-like retinopathy in the galactose-fed rat model. *Invest Ophthalmol VisSci*. 1995, 36(12), 2368-80.

Russell, ME; Utans, U; Wallace, AF; Liang, P; Arceci, RJ; Karnovsky, MJ; Wyner, LR; Yamashita, Y; Tarn, C. Identification and upregulation of galactose/N-acetylgalactosamine macrophage lectin in rat cardiac allografts with arteriosclerosis. *J Clin Invest*. 1994, 94(2), 722-30.

Sabeur, K; Ball, BA. Characterization of galactose-binding proteins in equine testis and spermatozoa. *Anim Reprod Sci*. 2007, 101(1-2), 74-84.

Schoeppner, HL; Raz, A; Ho, SB; Bresalier, RS. Expression of an endogenous galactose-binding lectin correlates with neoplastic progression in the colon. *Cancer*. 1995, 75(12), 2818-26.

Schulpis, KH; Karikas, GA; Bartzeliotou, A; Papakonstantinou, ED; Kalogerakou, M; Tsakiris, S. The effect of diet on Paraoxonase 1/Arylesterase activities in patients with disorders of galactose metabolism. *Clin Endocrinol (Oxf)*. 2007, 67(5), 687-92.

Shida, K; Misonou, Y; Korekane, H; Seki, Y; Noura, S; Ohue, M; Honke, K; Miyamoto, Y. Unusual accumulation of sulfated glycosphingolipids in colon cancer cells. *Glycobiology*. 2009, 19(9), 1018-33.

Shreeve, WW. Impaired oxidation of carbon-labeled galactose by alcoholic or diabetic liver in vivo. *Nuklearmedizin*. 1987, 26(4), 159-66.

Shu, X; Li, Y; Yan, W; Zhou, Y. Anti-oxidative effects of proanthocyanidins in mice induced by D-galactose. *Wei Sheng Yan Jiu*. 2002, 31(3), 191-2, 196.

Singh, R; Thapa, BR; Kaur, G; Prasad, R. Biochemical and molecular characterization of GALT gene from Indian galactosemia patients: identification of 10 novel mutations and their structural and functional implications. *Clin Chim Acta*. 2012, 414, 191-6.

Tötterman, TH; Forsbeck, K; Nilsson, K; Simonsson, B; Sundström, C; Sällström, J. Surface glycoprotein patterns of B type chronic lymphocytic leukaemia cells correlate with the clinical activity of the disease. *Scand J Haematol*. 1983, 30(1), 79-88.

Zoli, M; Cordiani, MR; Marchesini, G; Iervese, T; Labate, AM; Bonazzi, C; Bianchi, G; Pisi, E. Prognostic indicators in compensated cirrhosis. *Am J Gastroenterol*. 1991, 86(10), 1508-13.

In: Galactose
Editor: Vitor Hugo Pomin

ISBN: 978-1-63117-928-0

Chapter 3

GALACTOSE: DIET AND ITS IMPLICATION IN GALACTOSEMIA

Ana C. Ribeiro*[*]*, Maria J. Silva and Maria E. Figueira
Faculty of Pharmacy, University of Lisbon, Lisboa, Portugal

ABSTRACT

The aim of this chapter is to provide an update on recent developments in the field of Galactosemia and offer new perspectives into the as yet unknown.

Galactose is an energy-providing nutrient and also a basic substrate needed for the biosynthesis of many molecules in the body, where it forms part of glycolipids and glycoproteins in several tissues. Galactose is found in dairy products, sugar beets, and others gums and mucilage but also in some meats, vegetables and fruits, but in lesser amount. It is a monosaccharide which when combined with glucose, through a dehydration process, results in lactose, the prominent sugar in milk.

The liver plays an essential role in the metabolism of galactose. Diet derived carbohydrates, as disaccharides or polysaccharides, are broken down into simpler monosaccharides, which reach the liver via the portal blood system. The primary sugars in newborns and infants are derived from the breakdown of the disaccharide lactose in milk; lactose is broken down to glucose and galactose and when it reaches the hepatocytes, galactose is converted to glucose by a series of enzymatic reactions.

[*] acribeiro@ff.ul.pt.

Galactosemia is a relatively rare inherited enzyme deficiency with variable worldwide incidence. The deleterious potential of ingested galactose results from a defect in the galactose metabolic pathway, the Leloir pathway, which consists of three enzymes: galactose specific kinase (Galactokinase/GALK), galactose-1-phosphate uridyltransferase (GALT) and uridine diphosphate galactose - 4´- epimerase (GALE).

The most common cause of failure to convert galactose to glucose results from the deficit of galactose-1-P-uridyltransferase (GALT), the second enzyme of the pivotal Leloir pathway, and is known as classical galactosemia (OMIM 230400), a severe genetic disease of the newborns, an autosomal recessive condition that results in an acute toxicity syndrome. In this disease, galactose-1-phosphate accumulates inside hepatocytes causing a rapid liver failure with all its common associated symptoms: nausea, vomiting, hepatomegaly, jaundice, hypoglycemia and cataract. The clinical significance of establishing a diagnosis is clear: galactosemia could be fatal if undiagnosed. However, the treatment that consists in a severe restriction of dietary lactose/galactose and is considered life-saving, is not fully effective since long term follow-up of patients has shown that they may develop chronic complications, such as retardation and mental underdevelopment, verbal dyspraxia, motor abnormalities, and in young women hypergonadotrophic hypogonadism and premature ovarian failure.

Introduction

What Is Galactosemia?

Glucose is the primary metabolic fuel for humans and most other species. Hence, all the sugars from the diet, especially lactose and sucrose, are hydrolyzed by intestinal disaccharidases and reach the liver, via portal vein, where the absorbed monosaccharides (galactose and fructose) are converted into glucose.

Galactose metabolism occurs through an evolutionarily conserved pathway, known as the Leloir Pathway, in which galactose (Gal) and uridine diphosphoglucose (UDP-Glc) are converted to glucose-1-phosphate (Glc-1-P) and uridine diphosphogalactose (UDP-Gal) through the action of three sequential enzymes: galactokinase (GALK, EC 2.7.1.6), which phosphorylates α-D-galactose to produce galactose-1-phosphate (Gal-1-P); galactose-1-phosphate uridylyltransferase (GALT, EC 2.7.7.12), which transfers a uridine monophosphate group (UMP) from UDP-glucose to Gal-1-P, thereby releasing Glc-1-P and forming UDP-Gal; uridine phosphogalactose 4-epimerase

(GALE, EC 5.1.3.2), which interconverts UDP-Gal and UDP-Glc (Figure 1). Additionally, and before the any other metabolic transformation, β-D-galactose is firstly epimerized to α-D-galactose through the action of galactose mutarotase (GALM, EC 5.1.3.3) (Figure 1).

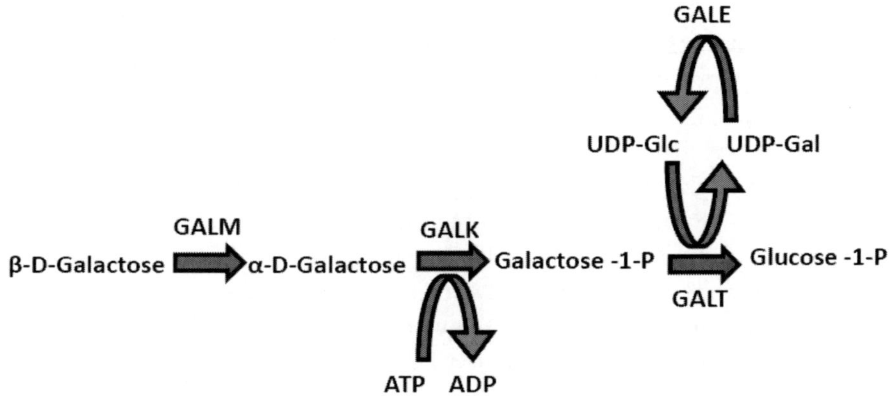

Figure 1. Leloir pathway; GALM: galactose mutarotase, GALK: galactokinase, GALT: galactose-1-phosphate uridylyltransferase, GALE: uridinephosphogalactose-4-epimerase.

The impairment of one of these enzymes results in what is known as galactosemia, which may be classified as type I, II and III.

GALT IMPAIRMENT

Galactosemia Type I or Classical Galactosemia (OMIM 230400)

Galactosemia type I is an autosomal recessive disorder of galactose metabolism, being the most common and the most severe form of galactosemia and is caused by deficiency of the GALT enzyme.

The reported frequencies of GALT deficiency galactosemia vary enormously in different populations throughout the world and range from 1 in 30,000–40,000 in European countries where neonatal screening is undertaken [1] to 1 in 1,000,000 in Japan [2,3].

Most patients present severe neonatal symptoms after ingestion of galactose, such as failure to thrive, hepatomegaly, jaundice, hepatosplenomegaly, hepatocellular insufficiency, intolerance to food, hypoglycaemia, renal tubular dysfunction, muscle hypotonia, bacterial sepsis, cataract that, if undiagnosed, can result in death.

GALT deficiency results in the accumulation of galactose and galactose derivatives, such as galactitol, galactonate, and Gal-1-P in the blood and/or tissues [4,5], and its excretion in the urine [6-8]. Besides the accumulation in erythrocytes, Gal-1-P can be elevated in liver, kidney, brain, tongue, adrenal, heart [9], ocular lens [10] and cultured skin fibroblasts [8,11] . It is important to note two reported cases [11,12] in which the Gal-1-P levels were augmented prior to birth.

The blood reference concentration for GALT in the newborn population is approximately in the range of 150-500μmol/L. A GALT value ≤ 32 μmol/L is typical in GALT-deficiency galactosemia, whereas GALT activity value of 41-120 μmol/L is common with clinically benign mutation [13].

When a severe GALT deficiency occurs, a marked elevation of galactose-1-phosphate in target tissues and a severe hipergalactosemia due to lactose ingestion is observed. A case reported by Berry [14] illustrates how critical can be an acute neonatal toxicity in infants with absent GALT activity. Galactose related metabolites are markedly elevated: erythrocyte galactose-1-phosphate level of 1307 μmol/L (NV<38 μmol/L), plasma galactitol level of 407 μmol/L (NV<1.0 μmol/L) and urine galactitol level was 4754 μmol/mmol creatinine (2≥NV ≤78 μmol/mmol creatinine for infants of one year of age). Associated with the anomalous biochemical parameters, the infant exhibited encephalopathy with consistent alterations identified with brain magnetic resonance imaging.

Two major hypothesis have been postulated in order to understand the potentially toxic effect of high levels of Gal-1-P: *i*) elevated levels of Gal-1-P could lead to useless phosphorylation reactions in which ATP is trapped in Gal-1-P, which then may be dephosphorylated to metabolites that have no energy-generating capability [15-18]; *ii*) the accumulation of Gal-1-P might inhibit essential glucose-metabolizing enzymes such as, glucose-6-phosphatase, glucose-6-phosphate dehydrogenase, phosphoglucomutase, glycogen phosphorylase, and/or UDP-Glc-pyrophosphorylase [19], all leading to changes in glucose pathways mainly with regard to energetic metabolism [8]. Additionally, it was reported that high concentrations of Gal-1-P inhibit galactosyl transferase, which could at least in part explain the glycosylation defects associated with classic galactosemia [20] and, more recently, the possible ability of Gal-1-P in inhibiting the function of inositol monophosphatase [21-24] affecting inositol production or metabolism in brain and other organs. However, other studies [25,26] that demonstrated the absence of a correlation between blood Gal-1-P and cognitive outcome in patients, led to the hypothesis of having a spectrum of Gal-1-P toxicity that may occur early in utero [8].

Concerning of the levels and ratios of UDP-Gal and UDP-Glc in patients with classic galactosemia, some authors claim that the levels of these sugar nucleotides are abnormally low in patients, whereas other reports argue the opposite [8].

Despite the controversial data, it is relevant to realize the change of UDP-Gal and UDP-Glc levels or ratios is an important question because both serve as key donors for the biosynthesis of glycoproteins and glycolipids. In this way, some authors [27] have postulated that abnormally low levels of UDP-Gal, in GALT patients, could preclude the galactosylation of cerebrosides in the brain by the blockage of cerebroside galactosyl transferase, the enzyme responsible for that metabolic step [8].

GALK IMPAIRMENT

Galactosemia Type II (OMIM 230200)

Partial to complete deficiency of GALK activity, or Galactosemia type II, is considered a rare autosomal recessive condition. However, the incidence of GALK deficiency vary by study and location, since a population-based study in the United States detected a frequency of approximately 1 in 1 million live births [28], whereas individuals of Romani descent in Europe demonstrate a frequency closer to 1 in 10,000 live births [8,29]. The only consistent clinical finding in GALK deficiency is the presence of bilateral cataracts, that have been reported by several authors [8] and for the first time by Gitzelmann in 1965 [30] in a GALK-deficient children as young as 4 weeks of age [31]. Other clinical symptoms have been described, such as mental retardation [32], macular deposits [33] and seizures with neurologic deterioration [34], but it could be coincidental. Since *pseudotumor cerebri*, that has been reported in more than one infant [35,36], has been postulated to occur by the same mechanism responsible for cataract formation [37] it could be, also, a possible but rare complication of GALK deficiency.

Patients with GALK deficiency, who are exposed to significant levels of environmental galactose, accumulate markedly elevated levels of galactitol in the blood, urine and brain [38]. Additionally and consequently, in GALK deficiency there is no elevation of Gal-1-P regardless of the diet [8].

GALE IMPAIRMENT

Galactosemia Type III (OMIM 230350)

Galactosemia type III, is the rarest form of these disorders. It results from the impairment of the third and final enzyme of the Leloir pathway, GALE, which functions as a homodimer to catalyze the interconversion of UDP-Gal and UDP-Glc.

GALE is a very important enzyme for the fact that it also allows the endogenous synthesis of UDP-Gal in the absence of exogenous sources of galactose, contributing to the endogenous galactose pool. Additionally, human GALE also catalyzes the interconversion of UDP-N-acetylgalactosamine (UDP-GalNAc), UDP-*N*-acetylglucosamine (UDP-GlcNAc) [39-41] and, as mentioned before, UDP-Gal and UDP-Glc, are essential substrates for the biosynthesis of glycoproteins and glycolipids in humans [8,20,42].

Epimerase deficiency galactosemia may comprise three forms: generalized, peripheral and intermediate; the first is characterized by a dramatically decreased in enzyme activity and a rise on Gal-1-P levels in all tissues tested [43, 44]; the benign peripheral form presents activity deficiency in red blood cells and circulating white blood cells, but normal or near normal in all other tissues; in the last one, enzyme activity is deficient in red blood cells and circulating white blood cells and less than 50% of normal levels in other cells, biochemical findings between those of the mild and severe forms [45,46]. The clinical findings, in children with deep generalized form who are on a regular milk diet, includes hypotonia, poor feeding, vomiting, weight loss, jaundice, hepatomegaly, liver dysfunction, aminoaciduria, and cataracts. On the contrary, infants with the peripheral or intermediate form generally remain clinically well even on a regular milk diet and are usually only identified by biochemical testing.

The major biochemical findings concerning peripheral, intermediate or generalized GALE deficiency are the accumulation of UDP-Gal and Gal-1-P in red blood cells, and an increase of galactitol plasmatic levels [47-51], which are associated to clinical symptoms as mentioned above.

Although the Leloir pathway is clearly the predominant route for galactose metabolism, several authors, namely the studies reported by Berry et col. [52,53], Ning et col. [54,55] and Yager et col. [56], provided strong evidences concerning a number of alternate pathways for the catabolism of galactose.

Alternative Pathways of Galactose Metabolism

There are three most important alternative pathways.

a) The reduction of galactose to galactitol (occuring with the accumulation of galactose in the blood or tissues of patients with galactosemia), makes galactitol a substrate for the enzymes that catalyze the first stage of the so-called polyol pathway of carbohydrate metabolism [57,58]. Although, this first reaction in this pathway may be catalyzed by either of two enzymes, aldose reductase (polyol NADP+ oxidoreductase, EC 1.1.1.21) or L-hexonate dehydrogenase (L-glucuronate: NADP+ oxidoreductase, EC 1.1.1.19). All current data point toward aldose reductase as the enzyme principally responsible for the direct reduction of galactose in mammals [8].

The fact that galactitol is not a substrate for the subsequent enzyme in the polyol pathway, causes a subsequent accumulation in tissues and/or excretion in the urine. However, this metabolic step does not seem to offer a significant form to eliminate galactose in the absence of GALT, being significant to galactosemic patients because of the negative clinical consequences attributed to galactitol accumulation, namely cataracts [8].

b) The oxidation of galactose to galactonate is another alternative route for galactose metabolization that has been identified by several authors [6,7,59-62]. However, how the reaction exactly takes place remains a controversial issue, but it is believed that the reaction reflects the activity of a soluble NAD^+-dependent galactose dehydrogenase (D-galactose: NAD^+ oxidoreductase, EC 1.1.1.48) that converts D-galactose to D-galactonolactone, which then spontaneously or enzymatically converts to galactonate, that may be further metabolized via the reactions of the pentose phosphate pathway [8].

c) The 'Pyrophosphorylase Pathway' (UGP) is believed to operate both as a GALT-independent bypass pathway for the conversion of Gal-1-P to UDP-Gal and also in the reverse direction (involving UGP, GALE, UGP again, and IMPase) to enable the endogenous synthesis of galactose from Glc-1-P and UTP, having been proposed as an explanation for the perceived ability of some patients with classic galactosemia to tolerate more dietary [63]. It has been referred that the pyrophosphorylase pathway can metabolize galactose at a rate of only about 1 percent of that of the Leloir pathway [64]. Nevertheless, in galactosemic patients who do not present a functional GALT enzyme, this small number may become significant [8].

The proposed pyrophosphorylase route (a GALT-bypass pathway) involves three different enzymes, consisting of four steps. The first, involves the phosphorylation of α-D-galactose by GALK to form Gal-1-P. Thereafter, a UTP-dependent glucose/galactose pyrophosphorylase (UGP), (EC 2.7.7.10), catalyzes the production of UDP-Gal (and PPi) from Gal-1-P and UTP. In the third step, occurs the conversion of UDP-Gal to UDP-Glc by GALE, and finally, UDP-Glc is recombined with PPi by the reversible UGP to generate Glc-1-P and UTP (Figure 2).

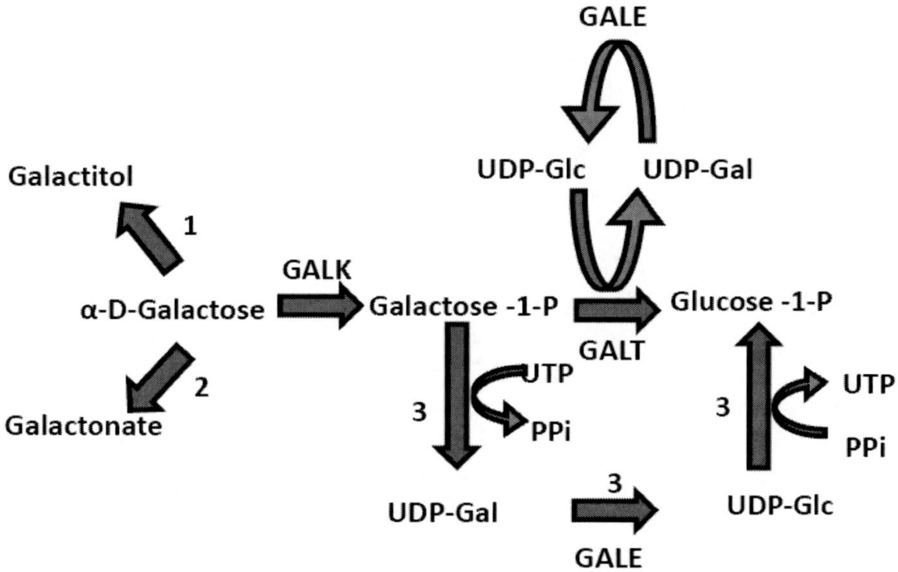

Figure 2. Leloir and alternative pathways: GALK: galactokinase, GALT: galactose-1-phosphate uridylyltransferase, GALE: uridinephosphogalactose-4-epimerase; UGP: UTP-dependent glucose/galactose pyrophosphorylase; 1: production of galactitol by aldose reductase; 2: production of galactonate by penthose phosphate pathway; 3: pyrophosphorylase pathway.

The metabolic relevance of these different alternative routes can be summarized if one considers that the reduction of galactose to galactitol and the oxidation of galactose to galactonate do not require any of the three Leloir enzymes: GALT, GALK or GALE. Additionally, the fact that some other routes may bypass one of the Leloir enzymes, namely GALT, has been a great deal of interest in patients with classic galactosemia, by the possibility of overcoming the metabolic blockage that results from the absence or impairment of GALT activity [8].

The dietary restriction of galactose produces a rapid clinical improvement in the neonate and infants, with the reversion of all clinical signs listed above. However, posterior findings revealed that this therapeutic approach may origin the development of several and serious consequences such as, neurological and intellectual disabilities, but also ovarian failure.

NATURAL SOURCES OF GALACTOSE AND DIET TO GALACTOSEMIC PATIENTS

Galactose is a monosaccharide epimer of glucose. It is a simple sugar, nonsoluble, and less sweet than glucose but it is considered a nutritive sweetener. Galactose is very important in the formation of lactose, sugar of the milk, because when combined with glucose, through a dehydration reaction, result in the disaccharide lactose. Lactose is produced by the mammary gland. To produce it, glucose is changed into galactose via hexoneogenesis in the animal body. The hydrolysis of lactose to glucose and galactose is catalyzed by the enzyme β-galactosidase (Figure 3).

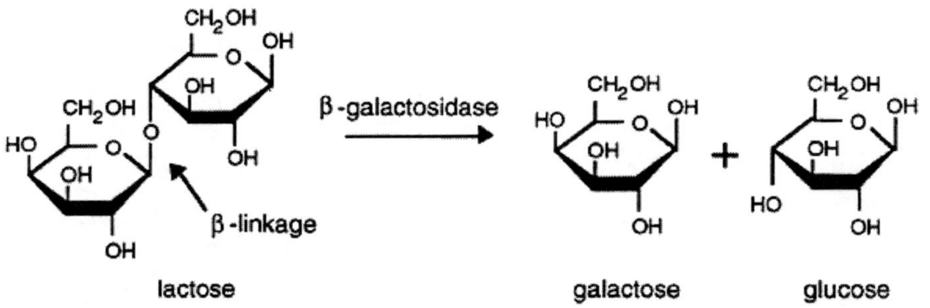

Figure 3. Hydrolyses of lactose.

In nature, galactose occurs in two structurally related forms (anomers), D-galactose and L-galactose. The main source of free galactose is milk and its derivatives, but it can also be found in a bound form in the viscera (brain, kidney, liver and spleen), and in lesser amounts in cereals, legumes (dried beans and peas) and fruit. Milk, yoghurts, hazelnuts and lentils are examples of food with a high galactose content (> 100 mg / 100g food). Papayas, bell peppers, persimmons, tomatoes and watermelons are food with a moderate galactose content (>10 mg /100g of fresh weigh) and cereals and bread without milk, rice and vegetable oils are low-galactose food (<10 mg/100 g food) [65,66].

Although meat is not traditionally thought as a dietary source of carbohydrate, small amounts may be present in free form and/or bound to proteins or lipids [67]. Therefore, it is important to know the amount of galactose in these foods.

In this regard, three types of galactose are found in foods. Free galactose, galactose as a part of lactose and galactose as part of a series of oligosaccharides, in combination with sucrose, sugars found in foods such as beans, nuts and cruciferous vegetables that can only be digested by gut bacteria [68]. Table 1 contemplates foods that contain higher amounts of galactose.

The free galactose content in fruit and vegetables varies with the variety, ripeness, time in storage and the type of processing [72] and, the amount of galactose in fruits and vegetables is much less than what exist in milk or cheese. Fruits and vegetables have 2 – 40 mg galactose/100g, milk has 2000 – 2500 mg/100g and Cheddar cheese 600 mg/100g. All dairy products contain lactose, which include milk, cream, cheese, yogurt and dairy frozen desserts.

Table 1. Food sources with higher concentration in Galactose

Food	Amount of Galactose (mg / 100g)	Food	Amount of Galactose (mg / 100g)
Garbanzo bean	443 b)	Tomato	5.6 e) – 13.3 c)
Kidney	153 b)	Pear	7.3 a)
Bean green	5.5 e)	Strawberry	4.6 f) – 10.7 e)
lentil	115.8 b)	Potato	1.2 a) – 10.7 e)
Soybean	44 b), g)	Banana	9.2 a)
Pea	11.8 e)	Brussels sprouts	9.2 a), d)
Watermelon	14.7 a)	Apple	8.3 a), d)
Papaya	28.6 a)	Lettuce	3.1 a) – 7.8 e)
Kiwi	9.8 a) – 27.1 e)	Broccoli	6.8 a)
Blueberry	26.2 c)	Carrot	6,2 a)
Pineapple	18.7 c)	Peach	5.5 b)
Onion	5.1 a) – 15.3 e)	Soy protein isolate	1.3 e)

a) [69]; b) [65]; c) [66]; d) [70]; e) [71]; f) [72]; g) [73].

The body also synthesizes galactose, namely as a constituent of glycolipids and glycoproteins in several tissues.

As already mentioned, patients with galactosemia require a treatment with a galactose-restricted diet (Figure 4). High levels of galactose in the blood are considered the main cause of the serious adverse symptoms associated to galactosemia.

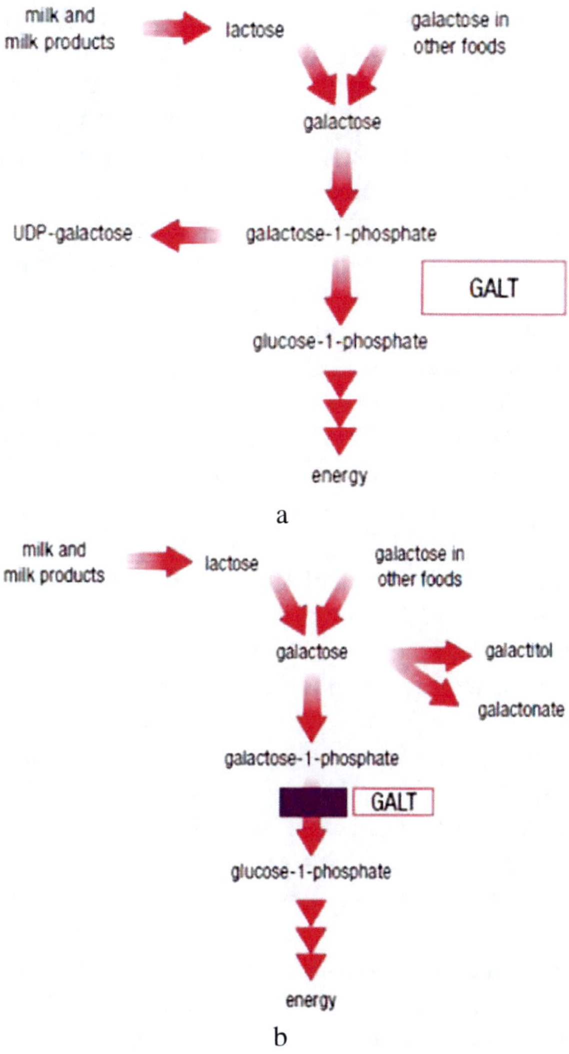

Figure 4. Conversion of galactose in energy. (A) Someone who does not have classical galactosemia. (B) Someone with classical galactosemia.

The disease is characterized by potentially lethal acute symptoms in the neonatal period that can be prevented or reversed through the immediate and rigorous restriction of dietary galactose.

Unfortunately there are no medicines available for the treatment of this condition, so a special diet is used to lower the blood galactose levels. Galactosemia is treated by lifelong galactose restriction that mandates strict avoidance of all milk and milk products and lactose-containing foods because lactose is hydrolyzed into galactose and glucose. Elimination diet is the only known treatment that reverses many of the clinical manifestations of acute phase in patients. In 1935, Mason and Turner [74] reported, for the first time, a study showing the successful use of the milk-free diet in an infant with galactosemia. A galactose-restricted diet free of lactose is lifesaving for galactosemic patients, but even with the use of this diet from the beginning, in early diagnosis, it is always not possible to prevent long-term complications such as the cognitive impairments. Physical and motor development should proceed normally but intellectual achievement may be depressed and ovarian failure is a recognized problem that affects about 95% of women with galactosemia [75]. The majority of patients, as reported in the literature, experience complications that can include cognitive disability, speech problems, neurological and/or movement disorders, and for females, ovarian dysfunction [76]. The dietary intervention alone does not eliminate long-term sequels of the disorder [77]. However early diagnosis of galactosemia and treatment with a galactose-restricted diet is very important since, for instance, cataracts can develop even in the first few weeks of life, making early diagnosis important in the prevention of severe cataracts. Therefore, newborn screening for galactosemia should improve morbidity [78].

Milk, which is rich in lactose, is a forbidden food in patients with galactosemia and therefore breastfeeding is contraindicated in children with this disorder [79]. Over time different strategies to feed this pediatric population with a diet without galactose were discussed. Nowadays, initiating the diet is much easier, since pediatric formulations of diets with a very limited amount of galactose are widely available. Nevertheless dietary treatment of galactosemia is not completely consensus and varies widely around the world [80]. Galactosemia is part of newborn screening programs in most countries. However, before knowing the outcome of the analysis, if babies do not eat well as expected, if they are lethargic and vomit with frequency, it is possible that they have this disorder. The first manifestations occur within the first 2 weeks of life and the symptoms developed a few days after the infant began to drink breast milk or formula, which contains galactose. So, if suspected, even before the results of the test, all galactose must be removed from the diet. After diagnosis, breastfeeding and milk formulation with lactose must be immediately removed and the infant should be fed with a galactose-free formula such as a formula based on hydrolyzed casein and dextrin maltose as carbohydrate source or soya milk. The safety of long-term use of soya milk has been much debated but there is no clinical evidence for its harmful effects

[81]. Although soya milks are typically made from the whole soya bean, which contains galactose, soya formulas are made from soya isolate protein, which has a very small amount of galactose. When transitioning from a milk and porridge base alimentation into the introduction of solid foods, it is almost impossible not to ingest small amounts of galactose, such as the trace amounts of galactose present in fruit and vegetables, bread, legumes, and offal [65].

In chronic treatments, treatment is not consensual and while some require an absolute restriction from any source of galactose, others advocate that the ingestion of small quantities contained in fruits and vegetables is possible but with limitations. In adulthood the treatment should continue, for the rest of their life, with lactose-restricted diet, but it is only natural that there is an increase of tolerance to exogenous galactose with age, because there is less endogenous production of galactose [82]. So, a lactose-restricted diet without limitations in intake of fruit and vegetables, with an increase of daily galactose intake, may be justified [80]. Effective galactose restriction requires careful reading of food product labels. Milk is added to many products, and lactose often appears in the coating of tablets [83]. Lactose is often used as pharmaceutical bulking agent or excipient. So, tablets, vitamin and mineral mixtures should be evaluated carefully for galactose content. Likewise it is necessary to be aware of hidden sources of lactose and galactose, which may exist, e.g. in flour, sausages and sauces [84].

GALACTOSE AND GALACTOSE-1-PHOSPHATE TOXICITY IN HUMANS *VS.* CONGENITAL DISORDERS

Congenital Disorders of Galactose Metabolism

In GALT-deficiency (Classic Galactosemia), galactose and galactose-1-P accumulate in patients, with galactose being further metabolized through two alternative pathways to form galactitol and galactonate [19, 85,86]. Among all the metabolites formed, gal-1-P and galactitol have received most attention. Various reports suggested that in vivo, gal-1-P competitively inhibited UDP-glucose pyrophosphorylase [22,87,88], inositol monophosphatase [22-24], phosphoglucomutase [89], glycogen phosphorylase [90], or even glucose-6-phosphatase [91]. If inhibition of UDP-glucose pyrophosphorylase occurs in vivo, it could potentially reduce UDP-glucose/UDP-galactose formation in the cell that could cause aberrant glycosylation of proteins and lipids. The reduction of of UDP-galactose concentration affects galactosylation to the level of glicolipids and complex glycoproteins. Galactocerebrosides and glucocerebrosides are the primary products of the enzyme UDP-galactose: cerebroside galactosyl transferase (CGT). In classic galactosemia, there is a consistent deficiency in cerebroside galactosylation, justified by an observation of deficient galactosylation coupled with an over glycosylation in the brain tissue specimens sampled from deceased classic galactosemia patients [27]. Yet, UDP-galactose serves as the product of GALT as well as a substrate for CGT. There are also reports showing abnormal circulating proteins, including transferrin (Tf), and follicle stimulating hormone (FSH) in the blood of GALT-deficiency patients with elevated erythrocyte Gal-1-P [92-94]. Because of these findings classic galactosemia has been regarded as a congenital disorder of glycosylation.

1. Glycosylation

Congenital disorders of glycosylation (CDG) are a group of diseases that affect glycoprotein biogenesis and that like much trafficking machinery is well conserved. CDGs can be divided into two groups based on the region of the glycosylation pathway affected [95]. Group I disorders result from defects in the assembly of the dolicholphosphate-linked oligosaccharide precursor [96] in the cytosol and the endoplasmic reticulum (ER) [97-100]. CDG-II disorders arise from defects in the processing of the glycans in the ER and the Golgi [99]. They result in apparently normal levels of glycan site occupancy; however, the glycoproteins contain aberrant glycan structures. Genetic deficiencies in *O*-glycosylation have been reported and in some cases associated with congenital muscular dystrophy. The deficiencies in the biosynthesis of oligosaccharide precursors or specific steps of *N*-glycan assembly, result in the absence or structural alteration of *N*-glycan chains. The low activity of one of the many enzymes, transporters or other functional proteins required in the glycosylation processing pathway are consistent with these diseases [101]. The CDG patients are identified based on clinical symptoms and deficiencies in multiple plasma glycoproteins. Patients had psychomotor retardation, low muscle tone, incomplete brain development, visual problems, coagulation disorders and endocrine abnormalities [102,103]. The common defect identified was the incomplete addition of sialic acid to a proportion of serum transferrin molecules (Tf), group I patients. In most cases, *N*- or *O*-glycosylation structural analysis provided the major clues to resolve the defect.

1.1. The Molecular Basis of Congenital Disorders of Glycosylation of Group I

Glycosylation is an essential process in eukaryotic cells. Many enzymatic activities contribute to the biosynthesis of *N*-linked glycans and deficiencies in this process leads to aberrant glycosylation [67].

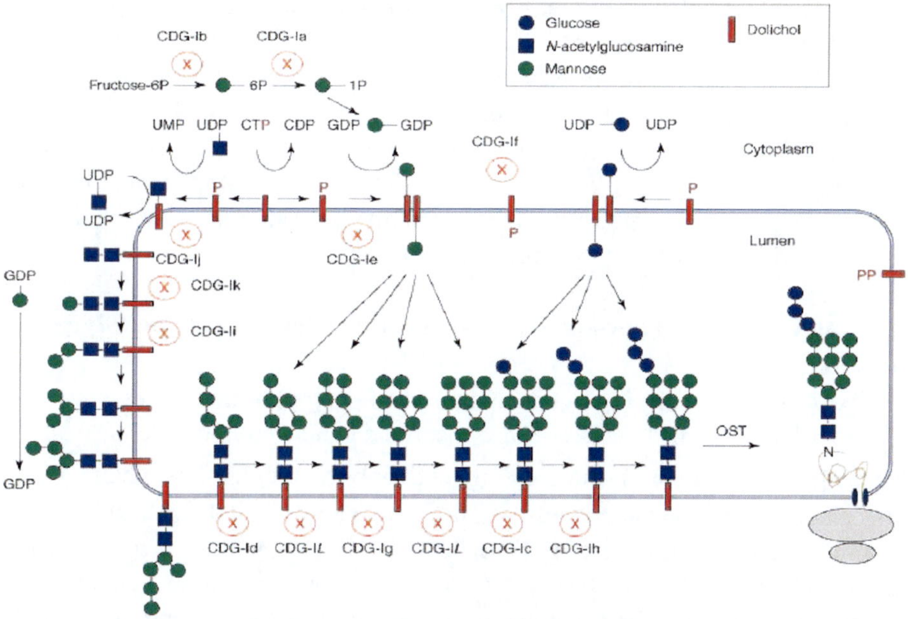

Reprinted from Current Opinion in Structural Biology, vol. 15, Freeze, HH and Aebi, M, Altered glycan structures: the molecular basis of congenital disorders of glycosylation, 490-498, 2005[96], with permission from Elsevier.

Figure 5. The pathway of *N*-linked protein glycosylation in the ER is affected in different forms of CDG type I. The assembly of the oligosaccharide and its transfer to nascent polypeptide chains are shown. This takes place at the membrane of the ER and polyisoprenoid lipid dolichol is used as the lipid anchor for oligosaccharide assembly. The initial steps occur on the cytoplasmic side of the ER membrane. Nucleotide-activated sugars (UDP-GlcNAc and GDP-Man) serve as donors in these reactions. Completion of the Glc3Man9GlcNAc2 oligosaccharide is achieved in the lumen of the ER. Dolichylphosphoglucose and dolichylphosphomannose are the monosaccharide substrates for the glycosyltransferases involved in this part of biosynthesis. Oligosaccharyltransferase (OST), an oligomeric membrane protein complex, catalyzes the transfer of the oligosaccharide to defined asparagine residues (N) of nascent polypeptide chains. CDG type I affects the assembly of the oligosaccharide substrate. The biosynthetic steps affected in the different CDG subtypes are indicated.

An incomplete structural LLO (lipid-linked core oligosaccharide) may result in deficiency in any of the step required for the assembly of LLO in the ER. As the oligosaccharyltransferases has specificity for the complete LLO, this results in hypoglycosylation of glycoproteins. Patients with a deficiency in the ER pathway generally display *N*-glycoproteins that lack, most of them, whole oligosaccharides. Studies concerning LLO assembly steps can be done using mutants defective in LLO assembly, which had been identified primarily in *Saccharomyces cerevisae* and in several mammalian cells [67] (Aebi and Hennet, 2001). This approach was detrimental for tracking the human defects that cause CGG Ic, Id, Ig, Ih, Ii, Ik and IL. Ie, If, Ia, Ib [105], Ie, Ij (Figure 5).

Detailed analysis of the mutation in different CGG type I cases has shown that there is always some residual enzymatic activity. The complete loss of any biosynthetic steps required for the assembly of the Glc3Man9GlcNAc$_2$ oligosaccharide results in embryonic lethality [106].

1.2. Congenital Disorders of Glycosylation of Complex-Type Glycans, Group II

The structural analysis of glycans on serum glycoproteins was essential to solve several group II defects as these disorders can affect multiple classes of glycans [96] (Figure 6). In these disorders a lack of complex-type chains with replacement with monosialylated hybrid chains can occurred, with loss of *N*-acetylglucosaminyl transferase II (GluNAcT-II) enzymatic activity and mutation of MGAT2 gene [105]. This enzyme is important in the synthesis of complex-type glycans chains. Also the loss of both galactose and sialic acid from Tf give a CDG-IId disorders consistent with of the loss ß 1,4-galactosyltransferase enzymatic activity and pathological mutations in ß 1,4-galactosyltransferase. The disorder called a CDG-IIc, also called leukocyte adhesion deficiency type II (LAD-II), was more complex [107,108] and more difficult to detect as Tf sialylation is normal and was not detected by the usual tests.

In these disorders *N*-glycosylation of IgM and *O*-linked glycans on leukocyte surface proteins was deficient in fucose. This defect results in greatly increased numbers of circulating leukocytes and leads to frequent infections.

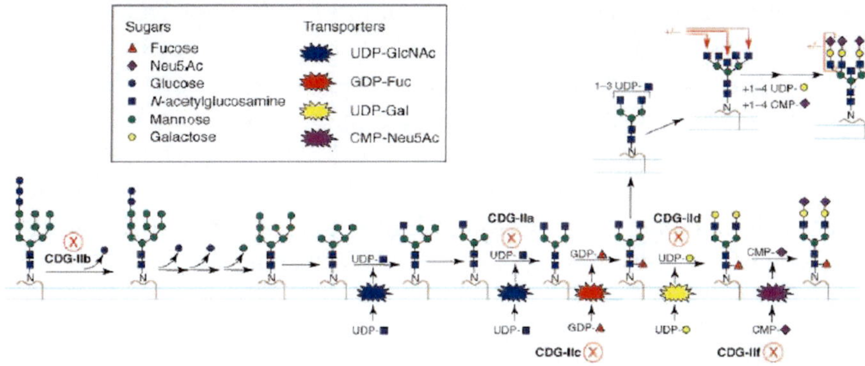

Reprinted from Current Opinion in Structural Biology, vol. 15, Freeze, HH and Aebi, M, Altered glycan structures: the molecular basis of congenital disorders of glycosylation, 490-498, 2005[96], with permission from Elsevier.

Figure 6. Type II CDG defects are caused by mutations that affect the processing of oligosaccharide chains after they are transferred to proteins in the ER. Initially, the three glucose residues are removed as part of the quality control of protein folding. Extensive removal of mannose residues is interspersed with the addition of multiple GlcNAc residues in a prescribed order, followed by capping of the multiple branches by galactose and sialic acid (Neu5Ac). In some cases, fucose is added near the protein linkage region or to the outer branches of the glycan. All the reactions, except the removal of the first mannose residue, occur in the Golgi and specific transporters are required to carry the nucleotide-sugars from the cytoplasm into the Golgi compartment. Defects that cause CDG-II are indicated.

In patients fibroblasts, the decreased of fucosylation is largely confined to the core region of biantennary *N*-glycans [109], not reflecting the full impact that glycosylation defect has in the others cells. The use of lectins, proteins with binding specificity to cellular glycosylated epitopes, in the decoding of this disorders reveal that CDG-IIc patients did not binding the α 1,3- and α 1,6- fucose-specific lectin from *Aleuria aurantia* (AAL), whereas normal cells have strong binding. The defect was identified as a deficiency in the GDP-fucose transporter, which provides fucose for both *N*- and *O*-linked glycans. An another type of CDG-IIf, with only one case reported, is caused by a defect in the CMP-sialic acid transporter [110] but *N*-linked glycans on serum glyproteins, including Tf, were sialylated normally. However, the patients completely lacked sialyl-Lewis^x on leukocytes due to a deficiency in sialic acid, which led to severe neutropenia, formation of giant platelets and abnormal platelets glycoproteins [111].

1.3. Biomarkers and Innovative Techniques to Study the CDG

The single Tf test does not identify all patients, but it remains the gold standard for detect group I patients. Additional serum markers may be useful and necessary. Analytical specific methods of proteomic coupled with glycomic such IEF-2D, ESI-MS combined with MALDI-MS and /or HPLC profiling of PNGaseF-released *N*-glycans from total serum can identify abnormal *N*-glycan branching and altered fucosylation. Lectins are also a specific method to identify the aberrant glycosylation of the molecules involved in CDG.

Current Therapeutic Approaches to Inborn Errors of Galactose Metabolism/Innovative Therapy for Classic Galactosemia

Enzyme deficiencies in the Leloir pathway, caused by bi-allelic amorphic or hypomorfic mutation in any of the genes coding for the GAL enzymes have been described [112-114]. Of these deficiencies, the most common disorder is Classic (Type I) Galactosemia, which is caused by bi-allelic amorphic mutation in the *GALT* gene. To date, the pathophysiology of the acute toxicity syndrome and the chronic complications remains largely unknown, but it is reasonable to assume that any blockage in a metabolic pathway will lead to (*i*) accumulation precursor(s), (*ii*) alternate metabolites normally not encountered, or (*iii*) absent metabolites past the enzymatic block. Any, or a combination of these possibilities, could be responsible for the phenotypes associated with the enzymatic blockage.

Inhibitors. New Drugs for Galactosemic Patients

For Human Galactokinase (GALK) (E.C.2.7.1.6)

In galactose metabolism, when an impairment of the second enzyme, the galactose-1-phosphate uridylyltransferase enzyme, of the Leloir pathway occurs, an accumulation of galactose-1-P is present. This is the fulcral point of galactosemia once this is a cytotoxic molecule. At present the subtraction of galactose for a patient´s diet is the only applicable treatment, but this is not enough since galactose is also produced endogenously, e.g. from the natural turnover of glycolipids and glycoproteins [113] and endogenous synthesis from UDP-glucose [52]. The development of an effective therapy through the application of inhibitors at the different enzyme levels of the Leloir pathway will be in the future a promissory strategy that could be complementary to dietary therapy for patients with CG.

As the most important pathogenic factor for developing long-term complications in Classic Galactosemia is Galactose-1-P, some authors [115,116] propose the pharmacological inhibition of GALK. Human GALK belongs to the GHMP small molecule kinase superfamily, which was named after the four characteristic family members: galactokinase (GALK), homoserine kinase (HSK), mevalonate kinase (MVK), and phosphomevalonato kinase (PMVK) [117].

Recently, there is an increasing interest in targeting GALK as a novel therapy to ameliorate the disease manifestation in patients with Classic Galactosemia as it would, in combination with galactose/lactose restriction reduce the accumulation of Gal-1-P. Research efforts have been done in order to understand the binding of small GALK inhibitors into the active site of the enzyme deprived of ATP. Using available crystallographic information [115], Wierenga and colleagues studied 34 compounds in a previous work [118], all of them with a preliminary characterization. These compounds contain at least 2 rings, at least 1 of which is aromatic, and all have at least 2 hydrogen-bond acceptor sites. A pair of aromatic rings separated by 1, 2 or 3 bonds is the most common recurring motif. Three small molecules, were selected, studied and characterized [119], which selectively inhibits GALK in vitro (Figure 7), with high potency of a IC_{50}s ranging from 0.7μM to 33.3μM. Experiments using SV40-transformed GALT-deficient fibroblasts cell line, GM00638A, from galactosemic patients [119], revealed that two of these selected compounds (1 and 24) lowered Gal-1-P concentration (Figure 7). By site-directed mutagenesis experiments, these authors identified one amino acid residue required for inhibitory function of two of the three selective compounds, and based in these results they generated binding models using a high precision docking software.

Unfortunately, long term exposure of these first-generation GALK inhibitors was too toxic for diploid cells (might also inhibit *N*-acetylgalactosamine kinase). These studies however, enable future development of non-toxic and more specific GALK inhibitors that might provide adjunct therapy for patients with Classic Galactosemia.

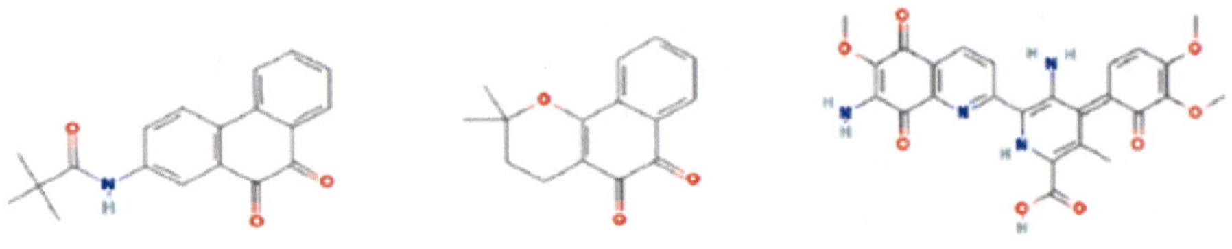

Compound 1 Compound 4 Compound 24

Reprinted from Chemico-Biological Interactions, vol. 188, Tang, M; Wierenga, K; Elsas, LJ; Lai, K. Molecular and biochemical characterization of human galactokinase and its small molecule inhibitors, 376–385, 2010[119], with permission from Elsevier.

Figure 7. Structure of three compounds specifically inhibit human GALK..

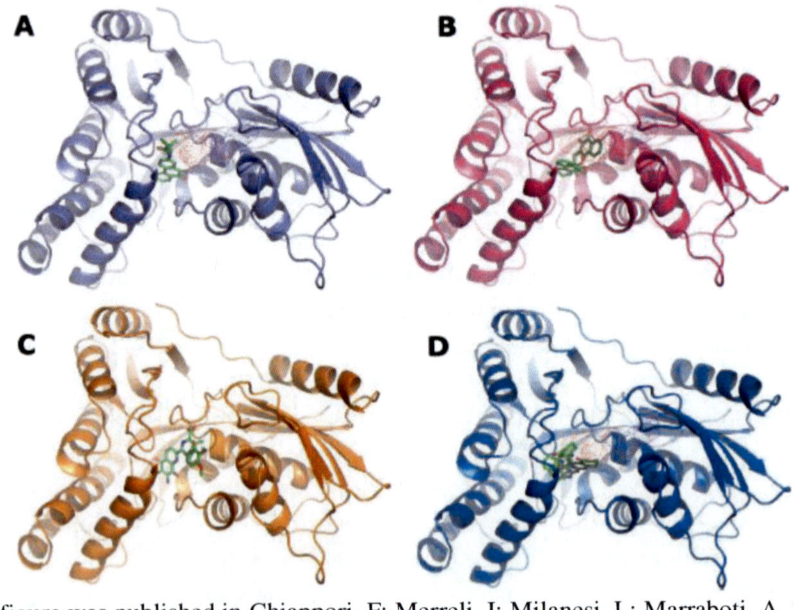

This figure was published in Chiappori, F; Merreli, I; Milanesi, L; Marraboti, A. Static and dynamic interactions between GALK enzyme and known inhibitors: Guidelines to design new drugs for galactose patients. Eur J Med Chem, 2013, 63, 423-434[120].Copyright © *year* Elsevier Masson SAS. All rights reserved."

Figure 8. Docking conformations of inhibitors in the canonical binding cavity from galactokinase. Docking pose of compound 1 (A), compound 4 (B), compound 24 (C) and ML152 (D). Ligands are shown in stick model and colored by atom type, carbons are colored based on docking results: conformations from simulations in the presence of ATP are in light green; conformation from simulations in the absence of ATP are in dark green. ATP volume is shown as dots.

Chiappori and colleagues [120] introduced static and dynamics simulation to analyze the interaction between GALK and its potential inhibitors taking in account the temporal evolution of the complex. This studies allow the introduction of the temporal dimension, taking account the conformational variability of protein [121]. Firstly, the authors redefined the binding sites of galactose, the natural substrate of galactokinase, by docking studies where two docking poses were obtained, one localized in the crystallographic binding site "canonical binding site", and a second pose that involve a secondary cavity alongside of the canonical binding site. For detail this type of interaction, docking poses were analyzed for identification of residues establishing H-bonds and hydrophobic interactions. In a second phase authors performed docking studies and the docking conformation of the GALK inhibitors previously identified [119,122] (Figure 8). Molecular dynamics simulations (MD) were performed after optimization of the best ligands with the best binding affinity to galactokinase.

Authors also compared the results to a structure-based pharmacophoric investigation to identify the spatial arrangement of chemical feature required of protein-ligand interaction. Despite the predicted binding affinity of all inhibitors (exception for one of them), achieved by docking simulation, the temporal evolution of the complex showed a modest affinity to galactokinase.

REFERENCES

[1] M. Murphy, B. McHugh, O. Tighe, P. Mayne, C. O'Neill, E. Naughten and D. T. Croke, *Eur. J. Hum. Genet.* 7, 549 (1999).

[2] H. Hirokawa, Y. Okano, J. Ashino, T. Imamura, I. Suyama and G. Ishiki, *Molecular characterization of galactosemia mutations (type 1) in Japanese*, The 7th International Congress of Inborn Errors of Metabolism, 1997 (Vienna, Austria), pp W123.

[3] L. Tyfield, J. Reichardt, J. Fridovich-Keil, D. T. Croke, L. J. Elsas II, W. Strobl, L. Kozak, T. Coskun, G. Novelli, Y. Okano, C. Zekanowski, Y. Shin and M. D. Boleda, *Hum. Mutat.* 13, 417 (1999).

[4] P. Schadewaldt, L. Kamalanathan, H. W. Hammen, and U. Wendel, *Rapid Commun. Mass Sp.* 17, 2833 (2003).

[5] C. T. Yager, J. Chen, R. Reynolds and S. Segal, *Mol. Genet. Metab.* 80, 283 (2003).

[6] P. Schadewaldt, H. W. Hammen, S. Stolpmann, L. Kamalanathan and U. J. Wendel, *J. Chromatogr. B.* 801, 249 (2004).

[7] C. Yager, S. Wehrli and S. Segal, *Clin. Chim. Acta,* 366, 216 (2006).
[8] J. Fridovich-Keil and J. H. Walter, *The Online Metabolic and Molecular Bases of Inherited Diseases (OMMBID)*: Galactosemia. New York: McGraw Hill (2008).
[9] V. Schwarz, *Arch. Dis. Child.* 35, 428 (1960).
[10] R. Gitzelmann, H. C. Curtius and I. Schneller, *Exp. Eye Res.* 6, 1 (1967).
[11] W. G. Ng, G. N. Donnell, W. R. Bergren, O. Alfi and M. S. Golbus, *Clin. Chim. Acta.* 74, 227 (1977).
[12] J. T. Allen, M. Gillett, J. B. Holton, G. S. King and B. R. Pettit, *Lancet,* 1 (8168 Pt 1), 603 (1980).
[13] D. E. Freer, C. Ficicioglu and D. Finegold, *Clin. Chem.* 56, 437 (2010).
[14] G. T. Berry, *Mol. Genet. Metabol.* 56, 437 (2012).
[15] J. S. Mayes and L. R. Miller, *Biochim. Biophys. Acta*, 313, 9 (1973).
[16] J. Forster, L. Schuchmann, C. Hans, H. Niederhoff, W. Künzer and D. Keppler, *Klin. Wochenschr.* 53, 1169 (1975).
[17] M. D. Kogut, T. F. Roe, W. Ng and G. N. Nonnel, *Pediatr. Res.* 9, 774 (1975).
[18] J. J. Starling and D. O. Keppler, *Eur. J. Biochem.* 80, 373 (1977).
[19] R. Gitzelmann, *Eur. J. Pediatr.* 154, S45 (1995).
[20] S. Roth, E. J. McGuire and S. Roseman, *J. Cell. Biol.* 51, 536 (1971).
[21] R. Parthasarathy, L. Parthasarathy and R. Vadnal, *Brain Res.* 778, 99 (1997).
[22] D. V. Mehta, A. Kabir and P. J. Bhat, *Biochim. Biophys. Acta,* 1454, 217 (1999).
[23] P. J.Bhat, *Med. Hypotheses*, 60, 123 (2003).
[24] T. I. Slepak, M. Tang, V. Z. Slepak and K. Lai, *Mol. Genet. Metabol.* 92, 78 (2007).
[25] D. D. Waggoner, N. R. Buis and G. N. Donnell, *J. Inherit. Metab. Dis.* 13, 802 (1990).
[26] M. A. Cleary, L. E Heptinstall, J. E. Wraith and J. H. Walter, *J. Inherit. Metab. Dis.* 18, 151 (1995).
[27] P. J. Lebea and P. J. Pretorius, *Med. Hypotheses,* 65, 1051(2005).
[28] H. Levy, *Inherited Disorders of Carbohydrate Metabolism.* Screening for galactosemia, D. Burman, J. Holton and C. Pennock, Lancaster, UK, MTP Press (1980).
[29] M. Hunter, E. Heyer, F. Austerlitz, D. Angelicheva, V. Nedkova, P. Briones, A. Gata, R. de Pablo, A. László, N. Bosshard, R. Gitzelmann, A. Tordai, L. Kalmar, C. Szalai, I. Balogh, C. Lupu, A. Corches, G.

Popa, A. Perez-Lezaun and L. V. Kalaydjieva, *Pediatr. Res.* 51, 602 (2002).

[30] R. Gitzelmann, *Lancet,* 2 (7414), 670 (1965).

[31] M. M. Kerr, R. W. Logan, J. S. Cant and J. H. Hutchison, *Arch. Dis. Child.* 46, 864 (1971).

[32] S. Segal, J. Y. Rutman and G. W. Frimpter, *J. Pediat.* 95, 750 (1979).

[33] B. L. Hodes, J. M. Schietroma, S.S. Lane, J. Sadeghi, D. Cunningham and D. Stambolian, *Metab. Pediatr. Syst. Ophthalmol.* 8, 39 (1985).

[34] W. R. Pickering and R. R. Howell, *J. Pediat.* 81, 50 (1972).

[35] N. Litman, A. I. Kanter and L. Finberg, *J. Pediat.* 86, 410 (1975).

[36] J. Colin, M. Voyer, D. Thomas, F. Schapira and P. Satge, *Arch. Fr. Pediatr.* 33, 77 (1976).

[37] P. R. Huttenlocher, R. E. Hillman and Y. E. Hsia, *J. Pediat.* 76, 902 (1970).

[38] G. T. Berry, J. V. Hunter, Z. Wang, S. Dreha, A. Mazur, D. G. Brooks, C. Ning, R. A. Zimmerman and S. Sega, *J. Pediatr.* 138, 260 (2001).

[39] F. Maley and G. F. Maley, *Biochim. Biophys. Acta.* 31, 577 (1959).

[40] F. Piller, M. H. Hanlon, R. L. Hill, *Biol. Chemis.* 258, 10774 (1983).

[41] J. M. Schulz, A. L. Watson, R. Sanders, K. L. Ross, J. B. Thoden, H M. Holden and J.L. Fridovich-Keil, *J.Biol. Chem.* 279, 32796 (2004).

[42] M. Amado, R. Almeida, T. Schwientek and H. Clausen, *Biochim. Biophys. Acta.* 1473, 35 (1999).

[43] R. Gitzelmann, B. Steinmann, B. Mitchell and E. Haigis, *Helv .Paediatr. Acta.* 31, 441 (1977).

[44] J. H. Walter, R. E. Roberts , G. T. Besley, J. E. Wraith, M. A. Cleary, J. B. Holton and R. MacFaul, *Arch. Dis. Child.* 80, 374 (1999).

[45] J. Chhay, C. Vargas, T. McCorvie, J. Fridovich-Keil and D. Timson, *J. Inherit. Metab. Dis.* 31, 108 (2008).

[46] K. K. Openo, J. M. Schulz, C. A. Vargas, C. S. Orton, M. P. Epstein, R. E. Schnur, F. Scaglia, G. T. Berry, G. S. Gottesman, C. Ficicioglu, A. E. Slonim, R. J. Schroer, C. Yu, V. E. Rangel, J. Keenan, K. Lamance and J. L. Fridovich-Keil, *Am. J. Hum. Genet.* 78, 89 (2006).

[47] R. Gitzelmann, *Inherited Disorders of Carbohydrate Metabolism.* Galactose metabolism, hereditary defects and their clinical significance, Burman D, J. Holton, C. Pennock, MTP Press, Lancaster, UK (1980).

[48] M. J. Henderson, J. B. Holton and R. J. MacFaul, *J. Inherit. Metab. Dis.* 6, 17 (1983).

[49] I. B. Sardharwalla, J. E. Wraith, C. Bridge, B. Fowler, S. A. Roberts, *J. Inherit. Metab. Dis.* 11, 249 (1988).

[50] C. Jakobs, A. C. Douwes, M. Brockstedt, F. Stellaard, W. Endres and Y. S. Shin, *J. Inherit. Metab. Dis.* 13, 517 (1990).
[51] N. Mizoguchi, H. Ono, T. Eguchi and N. Sakura, *Eur. J. Pediat.* 159, 851 (2000).
[52] G. T. Berry, I. Nissim, Z. Lin, A. T. Mazur, J. B. Gibson and S. Segal, S, *Lancet,* 346 (8982), 1073 (1995).
[53] G. T. Berry, N. Leslie, R. Reynolds, C. T. Yager and S. Segal, *Mol. Genet. Metab.* 72, 316 (2001).
[54] C. Ning, R. Reynolds, J. Chen, C. Yager, G. T. Berry, P. D. McNamara, N. Leslie and S. Segal, *Pediat. Res.* 48, 211 (2000).
[55] C. Ning, R. Reynolds, J. Chen, C. Yager, G. T. Berry, N. Leslie and S. Segal, *Mol. Genet. Metab.* 72, 306 (2001).
[56] C. Yager, J. Gibson, B. States, L. J. Elsas and S. Segal, *J. Inherit. Metab. Dis.* 24, 465 (2001).
[57] H. G. Hers, *Biochim. Biophys. Acta,* 37, 120 (1960).
[58] M. M. O'Brien and P. J. Schofield, *Biochem. J.* 187, 21 (1980).
[59] W. R. Bergren, W. G. Ng, G. N. Donnell and S. P. Markey, *Science,* 176 (4035), 683 (1972).
[60] N. J. Rancour, E. D. Hawkins and W. W. Wells, *Arch. Biochem. Biophys.* 193, 232 (1979).
[61] E. Wada, *Arch. Biochem. Biophys.* 25, 215 (1986).
[62] S. L. Wehrli, G. T. Berry, M. Palmieri, A. Mazur, L. Elsas III and S.Segal, *Pediat. Res.* 42, 855 (1997).
[63] K. J. Isselbacher, *Science,* 126, 652 (1957).
[64] H. D. Abraham and R. R. Howell, *J. Biol. Chem.* 244, 545 (1969).
[65] P. B. Acosta and K. C. Gross, *Eur. J. Pediatr.* 154, 87 (1995).
[66] S. S. Gropper, J. O. Weese, P. A. West and K. C. Gross, *J. Am. Diet Assoc.* 100, 573 (2000).
[67] S. J. Weese, K. Gosnell, P. West and S. S. Gropper, *J. Am. Diet Assoc.* 103, 373 (2003).
[68] L. K. Mahan and S. Escott-Stump, *Krause´s Food Nutrition and Diet Therapy*, Saunders, Elsevier, Philadelphia, USA (2004).
[69] K. C. Gross and P. B. Acosta, *J. Inherit. Metab. Dis.* 14, 253 (1991).
[70] C. H. Scaman, V. J. Jim and C. Hartnett, *J. Agric. Food Chem.* 52, 511 (2004).
[71] H. O. Kim, C. Hartnett and C. H. Scaman, *J Agric Food Chem.* 55, 8133 (2007).
[72] C. Hartness, H. O. Kim and C. H. Scaman, *Can. J. Diet Pract Res.* 68, 46 (2007).

[73] L. Gleason, M. Rasberry, S. van Calcar, *Understanding Galactosemia Diet Guide 3*, Abbot Nutrition, Columbus, Ohio, USA (2010).
[74] H. H. Mason and M. E. Turner, *Am. J. Dis. Child.* 50, 359 (1935).
[75] F. R.Kaufman, E. J. Horton, P. Gott, J. A. Wolf, M. D. Nelson, C. Azen and F. R. Manis, *J. Child. Neurol.* 10, 32 (1995).
[76] A. M. Bosch, *J. Inherit. Metab. Dis.* 29, 516 (2006).
[77] P. Jumbo-Lucioni, K. Garber, J. Kiel, I. Baric, G. Berry, A. Bosch, A. Burlina, A. Chiesa, M. L. Pico, S. Estrada, H. Henderson, N. Leslie, N. Longo. A. Morris, C. Ramirez-Farias, S. Scheweitzer-Krantz, C. Lynn, T. Silao, M. Vela-Amieva, S. Waisbren and J. Fridovich-Keil, *J. Inherit. Metab. Dis.* 35, 1037 (2012).
[78] N. Karadag, A. Zenciroglu, F. T. Eminoglu, D. Dilli, B. S. Karagol, A. Kundak. A. Dursun, N. Hakan and N. Okumus, *Clin. Lab.* 59, 1139 (2013).
[79] R. M. Lawrence, *Pediatr. Clinic. North. Am.* 60, 295 (2013).
[80] A. Bosch, *J. Inherit. Metab. Dis.* 34, 257 (2011).
[81] D. Turck, Curr. Opin. Clin. Nutr. Metab. Care, 10, 360 (2007).
[82] G. T. Berry, P. J. Moate and R. A. Reynolds, *Mol. Genet. Metab.* 81, 22 (2004).
[83] S. J. Weese, *Can. Vet. J.* 44, 982 (2003).
[84] J. Fernandes, J. Saudulbray, G. Bergh and J. Walter, *Inborne of metabolism*, Springer (2006).
[85] R. Gitzelmann, *Pediatr. Res.* 3, 279 (1969).
[86] R. Gitzelmann, H. J. Wells and S. Segal, *Eur. J. Clin. Invest.* 4, 79 (1974).
[87] K. Lai and L. J. Elsas, *Biochem. Biophys. Res. Commun.* 271, 392 (2000).
[88] K. Lai, S. D. Langley, F. W. Khwaja, E. W. Schmitt and L. J. Elsas, *Glycobiology,* 13, 285 (2003).
[89] R. S. Stempfel Jr, J. B. Sidbury Jr and C. J. Migeon, *J. Clin. Endocrinol. Met.* 20, 814 (1960).
[90] V. T. Maddaiah and N. B. Madsen, *J. Biol. Chem.* 241, 3873 (1966).
[91] H. M. Kalckar and E. S. Maxwell, *Physiol. Rev.* 38, 77 (1958).
[92] J. Jaeken, J. Kint and L. Spaapen, *Lancet*, 340, 1472 (1992).
[93] L. L. Prestoz, A. S. Couto, Y. S. Shin and K. G. Petry, *Eur. J. Pediatr.* 156, 116 (1997).
[94] J. Charlwood, P. Clayton, G. Keir, N. Mian and B. Winchester, *Glycobiology,* 8, 351 (1998).
[95] H. H. Freeze and M. Aebi, *Curr. Opin. Struct. Biol.* 15, 490 (2005).

[96] H. Carchon, E. Van Schaftingen, G. Matthijs, J. Jaeken, , *Biochim. Biophys. Acta, 1455, 155 (1999).*
[97] J. Jaeken, G. Matthijs, R. Barone and H. Carchon, *J. Med. Genet.* 34, 73 (1997).
[98] J. Jaeken, G. Matthijs, J. M. Saudubray, C. Dionisi-Vici, E. Bertini, P. de Lonlay, H. Henri, H. Carchon, E. Schollen and E. Van Schaftingen, *Am. J. Hum. Genet.* 62, 1535 (1998).
[99] H. Schachter and J. Jaeken, *Biochim. Biophys. Acta*, 1455, 179 (1999).
[100] T. Dupre, A. Barnier, P. De Lonlay, V. Cormier Daire, G. Durand, P. Codogno and N. Seta, *Glycobiology,* 10, 1277 (2000).
[101] K. J. Yarema and C. R. Bertozzi, *Genome. Biol.* 2, REVIEWS0004 (2001).
[102] J. Jaeken, M. Vanderschueren-Lodewyckx, P. Caeaer, L. Snoeck, L. Corbeel and E. Eggermont, *Pediatr. Res.* 14, 179 (1980).
[103] J. Jaeken, H. G. van Ejik, C. van der Heul, L. Corbeel, R. Eeckels and E. Eggermont, *Clin. Chim. Acta.* 144, 245 (1984).
[104] M. Aebi, and T. Hennet, *Trends Cell Biol.* 11, 136 (2001).
[105] M. Butler, D. Quelhas, A. J. Critchley, H. Carchon, H. F. Hebestreit, R. G. Hibbert, L. Vilarinho, E. Teles, G. Matthijs, E. Schollen, P. Argibay, D. J. Harvey, R. A. Dwek, J. Jaeken and P. M. Rudd, *Glycobyology*, 13, 601 (2003).
[106] K. J. Marek, I. K. Vijay and J. D. Marth, *Glycobiology,* 9, 1263 (1999).
[107] T. Lübke, T. Marquardt, A. Etzioni, E. Hartmann, K. von Figura and C. Körner, *Nat. Genet.* 28, 73 (2001).
[108] K. Lühn, M. K. Wild, M. Eckhardt, R. Gerardy-Schahn and D. Vestweber, *Nat. Genet.* 28, 69 (2001).
[109] L. Sturla, F. Fruscione, K. Noda, E. Miyoshi, N. Taniguchi, P. Contini and M. Tonetti, *Nat. Genet.* 15, 924 (2005).
[110] I. Martinez-Dunker, T. Dupre, V. Piller, F. Piller, J. J. Candelier, C. Trichet, G. Tchernia, R. Oriol and R. Mollicone, *Blood*, 105, 2671 (2005).
[111] T. B. Willig, J. Breton-Gorius, C. Elbim, V. Mignotte, C. Kaplan, R. Mollicone, C. Pasquier, A. Filipe, F. Mielot, J.P. Cartron, M.A. Gougerot-Pocidalo, N. Debili, J. Guichard, J.P. Dommergues, N. Mohandas and G. Tchernia, *Blood*, 97, 826 (2001).
[112] S. Segal, and G. T. Berry, *The Metabolic Basis of Inherited Disease*, Disorders of galactose metabolism, C. R. Sriver, A. L. D. Valle and W. S. Sly, McGraw-Hill, New York (1995).
[113] K. Lai, L. J. Elsas and K. J. Wierenga, *IUBMB Life*, 61, 1063 (2009).

[114] T. J. McCorvie and D. J. Timson, *IUBMB Life*, 63, 694 (2011).
[115] J. B. Thoden, D. J. Timson, R. J. Reece and H. M. Holden, *J. Biol. Chem*, 280, 9662 (2005).
[116] M. Tang, S. I. Odejinmi, H. Vankayalapati, K. J. Wierenga and K. Lai, *Mol. Genet. Metabol.* 105, 44 (2012).
[117] P. Bork, C. Sander and A.Valencia, *Prot. Sci.* 2, 31 (1993).
[118] K. Wierenga, K. Lai, P. Buchwald and M. Tang, *J. Biomol. Screen.* 13, 415 (2008).
[119] M. Tang, K. Wierenga, K, L. J. Elsas and K. Lai, *Chem. Biol. Interact.* 188, 376 (2010).
[120] F. Chiappori, I. Merreli, L. Milanesi and A. Marraboti, *Eur. J. Med. Chem.* 63, 423 (2013).
[121] J. D. Durrant and J. A. McCammon, *BMC Biol.* 9, 71 (2011).
[122] M. B. Boxer, M. Shen, C. Tanega, M. Tang, K. K. Lai and D. S. Auld, Toward improved therapy for classic galactosemia. Probe reports for the NIH Molecular Libraries Program (Internet), National Center for Biotechnology Information (US), Bethesda (MD), 2010.

In: Galactose
Editor: Vitor Hugo Pomin
ISBN: 978-1-63117-928-0

Chapter 4

GALACTO-OLIGOSACCHARIDES RECENT PROGRESS ON RESEARCH AND APPLICATION AS PREBIOTICS

Sheryl Lozel Arreola, Montira Intanon, Ngoc Hung Pham, Dietmar Haltrich and Thu-Ha Nguyen [•]
Food Biotechnology Laboratory,
Department of Food Sciences and Technology,
University of Natural Resources and Life Sciences,
(BOKU Wien), Vienna, Austria

ABSTRACT

Prebiotic oligosaccharides have attracted an increasing amount of attention because of their physiological importance and functional effects on human health, as well as their physico-chemical properties, which are of interest for various applications in the food industries. Galacto-oligosaccharides (GOS), one of the major groups of prebiotic oligosaccharides, are formed via the transgalactosylation reaction from lactose. This reaction is catalyzed by a number of β-galactosidases (lactases) in addition to their hydrolytic activity. GOS are complex mixtures of different oligosaccharides, and the spectrum of the oligosaccharides making up these mixtures strongly depends on the

[•] E-mail: thu-ha.nguyen@boku.ac.at.

source of the enzyme used for the biocatalytic reaction as well as on the conversion conditions used in their production. These oligosaccharides are of great interest because of their proven prebiotic (bifidogenic) characteristics. A plethora of GOS is also found in human milk, and these differently substituted oligosaccharides are associated with a number of beneficial effects for the breast-fed infant. This chapter reviews the production, the properties, the biological effects as well as the applications of galacto-oligosaccharides as prebiotics. The chapter also includes emerging trends in the production of novel, galactose-containing hetero-oligosaccharides, which are structurally more closely related to human milk oligosaccharides.

Introduction

The concept of 'probiotics' with the emphasis on the human host was described as 'a mono- or mixed-culture of live microorganisms which when applied to man or animal affects beneficially the host by improving the properties of the indigenous microflora' [1, 2]. Presently, there is a general acceptance that 'probiotics' refer to viable microorganisms which promote or stimulate beneficially the microbial population of the gastro-intestinal tract (GIT) [3, 4]. It was stated in different reviews that such microorganisms may not necessarily be constant inhabitants of the GIT but they should beneficially affect the health of man and animal [4-7]. Lactic acid bacteria (LAB) and bifidobacteria are the major representatives of probiotic microorganisms [4, 8]. LAB and bifidobacteria have long been used in the production of a wide range of foods without adverse effects on humans [8]. *Bifidobacterium* and *Lactobacillus* species, among LAB, receive special attention in the applications of probiotic products because of their GRAS (generally recognized as safe) status and beneficial effects on human health. Their beneficial roles on the host were summarized by Klaenhammer (1998) [9] including maintenance of the normal microflora, pathogen interference, exclusion and antagonism, immuno-stimulation and immuno-modulation, anti-carcinogenic and anti-mutagenic activities, deconjugation of bile acids, and lactase presentation *in vivo*. A number of *Lactobacillus* and *Bifidobacterium* strains are used for applications in probiotic products and these include for example *L. acidophilus*, *L. amylovorus*, *L. casei*, *L. crispatus*, *L. gasseri*, *L. johnsonii*, *L. paracasei*, *L. plantarum*, *L. reuteri*, *L. rhamnosus, B. bifidum, B. longum, B. infantis, B. breve*, or *B. adolescentis* [8, 10-13].

Since its first introduction [14], the concept of prebiotics has attracted an increasing amount of attention and stimulated both scientific and industrial interests. This concept was later revised [15, 16], and according to an updated definition of the prebiotic concept, 'a dietary prebiotic is a selectively fermented ingredient that results in specific changes, in the composition and/or activity of the gastrointestinal microbiota, thus conferring benefit(s) upon host health' [16]. Based on the criteria [15, 17] (i) resistance to gastric acidity, to hydrolysis by mammalian enzymes, and to gastrointestinal absorption; (ii) fermentation by intestinal microflora; and (iii) selective stimulation of growth and/or activity of intestinal bacteria associated with health/well-being, only inulin/fructo-oligosaccharides (FOS), galacto-oligosaccharides (GOS) and lactulose are fulfilling these requirements for prebiotics as documented and proven in several studies, although promise exists for several other dietary oligosaccharides [15, 17-20].

Prebiotic oligosaccharides can serve as fermentable substrates for certain members of the gut microbiota, and have been found to modulate the colonic flora by selective stimulation of beneficial bacteria such as bifidobacteria and lactobacilli as well as inhibition of 'undesirable' bacteria [4, 21, 22]. Galacto-oligosaccharides (GOS), the products of transgalactosylation reactions catalyzed by β-galactosidases when using lactose as the substrate, are non-digestible carbohydrates meeting the criteria of 'prebiotics'. GOS are of special interest to human nutrition because of the presence of structurally related oligosaccharides together with different complex structures in human breast milk [23-25].

PRODUCTION OF GALACTO-OLIGOSACCHARIDES

β-Galactosidases and Transgalactosylation of Lactose

Production of GOS (or sometimes referred to as TOS, transgalactosylated oligosaccharides) typically employs lactose as galactosyl donor and the transfer of the galactosyl moiety of lactose to suitable acceptor carbohydrates or nucleophiles using either glycoside hydrolases (EC 3.2.1.) or glycosyltransferases (EC 2.4.) [26-28]. Glycosyltransferases catalyze glycosidic bond formation employing sugar donors containing a nucleoside phosphate or a lipid phosphate leaving group, and are quite efficient as well as regio-and stereo-selective compared to glycoside hydrolases. However, due to limited supply, high price and necessity of specific sugar nucleotide as substrate of glycoside hydrolases, industrial GOS production favors the use of glycoside hydrolases [26].

Glycoside hydrolases (GH) are classified based on the stereochemical outcome of the hydrolysis reaction; they can be either *retaining* or *inverting* enzymes. Amino acid sequence similarities, hydrophobic cluster analysis, reaction mechanisms and the conservation of catalytic residues allow classification of β-galactosidases (β-gal; β-d-galactoside galactohydrolase E.C.3.2.1.23; lactase) in the GH families GH1, GH2, GH35, and GH42, indicating their structural diversity [28]. GH1 β-glycosidases are retaining enzymes of which the most commonly known enzymatic activities are myrosinases (thio-β-glucosidases), β-mannosidases, β-galactosidases, phospho-β-glucosidases and phospho-β-galactosidases. GH1 β-galactosidases are predominant in the plant kingdom and have been explored for their 3D conformation, active site residues, and mechanism of action with few reports from Archaea and recently also from the Eubacteria *Meiothermus ruber* DSM1279 [29]. The GH2 family, to which most of the β-galactosidases belong, comprises the LacZ and LacLM β-galactosidases as isolated and described from *E. coli*, lactic acid bacteria and bifidobacteria. GH1 and GH2 β-galactosidases use only lactose, β-(1→3) and β-(1→6) linked galactosides as their substrates while those belonging to families GH35 and GH42 act on different galactose-containing glycosides including higher oligosaccharides and polysaccharides [28]. Owing to the different substrate specificities, β-galactosidases of GH2 and GH42 are often found in the same organism [30-32].

β-Galactosidases catalyze the hydrolysis and transgalactosylation of β-D-galactopyranosides (such as lactose) [33-35] and are found widespread in nature. They catalyze the cleavage of lactose (or related compounds) in their hydrolysis mode, and are thus used in the dairy industry to remove lactose from various products. An attractive biocatalytic application is found in the transgalactosylation potential of these enzymes, which is based on their catalytic mechanism [33, 36]. Retaining β-galactosidases undergo a two-step mechanism of catalysis. First, this mechanism involves the formation of a covalently linked galactosyl-enzyme intermediate. Subsequently, the galactosyl moiety linked to the nucleophile is transferred to a nucleophilic acceptor. Water, as well as all sugar species present in the reaction mixture, can serve as a galactosyl acceptor. Hence, the resulting final mixture contains hydrolysis products of lactose, which are glucose and galactose, unconverted lactose as well as di-, tri- and higher oligosaccharides [37, 38]. Scheme 1 illustrates the possible lactose conversion reactions catalyzed by β-galactosidases, and structures of some galacto-oligosaccharides are given in Figure 1.

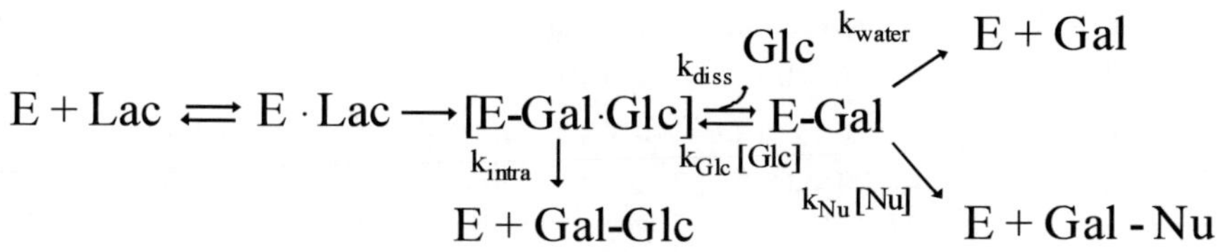

Scheme 1. Hydrolysis and galactosyl transfer reactions, both intra- and intermolecular, during the conversion of lactose catalyzed by β-galactosidases. E, Enzyme; Lac, lactose; Gal, galactose; Glc, glucose; Nu, nucleophile.

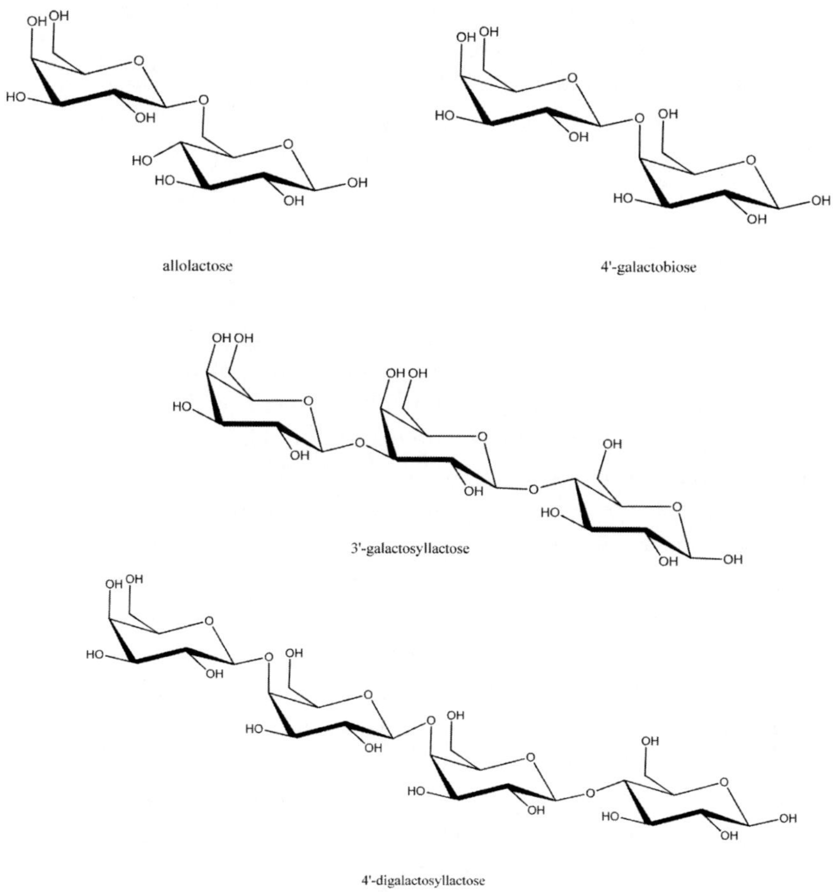

Figure 1. Structures of some galacto-oligosaccharides.

Transgalactosylation is described to involve intermolecular as well as intramolecular reactions. Intramolecular or direct galactosyl transfer to D-glucose yields regio-isomers of lactose. The glycosidic bond of lactose (β-D-Gal*p*-(1→4)-D-Glc) is cleaved and immediately formed again at a different position of the glucose molecule before it diffuses out of the active site. This is how allolactose (β-D-Gal*p*-(1→6)-D-Glc), the presumed natural inducer of β-galactosidases in certain microorganisms, can be formed even in the absence of significant amounts of free D-glucose [37, 39]. By intermolecular transgalactosylation, various di-, tri-, tetrasaccharides and eventually higher oligosaccharides are produced. Any sugar molecule in the reaction mixture can be the nucleophile accepting the galactosyl moiety from the galactosyl-enzyme complex, which is formed as an intermediate in the reaction. The GOS produced are not the product of an equilibrium reaction, but must be regarded as kinetic intermediates as they are also substrates for hydrolysis, and hence transgalactosylation reactions are kinetically controlled [39, 40]. For these reasons, GOS yield and composition change dramatically with reaction time, and the GOS mixtures thus obtained are very complex and can hardly be predicted.

Enzyme Sources

β-Galactosidases can be obtained from different sources including microorganisms, plants and animals. Microbial sources of β-galactosidase are of great biotechnological interest because of easier handling, higher multiplication rates, and production yield.

Table 1 presents some of the commercially available bacterial, fungal and yeast β-galactosidases. Recently, a number of studies have focused on the use of the genera *Bifidobacterium* and *Lactobacillus* for the production and characterization of β-galactosidases, including the enzymes from *L. reuteri, L. acidophilus, L. plantarum, L. sakei, L. pentosus, L. bulgaricus, L. fermentum, L. crispatus, B. infantis, B. bifidum, B. angulatum, B. adolescentis, and B. pseudolongum and B. breve* [41-55]. Bifidobacteria and lactobacilli have been studied intensively with respect to their enzymes for various different reasons, one of which is their 'generally recognized as safe' (GRAS) status and their safe use in food applications. It is anticipated that GOS produced by these β-galactosidases will have better selectivity for growth and metabolic activity of these bacterial genera in the gut, and thus will lead to improved prebiotic effects [56].

Table 1. Commercial β-galactosidases

Name	Manufacturer	Microorganism
BioLactase NTL-CONC	Biocon Ltd.,	*Bacillus circulans* [153, 154]
Lactozym pure 6500 L	Novozymes	*Kluyveromyces lactis* [154]
Lactase F "Amano"	Amano Enzyme Inc.	*Aspergillus oryzae* [154, 155]
Biolacta FN5	Daiwa Fine Chemicals Co., Ltd.	*Bacillus circulans* [155, 156]
Lactoles® L3	Biocon Ltd.,	*Bacillus circulans* [155]
Maxilact	DSM Food Specialties	*Kluyveromyces lactis* [157, 158]
Tolerase	DSM Food Specialties	*Aspergillus oryzae* [157, 158]

An extensive list of bacterial and fungal sources of β-galactosidases, as well as the lactose conversion reaction conditions and GOS yields, is given in [57].

Studies of thermostable glycosyl hydrolases have been conducted in pursuit of GOS production at high temperatures. These include β-glycosidases from *Pyrococcus furiosus* (F426Y), *Thermotoga maritima*, *Penicillum simplicissimum*, *Saccharopolyspora rectivirgula*, *Aspergillus niger*, *Bifidobacterium bifidum*, *Bacillus stearothermophilus*, *Alicyclobacillus acidocaldarius*, *Thermus aquaticus* YT-1, *Thermus thermophilus* KNOUC202, and *L. bulgaricus*, to name a few [47, 58-63]. The GOS yields as influenced by transgalactosylation of lactose at different temperatures were given in recent reviews [57, 64]. Cold-active β-galactosidases have also attracted attention because their applications in the industrial processes of lactose hydrolysis and oligosaccharides synthesis can lower the risk of mesophiles contamination. Cold-active β-galactosidases were isolated from *P. haloplanktis* TAE 79, *Planococcus* sp., *Arthrobacter psychrolactophilus*, *Arthrobacter* sp. 32c, *Alkalilactibacillus ikkense*, *Paracoccus* sp. 32d, *Halorubrum lacusprofundi,* and *Thalassospira frigidphilosprofundus* [65-72] and have been reported for their potential use to hydrolyze lactose in dairy products processed at low temperatures. Soluble cold-active β-galactosidases from *Paracoccus* sp. 32d and *Lactococcus lactis* IL 1403 were found to efficiently hydrolyze lactose in milk at 10°C [71, 73].

It is a well-known fact that β-galactosidases from different species possess very different specificities for building glycosidic linkages, and therefore produce different GOS mixtures. For example, the β-galactosidase from *Kluyveromyces lactis* produced predominantly β-(1→6)-linked GOS [74], the β-galactosidase from *Aspergillus oryzae* produced mainly β-(1→3) and β-(1→6) linkages in their GOS [75], *Bacillus circulans* β-galactosidase forms β-(1→2), β-(1→3), β-(1→4), β-(1→6) linked GOS [76], whereas β-galactosidases from *Lactobacillus* spp. showed preference to form β-(1→3) and β-(1→6) linkages in transgalactosylation mode [39, 43, 45, 47].

Microbial Production of GOS

GOS are produced from lactose by microbial β-galactosidases employing different enzyme sources and preparations including crude enzymes, purified enzymes, recombinant enzymes, immobilized enzymes, whole-cell biotransformations, toluene-treated cells, and immobilized cells. The enzyme sources, the process parameters as well as the yield and the productivity of these processes for GOS production are summarized in detail in recent reviews [25, 57, 64, 77]. The highest GOS productivity, 106 g L^{-1} h^{-1}, was observed when β-galactosidase from *Aspergillus oryzae* immobilized on cotton cloth was used for GOS production in a packed-bed reactor [78].

The choice of process technology either for lactose hydrolysis or GOS production depends on the nature of the substrate and the characteristics of the enzyme. The primary characteristic, which determines the choice and application of a given enzyme, is the operational pH range. Acid-pH enzymes, which are mainly from fungi, are suitable for processing of acid whey and whey permeate, while the neutral-pH enzymes from yeasts and bacteria are suitable for processing milk and sweet whey. Depending on the enzyme source, the pH value of the reaction mixture can be very acidic when using β-galactosidases from *A. oryzae* and *Bullera singularis* with optimum GOS yields at pH 4.5 and 3.7, respectively [79, 80]. Isobe and others studied the β-galactosidase from an acidophilic fungus, *Teratosphaeria acidotherma* AIU BGA-1, which was stable over the pH range of 1.5 to 7.0 and exhibited optimal activity at pH 2.5-4.0 and 70°C [81]. The maximum yield of GOS was observed at neutral pH for most bacteria and fungi though [44]. The time required to get maximum GOS depends inversely on the amount of enzyme. The highest GOS yields are generally observed when the reaction proceeds to 45 - 90% lactose conversion [57].

Despite the importance of LAB, and in particular *Lactobacillus* spp. and bifidobacteria, for food technology and dairy applications, and despite numerous studies on the gene clusters involved in lactose utilization by these bacteria, β-galactosidases from *Lactobacillus* and *Bifidobacterium* spp. have been characterized in detail pertaining to their biochemical properties or investigated for their ability to produce GOS in biocatalytic processes only recently. Previous studies reported the presence of multiple β-galactosidases in *B. infantis*, *B. adolescentis*, *B. bifidum,* as well as *B. breve* [51, 52, 55, 82-86], and revealed that these enzymes are very different with respect to substrate specificity and regulation of gene expression. Furthermore, these reports described the cloning and characterization of these enzymes and studied their transgalactosylation activity in detail, for example β-galactosidase BgbII from *B. adolescentis* showed high preference towards the formation of β-(1→4) linkages while no β-(1→6) linkages were formed [85]. In contrast, the β-galactosidase BgbII from *B. bifidum* showed a clear preference for the synthesis of β-(1→6) linkages over β-(1→4) linkages [32]. A recombinant β-galactosidase from *B. infantis* was found to be an excellent biocatalyst for GOS production giving the highest GOS yield of 63% (mass of GOS of the total sugars in the reaction mixture) [51].

β-Galactosidases of lactobacilli play an important role in a number of commercial processes, e.g., milk processing or cheese making [87, 88]. Recent studies of β-galactosidases, especially with respect to their enzymatic and molecular properties, from *L. reuteri*, *L. acidophilus*, *L. plantarum*, *L. sakei*, *L. pentosus*, and *L. bulgaricus* [39, 41-43, 45-47, 89, 90] revealed that these enzymes were found to be very well suited for the production of galacto-oligosaccharides. Maximum GOS yields at 30°C were 38% when using purified β-galactosidases from *L. reuteri* and *L. acidophilus* with initial lactose concentration of 205 g/L and at ~80% lactose conversion [39, 42]. When using purified β-galactosidases from *L. plantarum* and *L. sakei*, the yields at 30°C were 41% with similar initial lactose concentrations and at 77% and 85% lactose conversion, respectively [43, 45]. Purified β-galactosidase from *L. bulgaricus* gave the highest yield of 50% at 90% lactose conversion [47], and on the other hand, purified β-galactosidase from *L. pentosus* gave the lowest yields, 31%, compared to the above-mentioned β-galactosidases from lactobacilli [46]. In order to reduce enzyme costs by avoiding laborious and expensive chromatographic steps for the purification of the biocatalyst, crude β-galactosidase extract from *Lactobacillus* sp. directly obtained after cell disruption and separation of cell debris by centrifugation was used in lactose conversion for GOS production [90]. It was reported that there was no obvious difference in the obtained GOS yields using either purified or crude β-galactosidase at 37°C, and in addition, the crude enzyme was found to be equally stable as the purified one. Therefore, crude β-galactosidase extracts are suitable for a convenient and simple process of GOS production. Because of the GRAS status of most *Lactobacillus* spp., it is also safe to use these crude extracts in food and feed applications. The reduction of reaction temperature to 17°C to limit microbial growth and the use of a cheap lactose source such as whey permeate powder did not have significant adverse effects on the GOS yield [90].

Protein engineering is a powerful approach to favor transgalactosylation over hydrolysis, and hence improves transgalactosylation yields. A truncated β-galactosidase from *B. bifidum* enhanced the transgalactosylation activity of the enzyme towards lactose and as a result a normal, hydrolytic β-galactosidase was converted to a highly efficient transgalactosylating enzyme [91]. A mutagenesis approach was applied to the galactosidase BgaB of *Geobacillus stearothermophilus* KVE39 in order to improve its enzymatic transglycosylation of lactose into oligosaccharides. Exchange of one amino acid, arginine Arg109, in β-galactosidase BgaB to either lysine, valine or tryptophan improved significantly the formation of the main trisaccharide, i.e. 3'-galactosyl lactose. The yield of this trisaccharide increased from 2% to 12%, 21% and 23%, respectively, for these different variants compared to that of the native enzyme [92]. Enhancement of the production of GOS was achieved by mutagenesis of *Sulfolobus solfataricus* β-galactosidase LacS. Site-directed mutagenesis was performed to obtain two mutants of LacS, F441Y and F359Q, and the GOS yield was increased by 10.8 and 7.4%, respectively [93]. Although protein engineering strategies were successful to enhance transgalactosylation activities of different β-galactosidases, it has not been described for β-galactosidases yet that this approach was successful to alter also the linkage type of the GOS products [94].

Manufacturers of GOS

GOS are manufactured and commercialized mainly in Japan, the United States and Europe. The major manufacturers are Yakult Honsha (Japan) with their product Oligomate, Nissin Sugar Manufacturing (Japan) with Cup-Oligo,

Snow Brand Milk Products (Japan) with P7L, GTC Nutrition (United States) with Purimune, Friesland Foods Domo (the Netherlands) with Vivinal® GOS, Clasado Ltd. (UK) with Bimuno, and Dairy Food Ingredients (Ireland) with Dairygold GOS [23, 25, 57, 95-97].

Commercial GOS preparations typically are transparent syrups or white powders containing oligosaccharides of different DP, non-converted lactose and the monosaccharides glucose and galactose. They differ in purity of the GOS products and also in the linkages of the oligosaccharide chains, which depend on the enzymes used for the GOS productions. Oligomate contains mainly β-(1→6) linked GOS, Vivinal® GOS, Cup-Oligo and Purimune contain mainly β-(1→4) linkages, whilst Bimuno contains mainly β-(1→3) linked GOS [57]. Table 2 presents some commercial GOS and the enzymes used in their productions.

PROPERTIES AND BIOLOGICAL EFFECTS OF GALACTO-OLIGOSACCHARIDES

Properties of GOS

The physico-chemical properties of galacto-oligosaccharides are of significant interest for their application in the food industries. Generally, GOS are transparent/colorless water-soluble products (80% w/w solubility), and more viscous than high-fructose corn syrup [22, 57]. GOS are stable during treatment at elevated temperature of up to 160°C and as low as pH 2. They are also stable during long-term storage at room temperature under acidic conditions [38].The caloric value of GOS was estimated to be 1.7 kcal g^{-1}, this is approximately 30-50% of those of digestible carbohydrates such as sucrose [38]. GOS are low-calorie sweeteners since they pass through the human small intestine without being digested. GOS are undigested by pancreatic enzymes and gastric juice while passing the small intestine, which makes them suitable for low-calorie diets and for consumption by individuals with diabetes [57, 97]. They can be used as humectants because of their high moisture-retaining capacity to prevent excessive drying, hence to keep the foodstuff moist. They can alter the freezing temperature of frozen foods and reduce the amount of colouring due to Maillard reactions in heat-processed foods as relatively fewer reducing moieties are available [57, 97, 98]. These properties enable GOS to be applied in a wide variety of food products.

Table 2. Commercial galacto-oligosaccharides (GOS) in the market

Product	Company	Total GOS (% w/w)	Enzyme Source
Oligomate 55	Yakult Pharmaceutical Industry Co., Ltd. Tokyo, Japan	>55	*Sporobolomyces singularis*, *Kluyveromyces lactis* [159, 160]
Vivinal® GOS	Friesland Foods Domo, Amersfoort, The Netherlands	~60	*Bacillus circulans* [161, 162]
Purimune™	GTC Nutrition, Colorado, USA	≥ 90	*Bacillus circulans* [163, 164]
Bimuno® GOS	Clasado Ltd., Milton Keynes, England, UK	48-55	*Bifidobacterium bifidum* [165, 166]
Cup-oligo	Kowa Company Ltd., Tokyo, Japan	70	*Cryptococcus laurentii* [57, 167]

Apart from being used as sweeteners, GOS are nowadays incorporated in a wide range of products such as fermented milk products, breads, jams, snack bars, confectionery, beverages, infant milk formulas, and as sugar replacements [22, 23, 38].

Biological Effects

Prebiotic galacto-oligosaccharides can serve as fermentable substrates for certain members of the gut microbiota, and have been found to modulate the colonic flora [4, 21, 22]. The physiological importance and health benefits of prebiotic GOS have been reported extensively in several recent reviews on prebiotics and functional oligosaccharides [25, 99, 100]. The biological effects of GOS on human health are discovered in many different dimensions.

Positive Impact on the Intestinal Bifidobacteria and Lactobacilli Population

Galacto-oligosaccharides, like other prebiotics, are metabolized selectively in the gastrointestinal tract by beneficial bacteria associated with health benefits and well-being. These carbohydrates can thus positively modulate the colonic microbiota, which exerts an important influence on host health [15, 21, 22]. Bifidobacteria and lactobacilli play an important role in the eco-physiology of the colonic microbiota, although their population sizes and species composition vary among different groups of human population. The growth of these bacteria has been linked to beneficial health effects such as increased resistance to infection, stimulation of the immune system activity, protection against cancer, prophylactic and therapeutic benefits. Bifidobacteria are also known to excrete a range of water soluble vitamins such as folate, nicotinic acid, thiamine, pyridoxine, and vitamin B12 [22].

Different methods such as pure culture fermentations of single, selected strains [101, 102] and *in vitro* fermentations of mixed bacterial populations, particularly fecal bacteria, have been used as preliminary screening tools for prebiotic activities [103-105] whereas *in vivo* fermentations of non-digestible carbohydrates in animals and human subjects have been reported for evaluating the prebiotic effects of different oligosaccharide mixtures [15]. Pure culture fermentations are performed in appropriate basal media supplemented with the respective prebiotics, and the increase in cell numbers is quantified by turbidimetry of the cultures or by viable cell count. pH-controlled batch cultures are, however, better models to investigate the interactions between the gut populations in response to certain carbohydrates. Here, fermentation is again based on basal media, with the test carbohydrate being the sole fermentable substrate present, but the use of fecal bacterial populations allows for an investigation of the interactions, competition and cross-feeding during growth on the selected substrate. Changes in fecal bacteria concentrations are monitored using molecular techniques such as fluorescent *in situ* hybridization (FISH) or real-time PCR [106, 107]. Alternatively, *in vitro* colonic models and ^{13}C labelling of substrates can be used to study the prebiotic activity [108]. The ability of galacto-oligosaccharide uptake generally seems to vary within the genus of *Lactobacillus* and *Bifidobacterium*, and hence different growth rates on various oligosaccharides can be observed. In a recent study, growth of single strains of *Bifidobacterium*, *Lactobacillus* and *Streptococcus* on various trisaccharides including 4´-galactosyl-lactose and 6´-galactosyl-lactose was evaluated, and in general, these strains grew faster on the trisaccharides with a β-(1→6)-galactosyl moiety [109]. A plethora of GOS is also found in human milk, and these differently substituted oligosaccharides are associated with a number of beneficial effects for the breast-fed infant. Because of this, GOS are incorporated in infant formula to achieve a bifidogenic effect and to imply a "breast-fed-like" flora [110]. A recent study demonstrated the prebiotic attributes of a purified Vivinal® GOS formulation in an *in-vitro* colon model. The authors observed an increase in numbers of lactobacilli and bifidobacteria as well other beneficial bacteria, with a concomitant decrease in numbers of *Bacteroides species, Eubacterium halii, Prevotella,* and *Lactococcus* [108].

Prebiotic effects of GOS depend significantly on the degree polymerization, the linkage types as well as the composition of the GOS mixtures, and also vary between individuals. These differences are known to be important when it comes to GOS assimilation by beneficial bacteria in the colon. It was reported that the administration of a GOS mixture containing β-(1→3) as well as β-(1→4) and β-(1→6) linkages proved to have a better bifidogenic effect than a mixture containing GOS with β-(1→4) and β-(1→6) linkages [56]. Furthermore, bifidogenic properties of GOS are dose dependent. It is known that bifidobacteria populations generally increase as the GOS dosage and purity increase. However, it has been shown that even when GOS were administered for many weeks and at high doses, there were still some individuals for whom a bifidogenic response did not occur [111].

Protective Effect against Infections and Intoxications

The use of prebiotics to prevent non-antibiotic associated gut diseases is promising. GOS are dietary prebiotic oligosaccharides and increasingly used as new food ingredient, especially in infant formula. Infants are more susceptible to gastrointestinal pathogens than adults. It is well known that a higher number of bifidobacteria in the intestine of breast-fed infants has been associated with a better health compared with formula-fed infants. It was suggested that GOS administration reduced intestinal infections and lowered the incidence of gastroenteritis in healthy infants during the first year of age [112]. GOS are not only effective against enteric infections in infants but also against respiratory infections. A study, in which new-born infants were fed a mixture of 4 probiotic bacterial strains along with galacto-oligosaccharides, revealed no effect on the incidence of any allergic diseases and it seemed to increase resistance to respiratory infections during the first two years of life [113]. A similar result was found in another study of preterm infants in Finland, which concluded that early supplementation of prebiotics (GOS and polydextrose mixture) or probiotics reduce the risk of virus-associated respiratory tract infections during the first year of life [114].

The use of GOS as functional mimics for a cell-surface toxin receptor is continuing to be developed for treatment or prevention of an acute or chronic disease associated with the adhesion or uptake of a cholera toxin (Ctx), which is a significant cause of gastrointestinal disease globally. Ctx antiadhesive activity of GOS was shown in a study [115], in which GOS fractions containing more than 5% hexasaccharides (DP6) exhibited more than 90% binding to the cell-surface toxin receptor (GM1) and its competitive inhibition was dose dependent. Supplementation of the prebiotic GOS in enteral nutrition was also found to significantly improve the intestinal barrier function in secondary infectious complications associated with severe acute pancreatitis rats, which might be partly attributed to an increase in the population of probiotic bifidobacteria, stimulation of the production of sIgA in the intestinal mucus, decrease in the apoptosis of intestinal epithelial cells, and regulation of the expression of the tight junction protein occluding [116].

Protective mechanisms of GOS against enteric infections and intoxications are associated with the potential to inhibit pathogen infections by blocking or competing for bacterial adhesion sites as well as competitive inhibition of adhesion or uptake of bacterial toxin in intestinal cells. GOS showed the best adherence inhibition of *Escherichia coli* strain E2348/69 on HEp-2 and Caco-2 cells with the depletion in adherence on both HEp-2 and Caco-2 cells by 65 and 70%, respectively, when compares with FOS, inulin, lactulose, and raffinose [117]. A protective mechanism of GOS against other enteric pathogens such as *Salmonella* and *Listeria* was also reported. Purified GOS, derived from a mixture produced by the enzymatic activity of *Bifidobacterium bifidum*, were reported to reduce *Salmonella enterica* serovar Typhimurium adhesion and invasion both *in vitro* and *in vivo* [118]. It was demonstrated that ~2.5 mg GOS mL^{-1} significantly reduced the invasion of *S.* Typhimurium. The presence of GOS also prevented the adherence or invasion of *S.* Typhimurium to enterocytes, and thus reduced its associated pathology. It was also suggested that this protection appeared to correlate with significant reductions in the neutral and acidic mucins detected in goblet cells, possibly as a consequence of stimulating the cells to secrete the mucin into the lumen

[118]. In a recent study, it was demonstrated that galacto-oligosaccharides, obtained from transgalactosylation of lactose (GOS-La) or lactulose (GOS-Lu), and their derivatives caseinomacropeptide hydrolysates (hCMP:GOS-La and hCMP:GOS-Lu) significantly reduced adhesion *of Salmonella enterica* CECT 443 and *Listeria monocytogenes* CECT 935. GOS-Lu and hCMP:GOS-Lu also inhibited the production of IL-1β, inflammatory cytokines, by intestinal cells stimulated by the pathogens tested [119].

Immunomodulation for the Prevention of Allergies and Gut Inflammatory Conditions

Currently, there is increasing interest in the utilization of prebiotics to modulate the immune system and attenuate inflammations in the colon. Most of these data originate from animal models and were obtained in relation to FOS and its prebiotic effect. Nevertheless, there are some studies that either suggest or prove an effect of GOS on the immune system, suggesting either a direct or indirect modulatory effect [97].

Immunity consists of the innate and adaptive immune system. The innate immune system is the first line of defense for the body and it comprises a physical barrier such as the skin, phagocytic, inflammatory, dendritic and natural killer (NK) cell, as well as other soluble components such as cytokines and complement proteins. The adaptive immune system response occurs after activation of the innate system. It is more antigen-specific and it involves the T- and B-lymphocytes. Lymphocytes play an important role in this component of the immune system, either by modulating the function of other immune cells, or by directly destroying infected cells [22]. Several animal model studies on the immunomodulatory effects of GOS were reported. A study in mice revealed that $CD25^+$ regulatory T-cells have an important role in modulated Flu-vaccine responses induced by orally supplied prebiotic oligosaccharides containing GOS [120]. A recent study investigated the effect of GOS on colitis development and on immune variables in *Smad*3-deficient mice treated with the pathogen *Helicobacter hepaticus*. The results showed that GOS significantly reduced colitis severity in response to *H. hepaticus,* and it was suggested that GOS reduces colitis by modulating the function and trafficking of NK cells and may provide a novel therapeutic strategy for individuals with inflammatory bowel disease [121]. It is known that supplementation of non-digestible oligosaccharides during pregnancy has positive effects on hypertension as well as the metabolism, and may be used to ameliorate pregnancy-related metabolic disturbances. The effects of non-digestible oligosaccharides on the immune system during the pregnancy of mice supplemented with a specific mixture of short-chain galacto- and long-chain fructo-oligosaccharides (ratio of 9:1) was found to elicit a more tolerogenic immune reaction in pregnant mice [122].

In human studies, it has been suggested that GOS play a role in the development of the immune system in infants, and may consequently inhibit the onset of allergy. A specific prebiotic mixture of short-chain galacto-oligosaccharides and long-chain fructo-oligosaccharides (ratio of 9:1) has shown to reduce the incidence of atopic dermatitis at 6 months of age in infants at risk for allergy [123]. The synbiotic effect of several probiotic strains and GOS in preventing allergic diseases was demonstrated as well. High-risk pregnant women received probiotics for 2-4 weeks before delivery and their infants received a probiotic formulation with GOS for 6 months. It was shown that probiotics when taken together with GOS showed no effect on the incidence of all allergic diseases in high-risk children from birth to the age of two but significantly prevented eczema and especially atopic eczema [113].

Trophic Effects of Short-Chain Fatty Acids (SCFAs) on the Colonic Epithelium

Short-chain fatty acids (SCFAs), which are the end products of saccharolytic fermentations in the gut, are of interest as they are claimed to promote human health or may be antagonistic to intestinal competitors [15, 124]. The principal SCFAs that result from carbohydrate fermentations are acetate, propionate and butyrate. SCFAs stimulate colonic blood flow as well as fluid and electrolyte uptake [125], and inhibit proliferation and induce apoptosis in colon cancer cells [126]. SCFAs affect the synthesis of vitamins and essential amino acids, interaction with training of gut-associated lymphoid tissue; and resistance against colonization by enteric pathogens. Moreover, SCFAs affect colonic epithelial cell transport, energy transduction in colonocytes, growth and cellular differentiation [22, 127]. These trophic properties have important physiological implications, in addition to maintaining the mucosal defense barrier against invading organism. *In vitro* studies involving fecal microbiota are useful models for studying fermentation activity of oligosaccharides. FOS and GOS (at 10 g L^{-1}) were shown to increase acetate and butyrate formation, with transient accumulation of lactate and succinate [128]. It was also demonstrated that a GOS mixture derived from lactose with 6'-galactosyl-lactose and 4'-galactosyl-lactose as the main components exhibited a bifidogenic effect in fecal slurries similar or slightly higher than the commercial Vivinal® GOS, and enhanced the production of acetic acid and SCFAs [129].

Mineral Absorption

Consumption of GOS significantly increases calcium absorption in humans and GOS play a role in increasing bioavailability of calcium, which is a key to bone mass density [22]. Different studies in rats and human trials have shown positive effects of GOS in promoting calcium absorption. In a study on the dose-response effect of GOS supplementation on calcium and magnesium absorption, mineral retention, bone properties and gut microbiota in growing rats, beneficial effects on calcium and magnesium absorption and retention, femur calcium uptake, bone strength, and bone mineral density were observed. These effects either directly or indirectly were attributed to a decrease in cecal pH, an increase in cecal wall and content weight, and an increase in number of bifidobacteria [130]. A similar study reported that a diet containing GOS stimulated calcium absorption and the ingestion of GOS prevents osteopenia in partially gastrectomized rats [131]. Recently, the dose-response relationship of GOS supplementation on calcium absorption in adolescent girls was investigated. Significant improvement in calcium absorption with both low and high doses of GOS was observed, but it was not a dose-response relationship [132]. These observations may have particular importance because bone mass accretion is maximal during adolescence [133].

Other Health Benefits of GOS

Other additional health benefits of GOS such as effects on serum cholesterol and high-density lipoprotein (HDL) cholesterol levels, improving brain functions, maintenance of brain health, and adjunctive treatment of neuropsychiatric disorders were reported. It is believed that prebiotics can decrease serum cholesterol levels and increase HDL cholesterol levels when used in subjects with initial elevated serum cholesterol levels. However, the role of GOS regarding this health effect is still in question since it was demonstrated that 5.5 g of a B-GOS mixture administration to healthy elderly had no effect upon total serum cholesterol and HDL cholesterol levels [134].

In addition, it was shown that no differences in total cholesterol and low-density lipoprotein (LDL) cholesterol levels exist in infants receiving an infant formula supplemented with GOS and long-chain FOS in comparison with infants receiving a control infant formula [135]. More studies are required in order to demonstrate the underlying mechanisms of GOS in this respect.

Recently, evidence was presented that suggests effects of GOS in improving brain function with possible involvement of gut hormones. A study in rat reported that the effect of GOS on components of central *N*-methyl-D-aspartate receptor (NMDAR) signaling was greater than FOS, and it may reflect the proliferative potency of GOS on microbiota and increased brain derived neurotropic factor (BDNF) expression. This evidence suggested further investigations on the utility of prebiotics in the maintenance of brain health and adjunctive treatment of neuropsychiatric disorders [136]. In another recent study, it was reported that GOS or GOS-rich prebiotic yogurt could delay the onset of disease and prolong the lifespan in mice. They can attenuate motor neuron loss as well as muscle atrophy and dysfunction. Furthermore, they possess anti-inflammatory and anti-apoptotic effects through the regulation of related molecules. Altogether, GOS may have therapeutic potential for amyotrophic lateral sclerosis (ALS), and prebiotic yogurt may be considered as a nutritional therapy for this intractable disease [137].

EMERGING TRENDS IN THE PRODUCTION OF NOVEL HETERO-OLIGOSACCHARIDES

Human milk is known as the sole source of nourishment for breast-fed infants and for its promotion of a healthy development of newborns. Human milk is comprised of a complex mixture of oligosaccharides (5-10 g L^{-1} in addition to lactose) that are different in size, linkage and charge [138]. Human milk oligosaccharides (HMO) are a heterogenic group of about 200 molecular species consisting of mostly neutral and fucosylated oligosaccharides [139]. The potential health benefits of HMO have been studied with a special emphasis on prebiotic effects [138]. Recent studies have reported on the ability of HMO to selectively support the growth of specific strains of bifidobacteria thus providing insight on how HMO modulate the infant intestinal microbiota [140-142]. These results suggest that the prebiotic, bifidogenic effects of HMO are structure-specific and may vary depending on the HMO composition in milk [138, 140-142]. In addition, HMO are also considered as a mechanism to protect infants against exogenous infections [140, 143]. *In vitro* studies have shown that HMO bind and block the infection of pathogenic bacteria to animal cells by acting as receptor analogues to the intestinal cell glycans [140, 144, 145]. Because of these benefits, prebiotic HMO are of great interest for human nutrition.

HMO are composed of both neutral and anionic species with building blocks of 5 monosaccharides: D-glucose, D-galactose, *N*-acetyl-D-glucosamine, L-fucose, and *N*-acetylneuraminic acid (sialic acid). The basic structure of HMO includes a lactose core at the reducing end which is elongated by *N*-acetyl-lactosamine units with at least 12 different types of glycosidic bonds, wherein fucose and sialic acid residues are added to terminal positions [140, 143]. The terminal lactose is typically elongated by lacto-*N*-biose units (LNB; Gal-β-1,3-GlcNAc) in type I or *N*-acetyl-lactosamine units (LacNAc; Gal-β-1,4-GlcNAc) in the rarer type II structures. Both LNB and LacNAc are attached via a β-1,3-linkage to the galactosyl moiety of the terminal lactose, with an additional β-1,6-linkage in branched HMO. These LNB and LacNAc units can be repeated up to 25 times in larger HMO, forming the core region of these oligosaccharides. A further variation results from the attachment of fucosyl and sialic acid residues. Thus, the simplest structures following this general scheme (apart from certain trisaccharides such as galactosyl-lactose, fucosyl-lactose and sialyl-lactose) are the tetrasaccharides lacto-*N*-tetraose, Gal-β-1,3-GlcNAc-β-1,3-Gal-β-1,4-Glc (type I), and lacto-*N*-*neo*-tetraose, Gal-β-1,4-GlcNAc-β-1,3-Gal-β-1,4-Glc (type II) (Figure 2) [146-149]. Mono- and difucosyl-lactose, lacto-*N*-tetraose and its fucosylated derivatives, as well as sialyl-lactose and the sialylated forms of lacto-*N*-tetraose, are major oligosaccharides in human milk.

Some of the above-mentioned HMO structures or structurally related compounds can be accessed through different approaches. One such approach that has received some interest is based on β-galactosidase-catalyzed transglycosylation with lactose as donor (thus transferring galactose onto suitable acceptors) and GlcNAc as acceptor, thus obtaining *N*-acetyl-lactosamine (LacNAc) and its regioisomers. Using this approach and a hyperthermophilic β-galactosidase from *Sulfolobus solfataricus*, Gal-β-1,6-GlcNAc together with an unidentified sugar were the main products starting from a mixture of 1 M lactose and 1 M GlcNAc, while LacNAc and Gal-β-1,3-GlcNAc were formed as well, yet in lower concentrations [150]. This reaction was also optimized using β-galactosidase from *Bacillus circulans* as the biocatalyst. This enzyme is known for its propensity to synthesize β-1,4-

linkages in its transgalactosylation mode, and hence the main reaction product here was LacNAc together with smaller amounts of GlcNAc-containing higher oligosaccharides (one tri- and one tetrasaccharides) and Gal-β-1,6-GlcNAc. The total yield was 40% for these GlcNAc-containing oligosaccharides when starting from 0.5 M lactose and GlcNAc each [151]. This reaction and the β-galactosidase from *B. circulans* were also compared to the enzyme from *Kluyveromyces lactis* and the reaction conditions were optimized. The latter enzyme was shown to form predominately Gal-β-1,6-GlcNAc. Again, both enzymes formed a mixture of various di- to tetra-saccharides [152]. Since these structures resemble the core of HMO, they could be of interest as prebiotic compounds to be added to food.

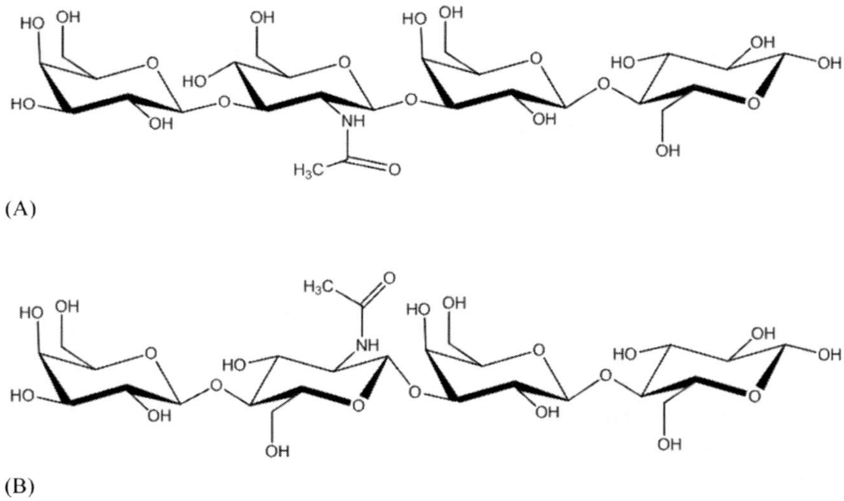

(A)

(B)

Figure 2. Some simple structures of human milk oligosaccharides: tetrasaccharides lacto-*N*-tetraose, Gal-β-1,3-GlcNAc-β-1,3-Gal-β-1,4-Glc (A), and lacto-*N*-*neo*-tetraose, Gal-β-1,4-GlcNAc-β-1,3-Gal-β-1,4-Glc (B).

Conclusion

The understanding of the relationship between certain oligosaccharide structures and prebiotic function already had an impact on novel prebiotic products that were brought to the market, and will have a more important impact in the future. The insights into the structures, production and biological effects of prebiotic galacto-oligosaccharides together with advancement in the area of biotechnology will certainly result in the enhancement of the production of GOS. The presence of structurally related oligosaccharides together with different complex structures in human breast milk makes GOS attract increasing interests from researchers and manufacturers. Since the structures of GOS or novel hetero-oligosaccharides resemble the core of human milk oligosaccharides, they could be of interest as prebiotic compounds to be added to food, and intensified research in this field is needed to open the door for commercial production of these novel functionally enhanced, prebiotic oligosaccharides.

REFERENCES

[1] J. H. J. Huis in't Veld and R. Havenaar, *Eur. J. Clin. Nutr.,* 45, 29-31 (1991).

[2] M. E. Sanders, *Int. Dairy J.,* 8, 341-347 (1998).

[3] W. H. Holzapfel, P. Haberer, R. Geisen, J. Bjorkroth, and U. Schillinger, *Am. J. Clin. Nutri.,* 73, 365s-373s (2001).

[4] W. H. Holzapfel and U. Schillinger, *Food Res. Int.,* 35, 109-116 (2002).

[5] R. Fuller, *J. Appl. Bacteriol.,* 66, 365-378 (1989).

[6] R. Havenaar, B. Ten Brink, and J. H. J. Huis in't Veld, in R. Fuller (ed.), Probiotics, the scientific basis, Chapman & Hall, London, pp. 209-221 (1992).

[7] S. Salminen, M. A. Deighton, Y. Benno, and S. L. Gorbach, in S. Salminen and A. Von Wright (eds.), Lactic acid bacteria: Microbiology and Functional aspects, Marcel Dekker Inc., New York, pp. 211-254 (1998).

[8] J. K. Collins, G. Thornton, and G. O. Sullivan, *Int. Dairy J.,* 8, 487-490 (1998).

[9] T. R. Klaenhammer, *Int. Dairy J.,* 8, 497-505 (1998).

[10] W. H. Holzapfel, P. Haberer, J. Snel, U. Schillinger, and J. H. J. Huis in't Veld, *Int. J. Food Microbiol.,* 41, 85-101 (1998).

[11] L. J. Fooks, R. Fuller, and G. R. Gibson, *Int. Dairy J.,* 9, 53-61 (1999).

[12] C. Shortt, *Trends Food Sci. Technol.,* 10, 411-417 (1999).

[13] G. W. Tannock, *Curr. Issues Mol. Biol.,* 1, 53-64 (1999).

[14] G. R. Gibson and M. B. Roberfroid, *J. Nutr.,* 125, 1401-1412 (1995).

[15] G. R. Gibson, H. M. Probert, J. Van Loo, R. A. Rastall, and M. B. Roberfroid, *Nutr. Res. Rev.,* 17, 259-275 (2004).

[16] ISAPP, 6th Meeting of the International Scientific Association of Probiotics and Prebiotics, London, Ontario (2008).

[17] M. Roberfroid, *J. Nutr.,* 137, 830S-837S (2007).

[18] M. Roberfroid, G. R. Gibson, L. Hoyles, A. L. McCartney, R. Rastall, I. Rowland, D. Wolvers, B. Watzl, H. Szajewska, B. Stahl, F. Guarner, F. Respondek, K. Whelan, V. Coxam, M. J. Davicco, L. Léotoing, Y. Wittrant, N. M. Delzenne, P. D. Cani, A. M. Neyrinck, and A. Meheust, *Br. J. Nutr.,* 104, S1-S63 (2010).

[19] H. Barreteau, C. Delattre, and P. Michaud, *Food Technol. Biotechnol.,* 44, 323-333 (2006).

[20] T. Barclay, M. Ginic-Markovic, P. Cooper, and N. Petrovsky, *J. Exci. Food Chem.,* 1, 27-50 (2010).

[21] R. A. Rastall, G. R. Gibson, H. S. Gill, F. Guarner, T. R. Klaenhammer, B. Pot, G. Reid, I. R. Rowland, and M. E. Sanders, *FEMS Microbiol. Ecol.,* 52, 145-152 (2005).

[22] G. T. Macfarlane, H. Steed, and S. Macfarlane, *J. Appl. Microbiol.,* 104, 305-44 (2008).

[23] R. G. Crittenden and M. J. Playne, *Trends Food Sci. Tech.,* 7, 353-361 (1996).

[24] P. K. Gopal, P. A. Sullivan, and J. B. Smart, *Int. Dairy J.,* 11, 19-25 (2001).

[25] V. Sangwan, S. K. Tomar, R. R. B. Singh, A. K. Singh, and B. Ali, *J. Food Sci.,* 76, R103-R111 (2011).

[26] B. M. de Roode, M. C. Franssen, A. van der Padt, and R. M. Boom, *Biotechnol. Prog.,* 19, 1391-1402 (2003).

[27] H. D. Ly and S. G. Withers, *Annu. Rev. Biochem.,* 68, 487-522 (1999).

[28] B. L. Cantarel, P. M. Coutinho, C. Rancurel, T. Bernard, V. Lombard, and B. Henrissat, *Nucleic Acids Res.,* 37, D233-238 (2009).

[29] R. Gupta, T. Govil, N. Capalash, and P. Sharma, *Appl. Biochem. Biotechnol.,* 168, 1681-1693 (2012).

[30] E. Yoshida, H. Sakurama, M. Kiyohara, M. Nakajima, M. Kitaoka, H. Ashida, J. Hirose, T. Katayama, K. Yamamoto, and H. Kumagai, *Glycobiology,* 22, 361-368 (2012).

[31] C. Schwab, K. I. Sørensen, and M. G. Gänzle, *Syst. Appl. Microbiol.,* 33, 300-307 (2010).

[32] T. Goulas, A. Goulas, G. Tzortzis, and G. R. Gibson, *Appl. Microbiol. Biotechnol.,* 84, 899-907 (2009).

[33] T. Nakayama and T. Amachi, in M. C. Flickinger and S. W. Drew (eds.), Encyclopedia of bioprocess technology: fermentation, biocatalysis, and bioseparation, John Willey and Sons, New York, pp. 1291-1305 (1999).
[34] L. F. Pivarnik, A. G. Senegal, and A. G. Rand, in J. E. Kinsella and S. L. Taylor (eds.), *Adv. Food Nutr. Res.*, Academic Press, pp. 33-41 (1995).
[35] J. E. Prenosil, E. Stuker, and J. R. Bourne, *Biotechnol. Bioeng.,* 30, 1019-1025 (1987).
[36] I. Petzelbauer, R. Zeleny, A. Reiter, K. D. Kulbe, and B. Nidetzky, *Biotechnol. Bioeng.,* 69, 140-149. (2000).
[37] R. R. Mahoney, *Food Chem.,* 63, 147-154 (1998).
[38] T. Sako, K. Matsumoto, and R. Tanaka, *Int. Dairy J.,* 9, 69-80 (1999).
[39] B. Splechtna, T. H. Nguyen, M. Steinböck, K. D. Kulbe, W. Lorenz, and D. Haltrich, *J. Agric. Food Chem.,* 54, 4999-5006 (2006).
[40] M. A. Boon, A. E. M. Janssen, and K. van `t Riet, *Enzyme Microb. Technol.,* 26, 271-281 (2000).
[41] T. H. Nguyen, B. Splechtna, M. Steinböck, W. Kneifel, H. P. Lettner, K. D. Kulbe, and D. Haltrich, *J. Agric. Food Chem.,* 54, 4989-4998 (2006).
[42] T. H. Nguyen, B. Splechtna, S. Krasteva, W. Kneifel, K. D. Kulbe, C. Divne, and D. Haltrich, *FEMS Microbiol. Lett.,* 269, 136-144 (2007).
[43] S. Iqbal, T. H. Nguyen, T. T. Nguyen, T. Maischberger, and D. Haltrich, *Carbohydr. Res.,* 345, 1408-1416 (2010).
[44] D. Gobinath and S. G. Prapulla, *Biotechnol. Lett.,* (2013) doi: 10.1007/s10529-013-1345-9.
[45] S. Iqbal, T. H. Nguyen, H. A. Nguyen, T. T. Nguyen, T. Maischberger, R. Kittl, and D. Haltrich, *J. Agric. Food Chem.,* 59, 3803-3811 (2011).
[46] T. Maischberger, E. Leitner, S. Nitisinprasert, O. Juajun, M. Yamabhai, T. H. Nguyen, and D. Haltrich, *Biotechnol. J.,* 5, 838-847 (2010).
[47] T. T. Nguyen, H. A. Nguyen, S. L. Arreola, G. Mlynek, K. Djinović-Carugo, G. Mathiesen, T. H. Nguyen, and D. Haltrich, *J. Agric. Food Chem.,* 60, 1713-1721 (2012).
[48] B. A. Black, V. S. Y. Lee, Y. Y. Zhao, Y. Hu, J. M. Curtis, and M. G. Ganzle, *J. Agric. Food Chem.,* 60, 4886-4894 (2012).
[49] G. X. Liu, J. Kong, W. W. Lu, W. T. Kong, H. Tian, X. Y. Tian, and G. C. Huo, *J. Dairy Sci.,* 94, 5811-5820 (2011).
[50] C. Nie, B. Liu, Y. Zhang, G. Zhao, X. Fan, X. Ning, and W. Zhang, *Protein Expr. Purif.,* 92, 88-93 (2013).
[51] M. N. Hung, Z. Xia, N. T. Hu, and B. H. Lee, *Appl. Environ. Microbiol.,* 67, 4256-4263 (2001).

[52] T. Goulas, A. Goulas, G. Tzortzis, and G. R. Gibson, *Appl. Microbiol. Biotechnol.,* 82, 1079-1088 (2009).
[53] K. Kawabata, Y. Sugiyama, T. Sakano, and H. Ohigashi, *Biofactors,* 39, 422-429 (2013).
[54] B. A. Rabiu, A. J. Jay, G. R. Gibson, and R. A. Rastall, *Appl. Environ. Microbiol.,* 67, 2526-2530 (2001).
[55] S. H. Yi, I. Alli, K. H. Park, and B. Lee, *New Biotechnol.,* 28, 806-813 (2011).
[56] F. Depeint, G. Tzortzis, J. Vulevic, K. I'Anson, and G. R. Gibson, *Am. J. Clin. Nutr.,* 87, 785-791 (2008).
[57] D. P. M. Torres, M. d. P. F. Gonçalves, J. A. Teixeira, and L. R. Rodrigues, *Compr. Rev. Food Sci. Food Safety,* 9, 438-454 (2010).
[58] T. Hansson, T. Kaper, J. D. Van Oost, W. M. De Vos, and P. Adlercreutz, *Biotechnol. Bioeng.,* 73, 203-210 (2001).
[59] J. B. Moore, P. Markiewicz, and J. H. Miller, *Gene,* 147, 101-106 (1994).
[60] W. Chen, H. Chen, Y. Xia, J. Zhao, F. Tian, and H. Zhang, *J. Dairy Sci.,* 91, 1751-1758 (2008).
[61] B. Di Lauro, A. Strazzulli, G. Perugino, F. La Cara, E. Bedini, M. M. Corsaro, M. Rossi, and M. Moracci, *Biochim. Biophys. Acta,* 1784, 292-301 (2008).
[62] E. S. Nam, M. S. Kim, H. B. Lee, and J. K. Ahn, *Prikl. Biokhim. Mikrobiol.,* 46, 562-571 (2010).
[63] J. Marín-Navarro, D. Talens-Perales, A. Oude-Vrielink, F. J. Cañada, and J. Polaina, *World J. Microbiol. Biotechnol.,* (2013), doi 10.1007/s11274-013-1517-8.
[64] D. O. Otieno, *Compr. Rev. Food Sci. Food Safety,* 9, 471-482 (2010).
[65] K. K. Pulicherla, P. S. Kumar, K. Manideep, V. P. B. Rekha, M. Ghosh, and K. R. S. Sambasiva Rao, *Prep. Biochem. Biotechnol.,* 43, 766-780 (2013).
[66] A. Hoyoux, I. Jennes, P. Dubois, S. Genicot, F. Dubail, J. M. François, E. Baise, G. Feller, and C. Gerday, *Appl. Environ. Microbiol.,* 67, 1529-1535 (2001).
[67] J. M. Hu, H. Li, L. X. Cao, P. C. Wu, C. T. Zhang, S. L. Sang, X. Y. Zhang, M. J. Chen, J. Q. Lu, and Y. H. Liu, *J. Agric. Food Chem.,* 55, 2217-2224 (2007).
[68] T. Nakagawa, R. Ikehata, T. Myoda, T. Miyaji, and N. Tomizuka, *Protein Expr. Purif.,* 54, 295-299 (2007).

[69] P. Hildebrandt, M. Wanarska, and J. Kur, *BMC Microbiol.,* 9, 151 (2009).
[70] M. Schmidt and P. Stougaard, *Environ. Technol.,* 31, 1107-1114 (2010).
[71] A. Wierzbicka-Woś, H. Cieśliński, M. Wanarska, K. Kozłowska-Tylingo, P. Hildebrandt, and J. Kur, *Microbial cell factories,* 10, 108 (2011).
[72] R. Karan, M. D. Capes, P. DasSarma, and S. DasSarma, *BMC Biotechnol.,* 13, 3 (2013).
[73] V. Vincent, N. Aghajari, N. Pollet, A. Boisson, S. Boudebbouze, R. Haser, E. Maguin, and M. Rhimi, *Antonie van Leeuwenhoek,* 103, 701-712 (2012).
[74] N. G. Asp, A. Burvall, and A. Dahlqvist, *Food Chem.,* 5, 147-153 (1980).
[75] T. Toba, A. Yokota, and S. Adachi, *Food Chem.,* 16, 147-162 (1985).
[76] S. Yanahira, T. Kobayashi, T. Suguri, M. Nakakoshi, S. Miura, H. Ishikawa, and I. Nakajima, *Biosci. Biotechnol. Biochem.,* 59, 1021-1026. (1995).
[77] A. R. Park and D. K. Oh, *Appl. Microbiol. Biotechnol.,* 85, 1279-1286 (2010).
[78] N. Albayrak and S. T. Yang, *Biotechnol. Bioeng.,* 77, 8-19. (2002).
[79] K.-i. Iwasaki, M. Nakajima, and S.-i. Nakao, *Process Biochem.,* 31, 69-76 (1996).
[80] H. J. Shin, J. M. Park, and J. W. Yang, *Process Biochem.,* 33, 787-792 (1998).
[81] K. Isobe, M. Yamashita, S. Chiba, N. Takahashi, and T. Koyama, *J. Biosci. Bioeng.,* 116, 293-297 (2013).
[82] M.-N. Hung and B. H. Lee, *Appl. Microbiol. Biotechnol.,* 58, 439-445 (2002).
[83] P. L. Moller, F. Jorgensen, O. C. Hansen, S. M. Madsen, and P. Stougaard, *Appl. Environ. Microbiol.,* 67, 2276-2283. (2001).
[84] K. M. J. Van Laere, T. Abee, H. A. Schols, G. Beldman, and A. G. J. Voragen, *Appl. Environ. Microbiol.,* 66, 1379-1384 (2000).
[85] S. W. A. Hinz, L. A. M. Van Den Broek, G. Beldman, J. P. Vincken, and A. G. J. Voragen, *Appl. Microbiol. Biotechnol.,* 66, 276-284 (2004).
[86] T. K. Goulas, A. K. Goulas, G. Tzortzis, and G. R. Gibson, *Appl. Microbiol. Biotechnol.,* 76, 1365-1372 (2007).
[87] E. M. Hébert, R. R. Raya, P. Tailliez, and G. S. De Giori, *Int. J. Food Microbiol.,* 59, 19-27 (2000).

[88] A. C. Adam, M. Rubio-Texeira, and J. Polaina, *Crit. Rev. Food Sci. Nutr.,* 44, 553-557 (2004).
[89] B. Splechtna, T. H. Nguyen, and D. Haltrich, *J. Agric. Food Chem.,* 55, 6772-6777 (2007).
[90] B. Splechtna, T. H. Nguyen, R. Zehetner, H. P. Lettner, W. Lorenz, and D. Haltrich, *Biotechnol. J.,* 2, 480-485 (2007).
[91] F. Jørgensen, O. C. Hansen, and P. Stougaard, *Appl. Microbiol. Biotechnol.,* 57, 647-652 (2001).
[92] G. Placier, H. Watzlawick, C. Rabiller, and R. Mattes, *Appl. Environ. Microbiol.,* 75, 6312-6321 (2009).
[93] Y. Wu, S. Yuan, S. Chen, D. Wu, J. Chen, and J. Wu, *Food Chem.,* 138, 1588-1595 (2013).
[94] J. Seibel and K. Buchholz, in H. Derek (ed.), *Advances in Carbohydrate Chemistry and Biochemistry*, Academic Press, pp. 101-138 (2010).
[95] L. Coulier, J. Timmermans, B. Richard, R. Van Den Dool, I. Haaksman, B. Klarenbeek, T. Slaghek, and W. Van Dongen, *J. Agric. Food Chem.,* 57, 8488-8495 (2009).
[96] M. J. Playne, Crittenden, R. G., in P. L. H. McSweeney, Fox, P. F. (eds.), Lactose, water, salts and minor constitutents, Springer, New York, pp. 121-201 (2009).
[97] G. Tzortzis and J. Vulevic, in D. Charalampopoulos and R. Rastall (eds.), Prebiotics and Probiotics Science and Technology, Springer New York, pp. 207-244 (2009).
[98] B. P. Lamsal, *J. Sci. Food. Agric.,* 92, 2020-2028 (2012).
[99] S. Patel and A. Goyal, *World J. Microbiol. Biotechnol.,* 27, 1119-1128 (2011).
[100] X. Qiang, C. YongLie, and W. QianBing, *Carbohydr. Polym.,* 77, 435-441 (2009).
[101] H. Kaplan and R. W. Hutkins, *Appl. Environ. Microbiol.,* 66, 2682-2684 (2000).
[102] J. Huebner, R. L. Wehling, and R. W. Hutkins, *Int. Dairy J.,* 17, 770-775 (2007).
[103] R. Palframan, G. R. Gibson, and R. A. Rastall, *Lett. Appl. Microbiol.,* 37, 281-2814 (2003).
[104] C. E. Rycroft, M. R. Jones, G. R. Gibson, and R. A. Rastall, *J. Appl. Microbiol.,* 91, 878-887. (2001).
[105] J. Vulevic, R. A. Rastall, and G. R. Gibson, *FEMS Microbiol. Lett.,* 236, 153-159 (2004).

[106] A. Cardelle-Cobas, M. Fernández, N. Salazar, C. Martínez-Villaluenga, M. Villamiel, P. Ruas-Madiedo, and C. G. De Los Reyes-Gavilán, *J. Dairy Res.,* 76, 317-325 (2009).

[107] A. Cardelle-Cobas, A. Olano, N. Corzo, M. Villamiel, M. Collins, S. Kolida, and R. A. Rastall, *J. Agric. Food Chem.,* 60, 2024-2032 (2012).

[108] A. J. H. Maathuis, E. G. van den Heuvel, M. H. C. Schoterman, and K. Venema, *J. Nutr.,* 142, 1205-1212 (2012).

[109] A. Cardelle-Cobas, N. Corzo, A. Olano, C. Peláez, T. Requena, and M. Ávila, *Int. J. Food Microbiol.,* 149, 81-87 (2011).

[110] P. M. Sherman, M. Cabana, G. R. Gibson, B. V. Koletzko, J. Neu, G. Veereman-Wauters, E. E. Ziegler, and W. A. Walker, *J. Pediatr.,* 155, S61-70 (2009).

[111] L. M. G. Davis, I. Martínez, J. Walter, and R. Hutkins, *Int. J. Food Microbiol.,* 144, 285-292 (2010).

[112] E. Bruzzese, M. Volpicelli, V. Squeglia, D. Bruzzese, F. Salvini, M. Bisceglia, P. Lionetti, M. Cinquetti, G. Iacono, S. Amarri, and A. Guarino, *Clin. Nutr.,* 28, 156-161 (2009).

[113] K. Kukkonen, E. Savilahti, T. Haahtela, K. Juntunen-Backman, R. Korpela, T. Poussa, T. Tuure, and M. Kuitunen, *J. Allergy Clin. Immunol.,* 119, 192-198 (2007).

[114] R. Luoto, O. Ruuskanen, M. Waris, M. Kalliomaki, S. Salminen, and E. Isolauri, *J. Allergy Clin. Immunol.,* (2013) doi:10.1016/j.jaci.2013.08.020.

[115] H. R. Sinclair, J. de Slegte, G. R. Gibson, and R. A. Rastall, *J. Agric. Food Chem.,* 57, 3113-3119 (2009).

[116] Y. Zhong, D. Cai, W. Cai, S. Geng, L. Chen, and T. Han, *Clin. Nutr.,* 28, 575-580 (2009).

[117] K. Shoaf, G. L. Mulvey, G. D. Armstrong, and R. W. Hutkins, *Infect. Immun.,* 74, 6920-6928 (2006).

[118] L. E. Searle, W. A. Cooley, G. Jones, A. Nunez, B. Crudgington, U. Weyer, A. H. Dugdale, G. Tzortzis, J. W. Collins, M. J. Woodward, and R. M. La Ragione, *J. Med. Microbiol.,* 59, 1428-1439 (2010).

[119] J. M. Laparra, O. Hernandez-Hernandez, F. J. Moreno, and Y. Sanz, *Food Res. Int.,* 54, 1096-1102 (2013).

[120] B. van't Land, M. Schijf, B. C. van Esch, J. van Bergenhenegouwen, J. Bastiaans, B. Schouten, L. Boon, and J. Garssen, *Vaccine,* 28, 5711-5717 (2010).

[121] A. Gopalakrishnan, J. F. Clinthorne, E. A. Rondini, S. J. McCaskey, E. A. Gurzell, I. M. Langohr, E. M. Gardner, and J. I. Fenton, *J. Nutr.,* 142, 1336-1342 (2012).
[122] N. van Vlies, A. Hogenkamp, S. Thijssen, G. M. Dingjan, K. Knipping, J. Garssen, and L. M. J. Knippels, *J. Reprod. Immunol.,* 94, 161-168 (2012).
[123] E. van Hoffen, B. Ruiter, J. Faber, L. M'Rabet, E. F. Knol, B. Stahl, S. Arslanoglu, G. Moro, G. Boehm, and J. Garssen, *Allergy,* 64, 484-487 (2009).
[124] J. H. Cummings, G. T. Macfarlane, and H. N. Englyst, *Am. J. Clin. Nutr.,* 73, 415S-420S (2001).
[125] D. L. Topping and P. M. Clifton, *Physiol. Rev.,* 81, 1031-1064 (2001).
[126] Y. Tang, Y. Chen, H. Jiang, and D. Nie, *Cell Death Differ.,* 18, 602-618 (2011).
[127] M. Blaut and T. Clavel, *J. Nutr.,* 137, 751S-755S (2007).
[128] M. J. Hopkins and G. T. Macfarlane, *Appl. Environ. Microbiol.,* 69, 1920-1927 (2003).
[129] A. Cardelle-Cobas, M. Fernandez, N. Salazar, C. Martinez-Villaluenga, M. Villamiel, P. Ruas-Madiedo, and C. G. de los Reyes-Gavilan, *J. Dairy Res.,* 76, 317-325 (2009).
[130] C. M. Weaver, B. R. Martin, C. H. Nakatsu, A. P. Armstrong, A. Clavijo, L. D. McCabe, G. P. McCabe, S. Duignan, M. H. C. Schoterman, and E. G. H. M. van den Heuvel, *J. Agric. Food Chem.,* 59, 6501-6510 (2011).
[131] E. F. dos Santos, K. H. Tsuboi, M. R. Araujo, N. A. Andreollo, and C. K. Miyasaka, *Rev. Col. Bras. Cir.,* 38, 186-191 (2011).
[132] C. M. Whisner, B. R. Martin, M. H. C. Schoterman, C. H. Nakatsu, L. D. McCabe, G. P. McCabe, M. E. Wastney, E. G. H. M. van den Heuvel, and C. M. Weaver, *Br. J. Nutr.,* 110, 1292-1303 (2013).
[133] L. Esterle, J. P. Sabatier, F. Guillon-Metz, O. Walrant-Debray, G. Guaydier-Souquieres, F. Jehan, and M. Garabedian, *Osteoporos. Int.,* 20, 567-575 (2009).
[134] J. Vulevic, A. Drakoularakou, P. Yaqoob, G. Tzortzis, and G. R. Gibson, *Am. J. Clin. Nutr.,* 88, 1438-1446 (2008).
[135] P. Alliet, P. Scholtens, M. Raes, K. Hensen, H. Jongen, J.-L. Rummens, G. Boehm, and Y. Vandenplas, *Nutrition,* 23, 719-723 (2007).
[136] H. M. Savignac, G. Corona, H. Mills, L. Chen, J. P. E. Spencer, G. Tzortzis, and P. W. J. Burnet, *Neurochem. Int.,* 63, 756-764 (2013).

[137] L. Song, Y. Gao, X. Zhang, and W. Le, *Neuroscience,* 246, 281-290 (2013).

[138] L. Bode, *Nutr. Rev.,* 67, S183-191 (2009).

[139] M. R. Ninonuevo, Y. Park, H. Yin, J. Zhang, R. E. Ward, B. H. Clowers, J. B. German, S. L. Freeman, K. Killeen, R. Grimm, and C. B. Lebrilla, *J. Agric. Food Chem.,* 54, 7471-7480 (2006).

[140] A. Marcobal, M. Barboza, J. W. Froehlich, D. E. Block, J. B. German, C. B. Lebrilla, and D. A. Mills, *J. Agric. Food Chem.,* 58, 5334-5340 (2010).

[141] R. G. LoCascio, M. R. Ninonuevo, S. L. Freeman, D. A. Sela, R. Grimm, C. B. Lebrilla, D. A. Mills, and J. B. German, *J. Agric. Food Chem.,* 55, 8914-8919 (2007).

[142] R. E. Ward, M. Niñonuevo, D. A. Mills, C. B. Lebrilla, and J. B. German, *Mol. Nutr. Food Res.,* 51, 1398-1405 (2007).

[143] D. S. Newburg, G. M. Ruiz-Palacios, and A. L. Morrow, *Annu. Rev. Nutr.,* 25, 37-58 (2005).

[144] G. M. Ruiz-Palacios, L. E. Cervantes, P. Ramos, B. Chavez-Munguia, and D. S. Newburg, *J. Biol. Chem.,* 278, 14112-14120 (2003).

[145] A. Cravioto, A. Tello, H. Villafan, J. Ruiz, S. Del Vedovo, and J. R. Neeser, *J. Infect. Dis.,* 163, 1247-1255 (1991).

[146] A. Kobata, *Proc. Jpn. Acad. Ser. B. Phys. Biol. Sci.,* 86, 731-747 (2010).

[147] C. Kunz, S. Rudloff, W. Baier, N. Klein, and S. Strobel, *Annu. Rev. Nutr.,* 20, 699-722 (2000).

[148] S. Wu, R. Grimm, J. B. German, and C. B. Lebrilla, *J. Proteome Res.,* 10, 856-868 (2011).

[149] S. Wu, N. Tao, J. B. German, R. Grimm, and C. B. Lebrilla, *J. Proteome Res.,* 9, 4138-4151 (2010).

[150] S. Reuter, A. Rusborg Nygaard, and W. Zimmermann, *Enzyme Microb. Technol.,* 25, 509-516 (1999).

[151] W. Li, Y. Sun, H. Ye, and X. Zeng, *Eur. Food Res. Technol.,* 231, 55-63 (2010).

[152] N. Bridiau and T. Maugard, *Biotechnol. Prog.,* 27, 386-394 (2011).

[153] S. A. Biocon Española, 2013 at http://www.biocon.es/en/productos-documentos.php?id=36.

[154] B. Rodriguez-Colinas, L. Fernandez-Arrojo, A. O. Ballesteros, and F. J. Plou, *Food Chem.,* 145, 388-394 (2014).

[155] Amano Enzyme Japan, 2007 at http://www.amano-enzyme.co.jp /eng/enzyme/23.html

[156] T. Palai, S. Mitra, and P. K. Bhattacharya, *J. Biosci. Bioeng.,* 114, 418-423 (2012).
[157] DSM Food Specialties, 2012 at http://www.dsm.com/le/en_US/maxilact/html/lactase.htm
[158] P. S. Panesar, S. Kumari, and R. Panesar, *Enzyme Res.,* Article ID 473137 (2010).
[159] Yakult Pharmaceutical Industry, at http://www.yakult.co.jp/ypi/en/product/ori.html
[160] US Food and Drug Administration, 2010 at http://www.accessdata.fda.gov/scripts/fcn/fcnDetailNavigation.cfm?rpt=grasListing&id=334
[161] Friesland Foods Domo, at http://vivinalgos.com/index.php?id=1
[162] US Food and Drug Administration, 2007 at http:// www.accessdata.fda.gov/scripts/fcn/fcnDetailNavigation.cfm?rpt=grasListing&id=236
[163] GTC Nutrition, at http://www.innovadex.com/Food/Detail/ 1698/101070/PURIMUNE
[164] US Food and Drug Administration, 2009 at http:// www.accessdata.fda.gov/scripts/fcn/fcnDetailNavigation.cfm?rpt=grasListing&id=286
[165] Clasado, at http://www.bimuno.com/
[166] EFSA Panel on Dietetic Products Nutrition and Allergies (NDA), *EFSA J.,* 11, 3259 (2013).
[167] R. Hartemink, K. M. Van Laere, C. C. Peeters, M. J. Nout, and F. M. Rombouts, *Lett. Appl. Microbiol.,* 25, 38-42 (1997).

In: Galactose
Editor: Vitor Hugo Pomin

ISBN: 978-1-63117-928-0

Chapter 5

GALACTOSE CONFIGURATIONS IN NATURE WITH EMPHASIS ON THE BIOSYNTHESIS OF GALACTOFURANOSE IN GLYCANS

Carla Marino and Rosa M. de Lederkremer*
CIHIDECAR-CONICET-UBA, Departamento de Química Orgánica, Facultad de Ciencias Exactas y Naturales, Universidad de Buenos Aires, Pabellon II, Ciudad Universitaria, Buenos Aires, Argentina

ABSTRACT

Glycosylated D-galactose is widely distributed in nature. Less common, L-galactose was found in snail and plant galactans. The difference with the most abundant monosaccharide, D-glucose, is that D-galactose may be found in pyranosic and furanosic configurations. In the animal kingdom, free D-galactose is not present but is a common constituent of glycoproteins and glycolipids, always as pyranose. In fact, D-galactose is incorporated into human milk oligosaccharides in larger quantities than glucose. The β-(1,4)- galactosyltransferase links galactose to glucose to form lactose, the core for human milk oligosaccharides (HMO). Interestingly, the furanose form has been identified in important human pathogens like *Mycobacterium tuberculosis, Aspergillus fumigatus and Trypanosoma cruzi*, the agent of Chagas disease. In both

* e-mail: lederk@qo.fcen.uba.ar.

configurations, the β-anomer predominates in the glycans. The absence of galactofuranose (Gal*f*) in mammals and the important role that Gal*f*-containing molecules play in host cell recognition led to the enzymes involved in the Gal*f* metabolic pathways as targets for the development of drugs. Both, Gal*p* and Gal*f* must be activated as the nucleotides UDP-Gal*p* and UDP-Gal*f* for their incorporation into glycans. The nucleotide precursor for L-galactose is GDP-L-galactose, which is formed from GDP-mannose by the action of a 3',5'-epimerase. Also, whereas UDP-Gal*p* may be synthesized from the free monosaccharidesgalactose or glucose, in the latter case through the action of a UDP-Glc-4-epimerase, UDP-Gal*f* is produced from UDP-Gal*p* by the action of a unique enzyme, UDP-Gal*p* mutase (UGM), which catalyzes its conversion into UDP-Gal*f*. In the last two decades several laboratories have been committed to understand the mechanism of action of UGM and its properties. The achievements in this area are presented in this chapter.

INTRODUCTION

Glycosylated D-galactose (D-Gal) is widely distributed in nature. Less common, L-galactose (L-Gal) (Figure 1) was found in snail, alga and plant galactans and will not be discussed in this review.

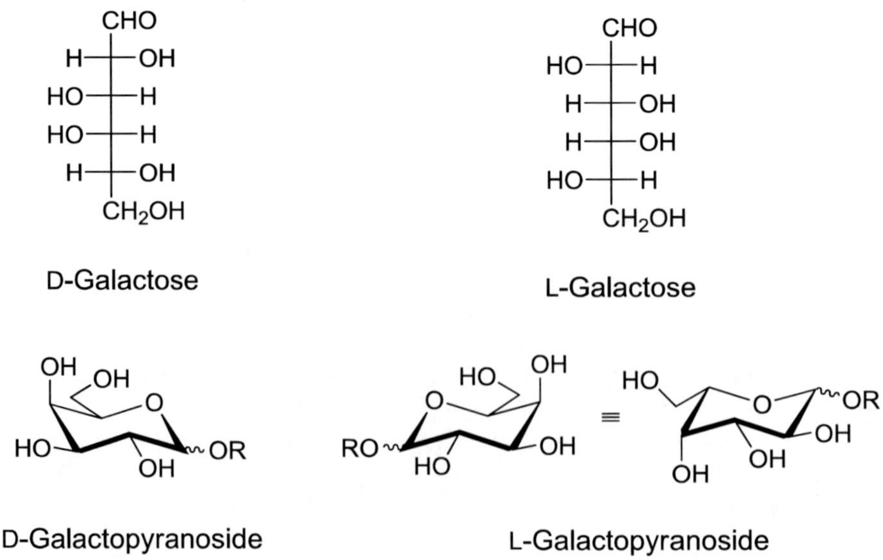

Figure 1. Enantiomeric forms of galactose.

In the animal kingdom, free D-galactose is not present, but in glycosidic linkage to glucose forms lactose, the milk disaccharide. It is also a common constituent of glycoproteins and glycolipids, always as pyranose (Taylor and Drickamer 2011).The difference with the most abundant monosaccharide, D-glucose, is that D-galactose may be found in pyranosic and furanosic configurations (Figure 2). In both configurations, the β-anomer predominates in the glycans. Interestingly, the furanose form has been identified in important human pathogens like *Mycobacterium tuberculosis, Aspergillus fumigatus and Trypanosoma cruzi*, the agent of Chagas disease (Marino et al. 2012, Richards and Lowary 2009). Methods to study the biosynthesis of bacterial galactofuranosides have been described (Poulin and Lowary 2010), and the biosynthesis of Gal*f* in kinetoplastids has been reviewed (Oppenheimer et al. 2011a). A review on the biosynthesis, metabolism, and chemo-enzymatic synthesis of furanosyl-containing conjugates including β-D-galactofuranosides has been published (Chlubnova et al. 2012).

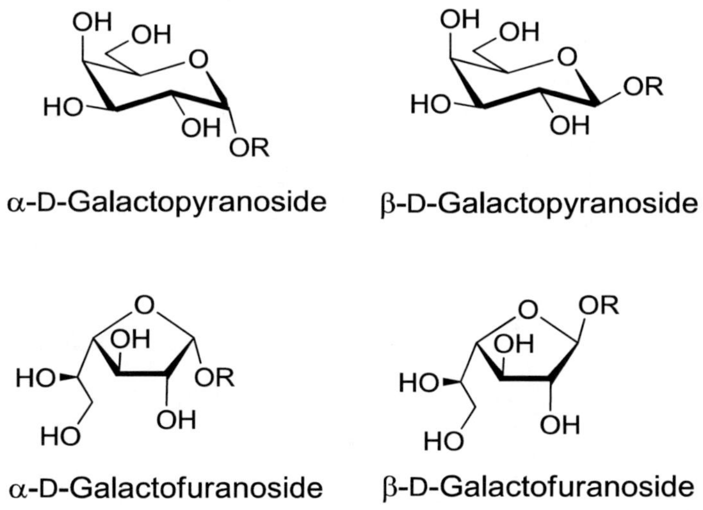

Figure 2. Configurations of D-galactosides.

Being galactofuranosides absentin mammals the enzymes involved in their biosynthesis are good targets for chemotherapy. D-Galactose is incorporated into glycans from the nucleotide activated sugar donors. Uridine diphosphate galactopyranose (UDP-Gal*p*) may be originated from glucose by *the novo* synthesis or by galactose salvage pathway (Scheme 1) (Thibodeaux et al. 2008). In the first pathway the glycolytic intermediate glucose 6-phosphate is converted to glucose 1-phosphate by a phosphoglucosemutase prior to uridine transfer by the uridyltransferase GPUT, an essential enzyme for all organisms. In species ranging from *Escherichia coli* to human, UDP-glucose-4-epimerase (UGE, also called UDP-galactose-4-epimerase) catalyzes the interconversion of UDP-glucose and UDP-galactose which may be also formed from free galactose via the galactose salvage pathway (Scheme 1) (Allard et al. 2001, Holden et al. 2003). Some eukaryotes like the protozoo *Trypanosoma cruzi* depend on UGE (encoded by TcGALE) for growthsince its hexose transporter is unable to transport galactose for the synthesis of its glycoconjugates (MacRae et al. 2006). The *A. fumigatus* genome contains three genes encoding for putative UDP-glucose-4-epimerases and studies on their function were reported (Lee et al. 2013).

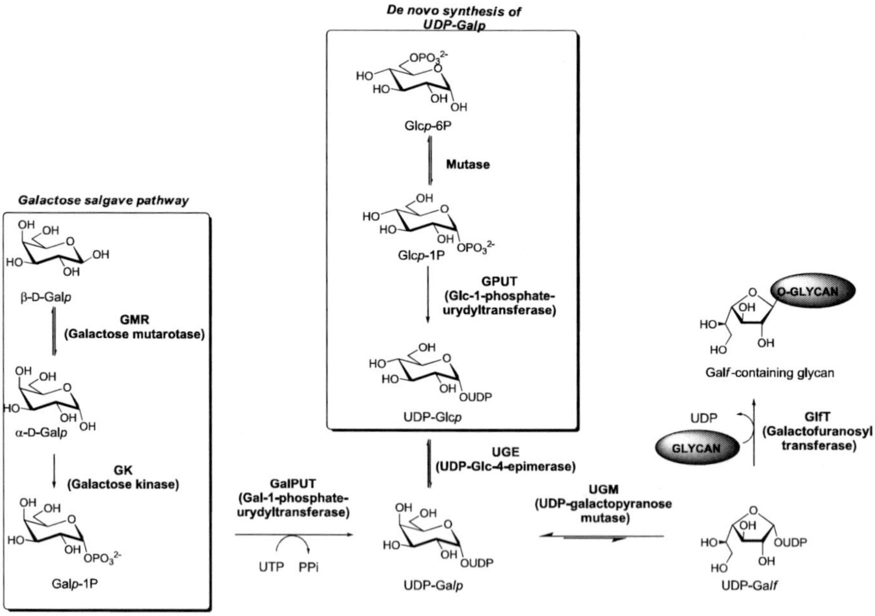

Scheme 1. Biosynthesis of UDP-Gal*p*, UDP-Gal*f* and Gal*f*-glycan.

For the production of the Gal*f* nucleotide, UDP-Gal*p* must be first synthesized to be then converted to UDP-Gal*f* by the action of UDP-Gal*p*mutase (UGM, Scheme 1).

The final coupling of the monosaccharide to the growing glycan is performed by galactosyltransferases. Galactopyranosyltransferases have been extensively studied, in particular those involved in the biosynthesis of important mammal glycolipids and glycoproteins. The expression of many of these transferases is altered in various diseases (Ram and Munjal 1985, Brockhausen 2006). In contrast, fewer studies on galactofuranosyltransferases have been reported, mostly in the last decade.

Biosynthetic studies require the chemical synthesis of oligosaccharides, glycoconjugates and mimetics of D-Gal*f* as probes. The diverse strategies developed for the synthesis of such molecules have been extensively reviewed (Richards and Lowary 2009, Peltier et al. 2008, Marino et al. 2012, Marino and Baldoni 2014, Imamura and Lowary2011, Taha et al. 2012).

UDP-GALACTOPYRANOSE MUTASE (UGM)

It was first established in *Salmonella thyphimurium* that UDP-Gal*p* is a precursor for the incorporation of Gal*f* (Nikaido and Sarvas 1971). It was only after two decades that the enzyme responsible for the conversion of UDP-Gal*p* to UDP-Gal*f* (Scheme 2) was identified in *E. coli* and is known as UDP-Gal*p* mutase (UGM) (Stevenson et al. 1994, Nassau et al. 1996).

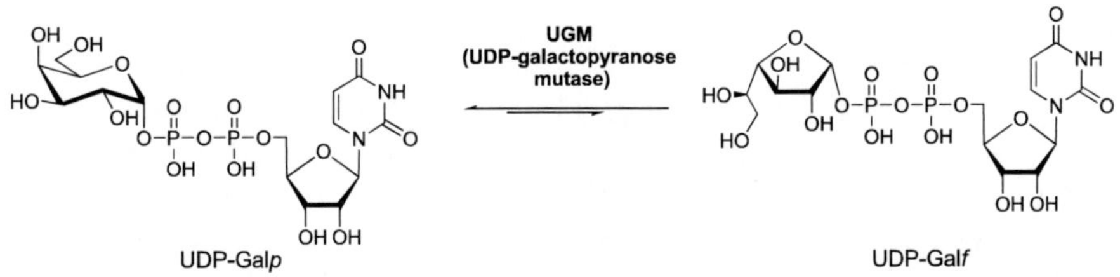

Scheme 2. Biosynthesis of UDP-Gal*f* catalyzed by UDP-galactopyranosemutase.

The reaction is reversible and favors the more stable pyranose nucleotide (93:7 ratio at equilibrium). UGM was later described in other bacteria such as *Klebsiellapneumoniae* (Köplin et al. 1997) and *M. tuberculosis* (Weston et al. 1998), in fungilike *Aspergillus* spp. (Damveld et al. 2008, Schmalhorst et al. 2008, El-Ganiny et al. 2008), in protozoa such as *Leishmania major* (Beverley et al. 2005, Bakker et al. 2005, Oppenheimer et al. 2011b) and recently in nematodes (Wesener et al. 2013). UGM is a flavoenzyme only active when the flavin adenine dinucleotide (FAD) cofactor is in the reduced form. Whereas the bacterial enzyme is dimeric and the fungal UGM is tetrameric, the enzyme in the kinetoplastids *Leishmania* and *T. cruzi*, function as a monomer (Sanders et al. 2001, Oppenheimer et al. 2010, Oppenheimer et al. 2011b, Oppenheimer et al. 2012, Da Fonseca et al. 2013, Dhatwalia et al. 2012b). Eukaryotic enzymes show about 50% sequence identity but only share less than 20% sequence homology with their prokaryote orthologs, being the catalytic region very similar in all UGMs. A UGM homolog (glf-1) was identified in the nematode *Caenorhabditis elegans* (Novelli et al. 2009) although the Gal*f*-containing glycan has not yet been described. Kinetic parameters obtained for the gen product CeUGM, are in the range of other eukaryotic homologues (Wesener et al. 2013).

It was shown that UGM is a virulence factor in the microorganisms with glycans containing Gal*f*. For instance, biosynthesis of the Gal*f* in *Mycobacteria* is essential for growth (Pan et al. 2001). Also, in pathogenic eukaryotes the role of UGM in thepathogenesis has been shown. GIPLs containing Gal*f* in *Leishmania major* are important for establishing the infection (Suzuki et al. 2008). Deletion of the UGM gene resulted in attenuated virulence (Kleczka et al. 2007, Madeira da Silva et al. 2009). In *A. fumigatus*, the contribution of Gal*f* to its virulence was also described (Schmalhorst et al. 2008).

Crystal Structure of UGM

A total of twenty nine structures of UGM from six microorganisms have been deposited in the Protein Data Bank (Tanner et al. 2013). They include bacterial and eukaryotic UGMs, in both the oxidized and reduced states, as well as structures of the enzyme complexed with UDP, UDP-Gal*p*, UDP-Glc, UDP-phosphono-galactopyranose (a nonhydrolyzable C-glycosidicphospho nate), NADH, and NADPH.

The group of Sanders was pioneer in studies of the crystal structure of UGM. In the first reports, the enzyme from *E. coli* (ecUGM), *K. pneumoniae* (kpUGM) and *M. tuberculosis* (mtUGM) were crystallized without substrate or inhibitor and their structures have been determined (Sanders et al. 2001, Beis et al. 2005). The structures revealed that the overall architecture of UGM consists of three domains, a FAD binding domain, an α-helix which functions in binding the uridine group of the substrate and a β-sheet domain (Figure 3A) (Tanner et al. 2013). The structures of all the bacterial UGMs are very similar, with the only differences occurring in the positioning of a mobile loop located next to the active site. On the basis of this structural information and sequence of aminoacids, active site residues were identified and site directed mutagenesis of these residues was found to affect the substrate binding and catalytic activity. Mutation of a conserved arginine (Arg174 in kpUGM) in a mobile loop located away from the active site resulted in an inactive enzyme (Chad et al. 2007). The functional role of this conserved arginine and the possible movement of this mobile loop were studied through molecular dynamics simulations. The binding affinities of the substrate UDP-Gal*p* and of the inhibitor UDP were explored by saturation transfer difference-NMR spectroscopy (STD-NMR) and molecular modeling (Yuan et al. 2005).

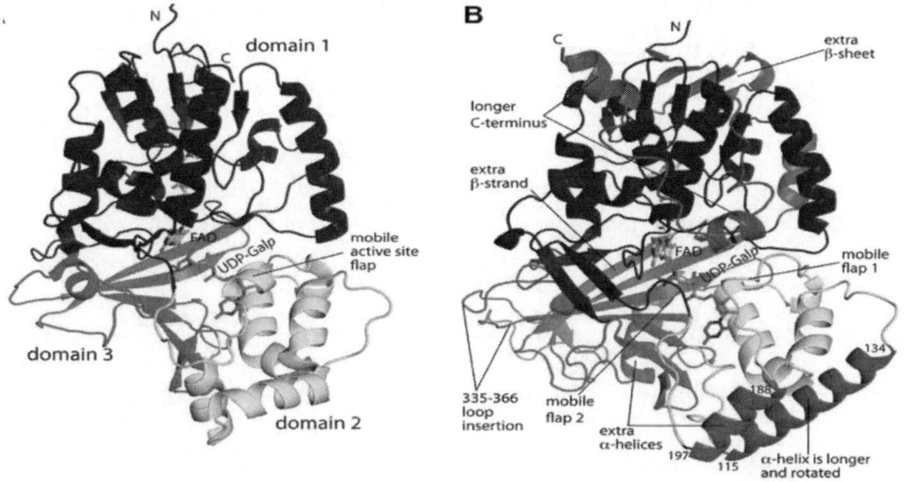

Figure 3. Structures of UGM. A) Protomer structure of *Deinococcus radiodurans* UGM (drUGM). B) Protomer structure of the eukaryotic AfUGM (Tanner et al. 2013).

The first crystal structures of UGM in complex with the natural substrate UDP-Gal*p* and UDP were obtained with the UGM from *Deinococcus radiodurans* (drUGM) (Partha et al. 2009). Analysis of these structures confirmed that the active site of UGM closes around the substrate as it binds through its diphosphate.

In spite of the low sequence identity of bacterial and eukaryotic UGMs most residues required for substrate and FAD binding are conserved (Beverley et al. 2005, Chad et al. 2007). Reports from two laboratories on the first crystal structure of a eukaryotic UGM from *A. fumigatus* (AfUGM) were published simultaneously. Both groups reported almost identical structures (Dhatwalia et al. 2012a, van Straaten et al. 2012a). The structures for the complex with NADP(H) have been solved and the binding domain was identified (Dhatwalia et al. 2012c).

Analysis of the data showed that AfUGM has several extra secondary and tertiary structural elements that are not found in bacterial UGMs and are important for substrate recognition and tetramerization (Figure 3B) (Tanner et al. 2013). The UGMs of pathogenic protozoa like *L. major* and *T. cruzi* have been also studied. The *L. major* UGM has been crystallized after purification by Ni^{2+} affinity chromatography and structure determinations were reported (van Straaten et al. 2012b). Analysis of the crystal structure of the UGM from *T. cruzi* (45% identical to AfUGM) showed that substrate recognition in eukaryotes is different from that of bacterial UGMs (Dhatwalia et al. 2012b). There were also differences in the conformational changes produced via reduction of the FAD in the UGM of the fungus with respect tothe TcUGM, that could be responsible for the different oligomericstate in solution. The data suggest that TcUGM is monomeric in solution which confirms previos results of size exclusion chromatography (Oppenheimer et al. 2010). Also, neither the AfUGM-type tetramer nor any of the previously observed bacterial UGM dimers are present in the TcUGM crystal lattice (Tanner et al. 2013).

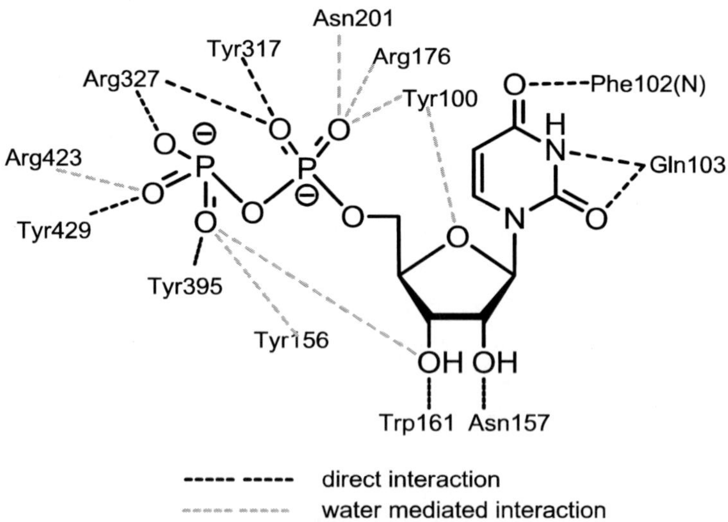

Figure 4. Protein-UDP interactions in TcUGM (Dhatwalia et al. 2012b).

TcUGM and AfUGM complexed with UDP showed that the UDP binding sites are identical but different than in bacteria. Electron density maps clearly indicate that all three chemical groups of UDP (base, ribose, and pyrophosphate) establish stabilizing electrostatic interactions with several aminoacids of the enzyme (Figure 4) (Dhatwalia et al. 2012b). However, all UGMs showed the Gal*p* unit next to the flavinisoalloxazine such that the N_5FAD and C_1Gal*p* atoms are close. This is consistent with the mechanism of isomerization discussed below. Also, all UGMs share the same type of pyrophosphate recognition in domain 3. Tyrosine residues form hydrogen bonds with the pyrophosphate and an ion pair of Arg and Asn stabilizes the pyrophosphate.

Catalytic Mechanisms of UGM

Many efforts have been devoted to understand the mechanism of tautomerization of UDP-Gal*p* to UDP-Gal*f*. UGM is a unique flavoprotein, the flavin acting as a nucleophile that attacks the anomeric carbon atom of the galactose moiety (Scheme 3). Enzymatic activity requires the FAD cofactor in the reduced state (FADH) in order to catalyze a non-redox reaction. Three different mechanisms were proposed, S_N2, S_N1, and a single transfer electron mechanism, for the formation of the FAD-galactose intermediate I (Soltero-Higgin et al. 2004, Gruber et al. 2009, Itoh et al. 2007, Fullerton et al. 2003). The formation of the covalent adduct was supported by chemical reduction of the iminium form III and characterization of the product by mass spectroscopy (Soltero-Higgin et al. 2004). Participation of N-5 of FAD in the reaction was consistent with the lack of activity observed with the enzyme reconstituted with 5-deaza-FAD. Further studies indicated that formation of the adduct I occurs via a direct attack of the flavin (S_N2 mechanism) rather than formation of an oxocarbenium ion, followed by flavin attack (S_N1 mechanism) (Sun et al. 2012, Oppenheimer et al. 2012). A flavin semiquinone intermediate was not observed in time resolved spectroscopy of the reaction of UDP-Gal*f* with reduced *T. cruzi* UGM, suggesting that a single electron transfer mechanism is not working.

Deprotonation of the N-5 FAD to produce the flavin-iminium ion was explained by quantum mechanical calculations. The C-4=O of the flavin accepts the proton from the N-5 FAD(I→II) and transfers it to the O-5 Gal*p*, facilitating ring opening and formation of the iminium ion III (Scheme 3). The simulations also predicted that during ring contraction, the proton from the hydroxyl group at C-4Gal*p* is transferred to the C-4=O of the flavin (IV, Scheme 3) (Huang et al. 2012). This activation is only possible if the OH-4 of the sugar is axial, thus explaining why UDP-Glc despite binding to UGM of *K. pneumonie* is not a substrate for this enzyme (Gruber et al. 2009). After recyclization, the final step in the reaction involves an attack on the anomeric carbon of IV by UDP, leading to the formation of UDP-Gal*f*. This mechanism was established by data obtained from studies on prokaryotic UGMs. It was proposed that recyclization to the furanose is the rate-determining step (Oppenheimer et al. 2012).

It was proved that in the eukaryotic UGMs the flavin is activated by reduction with NADPH (Oppenheimer et al. 2012, Dhatwalia et al. 2012c, Da Fonseca et al. 2013). The mechanism starts with binding of NADPH followed by hydride transfer and UDP-Gal*p* binding. Conformation of the polypeptide chain near the flavin changed dramatically in response to flavin reduction whereas no changes were observed in the protein conformation on reduction of bacterial UGM (Partha et al. 2009; Gruber et al. 2009).

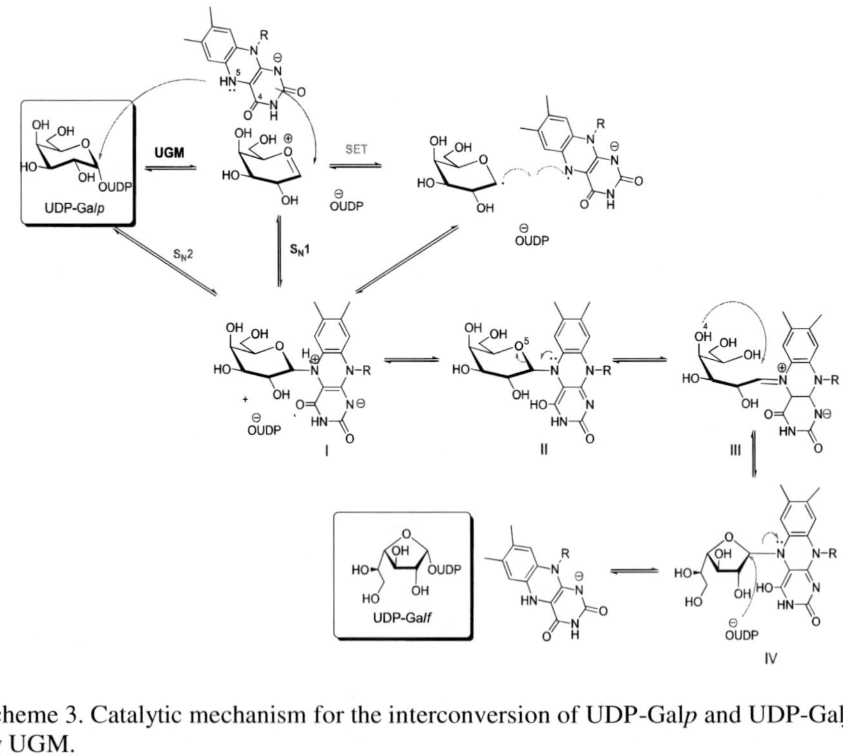

Scheme 3. Catalytic mechanism for the interconversion of UDP-Gal*p* and UDP-Gal*f* by UGM.

None of the residues that contact the ADP of NADPH in AfUGM are present in the sequences of bacterial UGMs, suggesting that the identified NAD(P)H site is not present in bUGMs. However, bacterial UGMs can also be activated by NAD(P)H although excess coenzyme and longer incubation times are required, suggesting that NAD(P)H may not be the physiological hydride donor in bacteria.The different conformations of the active site flaps which contain residues that directly contact the substrate indicate that these regions are highly flexible. Protein flexibility is a fundamental aspect of UGM catalysis, particularly for eUGMs, which have an additional mobile active site flap and a highly flexible histidine loop. Bacterial UGMs haveone active site flap whereas eUGMs have two mobile flaps. Molecular dynamic (MD) simulations of a prokaryotic substrate-bound UGM structure predicted that the flexible flap changed from an open conformation to a closed conformation in the presence of the substrate (Yao et al. 2009, Yuan et al. 2008). Molecular dynamic simulations have also been used to study substrate-associated active site motion in TcUGM (Boechi et al. 2013). It was observed that both flaps open in the absence of ligand, thus creating a channel for ligand uptake. When UDP-Gal*p* is bound, intramolecular interactions help maintain both flaps closed. MD simulations show that UMP is essential for closure of the active site. The mechanism for product release is unclear. Studies of the crystallinestructure of UGM complexed with UDP-Gal*f* may help to elucidate this step of the mechanism.

GALACTOFURANOSYLTRANSFERASES

The galactofuranosyltransferases (Gal*f*Ts), working *in vivo* after UGM for the introduction of Gal*f* in glycans were less studied than the mutases, probably due to the difficulties in obtaining the activated donor UDP-Gal*f*. Several chemical syntheses of the Gal*f* nucleotide have been reported (Zhang and Liu 2000, Tsvetkov and Nikolaev 2000, Marlow and Kiessling 2001). An effective chemoenzymatic procedure for the preparation of UDP-Gal*f* and derivatives was originally developed by Field and coworkers using three enzymes (Errey et al. 2004) and described in detail by Lowary (Scheme 4) (Poulin and Lowary 2010). This method was able to form UDP-α-D-Gal*f* with 79% yield and it is so far the most efficient enzyme-catalyzed route to UDP-α-D-Gal*f*.

The chemical and enzymatic methods start from Gal*f*-α-1-phosphate, prepared for the first time by Lederkremer et al. (1994). Starting from [6-^{3}H]-Gal-α-1-phosphate the radioactive nucleotidewas chemically synthesized (Mariño et al. 2005). For the preparation of derivatives of UDP-Gal*f*, useful for mechanistic studies and as potential inhibitors, the starting compound is a conveniently modified Gal*f*-α-1-phosphate (Peltier et al. 2010). However, the three-enzyme system failed to produce any of the desired sugar nucleotides when incubated with either 2-acetamido-2-deoxy-α-D-galactofuranose-1-phosphate or 2-azido-2-deoxy-α-D-galactofuranose-1-phosphate and the respective nucleotides had to be chemically synthesized (Snitynsky and Lowary 2014).

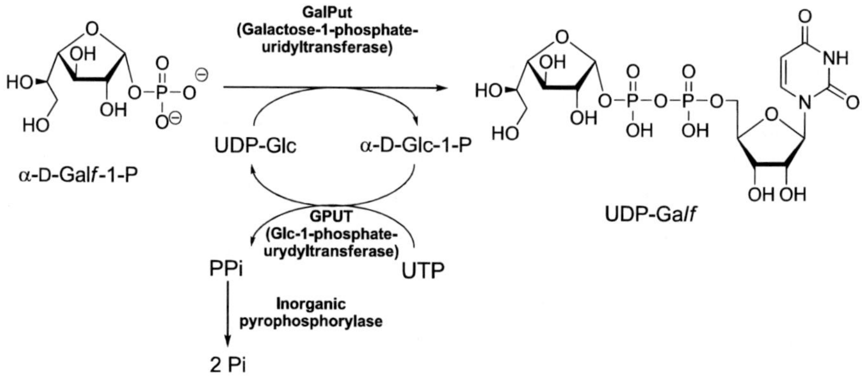

Scheme 4. Chemoenzymatic synthesis of UDP-Gal*f* from Gal*f*-α-1-phosphate.

Galactofuranosyltransferases in Trypanosomatids

The first Gal*f* transferase in a eukaryote was described in *Leishmania*. This protozoan parasite incorporates Gal*f* in two surface glycoconjugates, the abundant lipophosphoglycan (LPG) and the smaller glycoinositol phospholipids (GIPLs) (Figure 5) (Lederkremer and Colli 1995, Zhang et al. 2004). The Gal*f* transferase, LPG1, is localized in the Golgi where it adds the β-Gal*f* to the core LPG structure (Spath et al. 2000). Later studies showed that LPG1 is a metal glycosyltranferase with typical conserved motifs, including a cytoplasmic tail, a transmembrane domain, and a DXD metal-binding motif (Zhang et al. 2004). Mutants resulting from the deletion of *lpg*1 gene in both *L. major* and *L. donovani*, show LPG1 to beimportant for LPG formation. Due to the lack of LPG, the mutant strains with deletion of *lpg1* gene in *L. major* showed attenuated virulence. *Leishmania* species show different response to lpg1 deletion (Spath et al. 2003). Three related genes were identified in *L. major* and termed LPG1L, LPG1R and LPG1G (Zhang et al. 2004). The genes *lpg1*, are only responsible for the addition of Gal*f* to LPG and not to the

GIPLs. The function of the *lpg1g gen* was not described. Homologs of *lpg1l* and *lpg1r* were detected in other trypanosomatids.

A β(1→3) galactofuranosyltransferase (TrGALFT) of 45 kDa was described in non virulent *Trypanosoma rangeli* (Stoco et al. 2012).

Different from *L. major*, where a transmembrane protein domain is found in all GALFTs (Zhang et al. 2004), this domain was absent in the *T. rangeli* GALFT. Furthermore, TrGALFT sequence contains a modification of the luminal C-terminal domain with the presence of a DXE motif instead of the canonical DXD motif found in glycosyltransferases.

Although genes encoding β-(1→3) galactofuranosyltransferases have been detected in the genoma of pathogenic *T. cruzi* (El-Sayed et al. 2005), their expression and protein characterization were not reported. Antibodies raised against TrGALFT did not recognize any protein in *T. cruzi* extracts (Stoco et al. 2012).

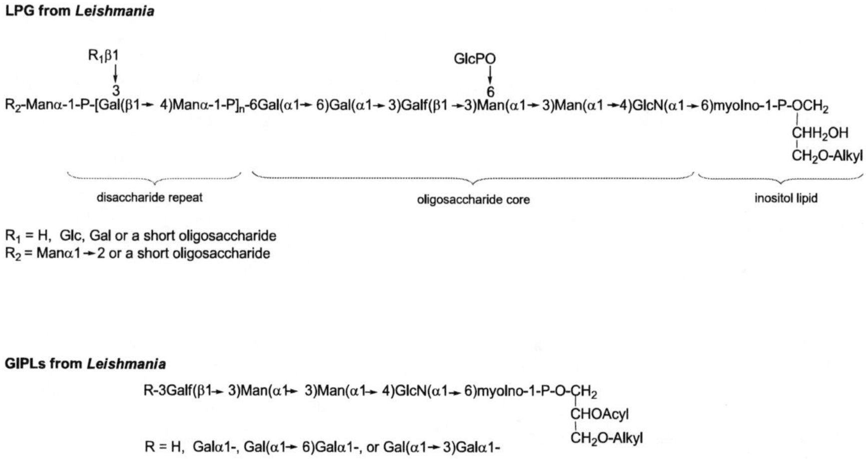

Figure 5. Structure of LPG and GIPLs from *Leishmania s*pp.

Galactofuranosyltransferases in Aspergillus

The cell walls of filamentous fungi in the genus *Aspergillus* have galactofuranose-containing polysaccharides and glycoconjugates, including O-glycans, N-glycan and fungal-type galactomannan, which are important for cell wall integrity (Figure 6) (Latgé 2009, Latgé 2010, Tefsen 2012, Fontaine et al. 2011, Jin 2012). Agalactofuranosyltransferase, GfsA, encoded by the gene AN8677 was identified in *Aspergillus nidulans* using reverse-genetic and biochemical approaches. The enzyme, which requires a divalent manganese cation for activity, is localized in the Golgi and has β-(1→5)- or β-(1→6)-galactofuranosyltransferase activity for *O*-glycans in glycoproteins of *A. nidulans*. Several *gfs*A orthologues were found in members of the *Pezizomycotina* subphylum of *Ascomycota*, including the human pathogen *Aspergillus fumigatus* in which the putative orthologue named Af*gfsA* was identified (Komachi et al. 2013). Noorthologues of *gfsA* were found in thegenomes of *C. elegans*, *T. cruzi*, or bacteria. *GfsA* has 87% sequence identity with *Aspergillus flavus* NRRL 3357 (AFL2G_12474), 84% with *A. niger* CBS 513.88 (An12g08720), 84% with *A. fumigatus* A1163 (AFUB_096220), 84% with Af293 (Afu6g02120), 83% with *Aspergillus oryzae* RIB40 (AO090120000096), 76% with *Penicillium chrysogenum* Wisconsin 54-1255 (Pc22g24320), 62% with *Ajellomyces capsulatus* NAm1 (HCAG_03193), 57% with *Coccidioides immitis* RS(CIMG_05833), 56% with *Paracoccidioides brasiliensis* Pb03 (PABG_06492), 55% with *Trichophyton rubrum* CBS118892 (TERG_00129), 32% with *Neurospora crassa* OR74A (NCU02213) and 32% with *Fusarium graminearum* PH-1 (FGSC_05770). The disruption of *gfsA* inhibited hyphal extension and conidial formation (Komachi et al. 2013).

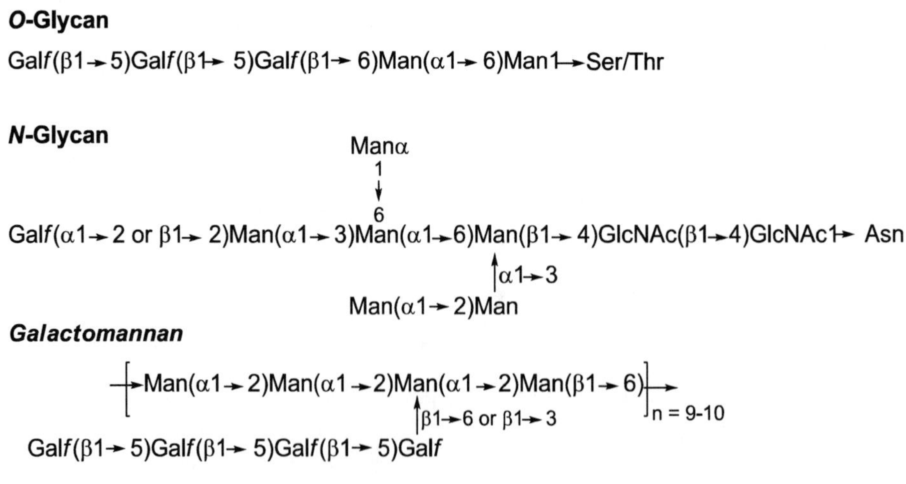

Figure 6. Structure of Gal*f*-containing molecules in *Aspergillus*spp.

Galactofuranosyltransferasesin prokaryotes

Galactofuranosyltransferases are essential for mycobacterial cell wall biosynthesis. In Mycobacteria, Gal*f* residues are found in the mycolyl-arabinogalactan (mAG) complex molecule (Figure 7). The core of the mAG is a galactan composed of 30-35 D-Gal*f* residues connected through alternating β-(1→5) and β-(1→6) linkages. The biosynthesis of mAGgalactan involves two bifunctional galactofuranosyltransferase enzymes, GlfT1 and GlfT2 (Beláňová et al. 2008). GlfT1 encoded by *Rv3782* is responsible for adding the first and second Gal*f* residues to the α-L-Rha*p*-(1→3)-α-D-Glc*p*NAcdecaprenyl-pyrophosphate acceptor substrate(Alderwick et al. 2008, Beláňová et al. 2008). The final product of the GlfT1-catalyzed reaction is the GlfT2 acceptor substrate. GlfT2 encoded by *glfT2* (*Rv3808c*), adds approximately 30 Gal*f* residues to the β-D-Gal*f*-(1→5)-β-D-Gal*f*-(1→4)-α-L-Rha*p*-(1→3)-α-D-Glc*p*NAc-decaprenyl-pyrophosphate acceptor substrate (Figure 7) (Kremer et al. 2008). The α-stereochemistry in UDP-Gal*f* and the β-stereochemistry of the glycosidic linkages in the products generated by GlfT1 and GlfT2 indicate that catalysis follows an inverting mechanism. GlfT2 has been more extensively studied than GlfT1. Recombinant GlfT2 has been expressed and purified (Alderwick et al. 2008, Rose et al. 2006). Subsequent studies on the enzyme have demonstrated that GlfT2 synthesizes both β-Gal*f*-(1→5)-Gal*f* and β-Gal*f*-(1→6)-Gal*f* linkages using a single active site (Szczepina, et al. 2009, May et al. 2012). Crystal structures of free and UDP-bound GlfT2, reveal a homotetrameric architecture (Wheatley et al. 2012). For studying specific protein–carbohydrate interactionsinvolved in substrate recognition and turnover, methylatedand deoxygenated carbohydrate analogs of the donor UDP-Gal*f* were prepared by chemoenzymatic methods (Poulin and Lowary 2010) to prove the donor specificity of GlfT2, and to explore their effect on galactanpolymerization (Poulin et al. 2012). The isomeric trisaccharidesoctyl β-D-Gal*f*-(1→5)-β-D-Gal*f*-(1→6)-β-D-Gal*f* and octyl β-D-Gal*f*-(1→6)-β-D-Gal*f*-(1→5)-β-D-Gal*f* were used as acceptor substrates for kinetic analysis. The addition of a Gal*f* residue deoxygenated at C-5 or C-6 to the growing galactan chain resulted in products which no longer act as acceptors for the enzyme, showing that both, the terminal C-5 and C-6 hydroxyl groups of the acceptor substrate are required for GlfT2 activity. Gens responsible for the coupling of Gal*f* to other monosaccharides have been also described. For instance, WbbI in *E. coli* performs β-(1→6) coupling of Gal*f* to α-glucose (Wing et al. 2006) andWbbO in *K. pneumoniae* couples Gal*f* to Gal*p* by a β-(1→3)-linkage (Guan et al. 2001).

UDP-GALACTOFURANOSE TRANSPORTER

UDP-Gal*f*, synthesized in the cytosol (Kleczka et al. 2007) must be transported into a compartment of the secretory pathway prior to incorporation of the Gal*f* into a glycan (Figure 8).

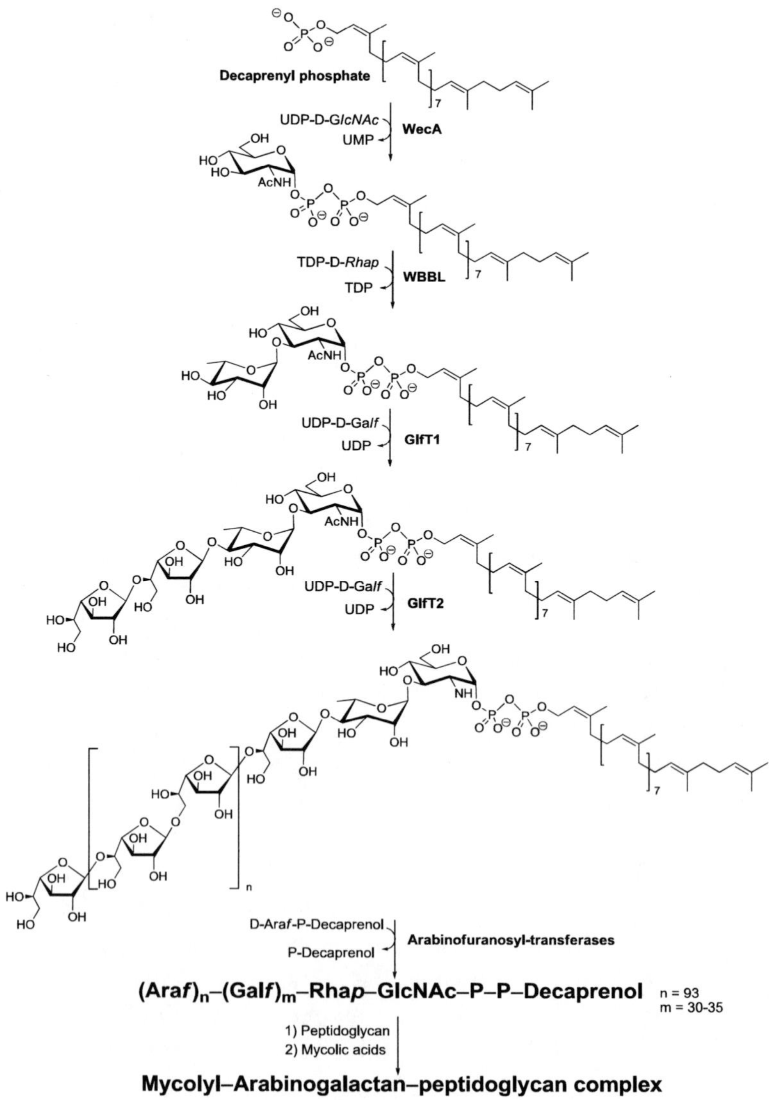

Figure 7. Proposed pathway for the biosynthesis of mycobacterial arabinogalactan.

Nucleotide sugar transporters (NSTs) aremulti-transmembrane proteins present in all kinds of eukaryotic organisms (Hirschberg 1998, Gerardy-Schahn et al. 2001). A Golgi localized nucleotide sugar transporter with specificity for UDP-Gal*f* was first described in *A. fumigatus* and named GlfB (Engel et al. 2009). Gene deletion experiments showed that *glf*B is most probably required for fullvirulence of the fungus. A BLAST search of the *A. fumigatus* genome with various characterized NST protein sequences identified the gene adjacent to the UDP-Gal mutase gene (*glf*A). Interestingly, all fungi from the subphylum *Pezizomycotina* whose genome has been fully sequenced display a homolog of *glf*B clustered with *glf*A. The role of the *A. nidulans* UDP-galactofuranose transporter named UgtA in cell wall architecture, conidiation, and drug sensitivity was inferred by comparing wild type strains with mutants produced by deletion of *ugt*A (Afroz et al. 2011).

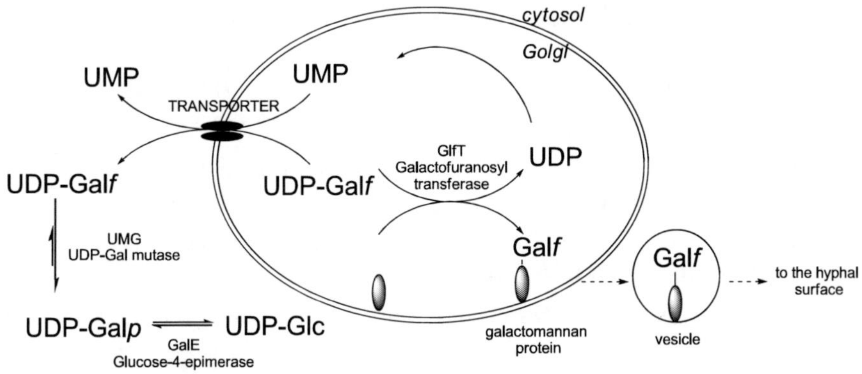

Figure 8. Biosynthesis of *Galf*-containing glycans. UDP-Galactofuranose (UDP-Gal*f*) is synthesized from UDP-Galactopyranose (UDP-Gal*p*) and translocated via a transporter into the Golgi in exchange for UMP. Galactofuranosyltransferases transfer Gal*f* moieties from UDP-Gal*f* on various glycoconjugates and UDP is converted to UMP by a nucleoside diphosphatase.

Chemical Inhibition of UGM

Most efforts to inhibit incorporation of Gal*f*in glycoconjugates, essential for cell viability, have chosen UGM as the target. Several compounds showed *in vitro* inhibition of the enzyme and the effect of some of them on *Mycobacteria* growth was assayed (Caravano et al. 2006, Liautard et al. 2006,

Ghavami et al. 2004, Lee et al.1999, Scherman et al. 2003, Veerapen et al. 2004, Itoh et al. 2007).

A library of 62 aminothiazoles was synthesized and screened against the UGM from *K. pneumoniae* or *M. tuberculosis* (Dykhuizen et al. 2008) using a fluorescence polarization assay (Soltero-Higgin et al. 2004).Twentyfive2-aminothiazoles were identified as UGM ligands (Kd< 60μM), from which two of them, **1** and **2** (Figure 9), were most effective as competitive inhibitors. The UGM inhibitors also blocked mycobacterial growth. The two aminothiazoles**3** and **4** were also effective inhibitors of the *C. elegans* UGM (Wesener et al. 2013). The pyrazole compound **5** and compound **2** (Figure 9) were analyzed as inhibitors of *M. tuberculosis* (tb) and *K. pneumonia* (kp) UGMs. IC_{50} values of 62μM and 44μM against tbUGM and kpUGM, respectively were obtained for compound **5** (Borrelli et al. 2010). The aminothiazole **2** gave IC_{50} values of37μM and 7.2μM. The antimicrobial activity was measured by the minimum inhibitory concentration (MIC) of the compounds against *Mycobacterium* strains. MICs for the pyrazole**5** were 3.3μg/mL and 6.7 μg /mL for two strains of *M. smegmatis* tested and 6.5μg /mL for *M. bovis* BCG. MICs for the aminothiazole **2** were 12.5μg /mL for both *M. smegmatis* strains, whereas it was ineffective against *M. bovis* BCG at the higher concentration (50μg /mL) tested. The pyrazole **5** also showed activity against *M. tuberculosis* H37Rv as evidenced by growth inhibition zones at 2.5μg, increasing with the amount of inhibitor. The aminothiazole **2** did not inhibit the growth of *M. tuberculosis* H37Rv at any of the concentrations tested up to 100μg. Pyrazole **5** has moderate toxicity for mammalian cells, similar to that of quinine, but less toxic than the aminothiazole **2** (Borrelli et al. 2010).

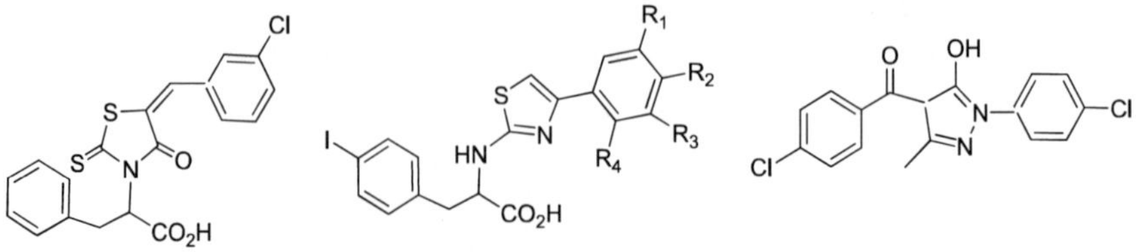

1

2 $R_1 = R_2 = Cl, R_3 = R_4 = H$
3 $R_1 = H, R_2 = Cl, R_3 = H, R_4 = Cl$
4 $R_1 = H, R_2 = Cl, R_3 = Cl, R_4 = H$

5

Figure 9. Pyrazol, 2-aminothiazole and thiazolidinone derivatives tested as inhibitors of UGM.

The tetrafluoro derivatives of UDP-Gal*f* **6** and UDP-Gal*p* **7** (Figure 10) were synthesized and analyzed as inhibitors of UGM from *K. pneumoniae*. The fluorinated derivatives were better inhibitors than UDP in a standard competition assay of conversion of UDP-Gal*f* to UDP-Gal*p* (N'Go et al. 2014).

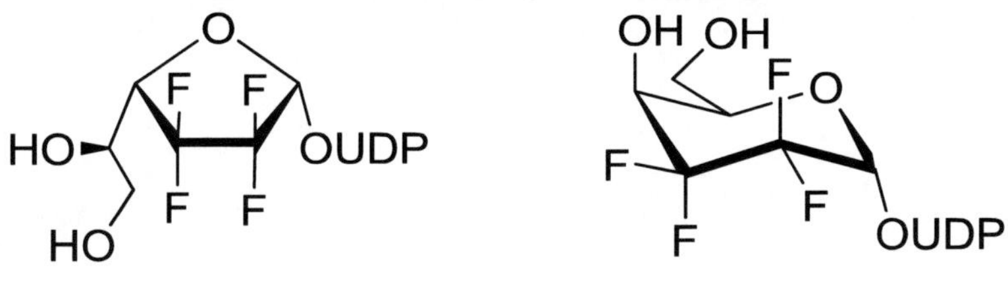

Figure 10. Fluorinated analogues of UDP-Gal*p* and UDP-Gal*f* evaluated as inhibitors of UGM from *K. pneumonia.*

Inhibitors of UDP-GalfTransferases

The search for inhibitors of the galactofuranosyltransferases had mainly the purpose to find new antituberculosis drugs, since D-galactofurans are key components of the *M. tuberculosis* cell wall. Iminosugars, analogues of monosaccharides where the ring oxygen has been replaced by nitrogen, were described as potent inhibitors of glycosidases and glycosyltransferases (Lillelund et al. 2002). Compounds **8** and **9** (Figure 11) inhibited the biosynthesis of the mycobacterial galactan (Lee et al. 1997). The 1-N-iminosugar **10** showed moderate inhibitory activity against proliferation, however, it did not show significant inhibitory activity against UDP-Gal*p* mutase (*M. smegmatis*), suggesting that inhibition of galactan biosynthesis was due to the biological action on the UDP-Gal*f* transferase (Cren et al. 2004).

UDP-Gal*f* synthetic analogs, modified at C-5 and C-6 of the Gal*f* unit, were prepared using a chemoenzymatic route and their effect on mycobacterial galactan biosynthesis was studied (Peltier et al. 2010). The 6'-F nucleotide **12** and the deoxy nucleotides **13** and **14** (Figure 11) in a concentration of 100 μg/ml almost completely abolish cell-free production of the galactan polymer. The incorporation of these analogs into the growing galactan chain by GlfT1, leading to modified dead-end glycolipid intermediates, appears to be the predominant mechanism by which polymer production is halted. However, GlfT2 may also introduce 6-deoxy-Gal*f* residues into the polymer chain leading to similar "dead-end" intermediates. In addition, compounds **12-14** served also as weak inhibitors of GlfT2. Inhibition of this enzyme by the bicycle imino structure linked to a uridine nucleoside in compound **11** was also described (Trunkfield et al. 2010). The unnatural 1,2-*trans* UDP-6-NHAc-Gal*f* (**15**) strongly inhibited the growth of *L. donovani* promastigotes (Dureau et al. 2010).

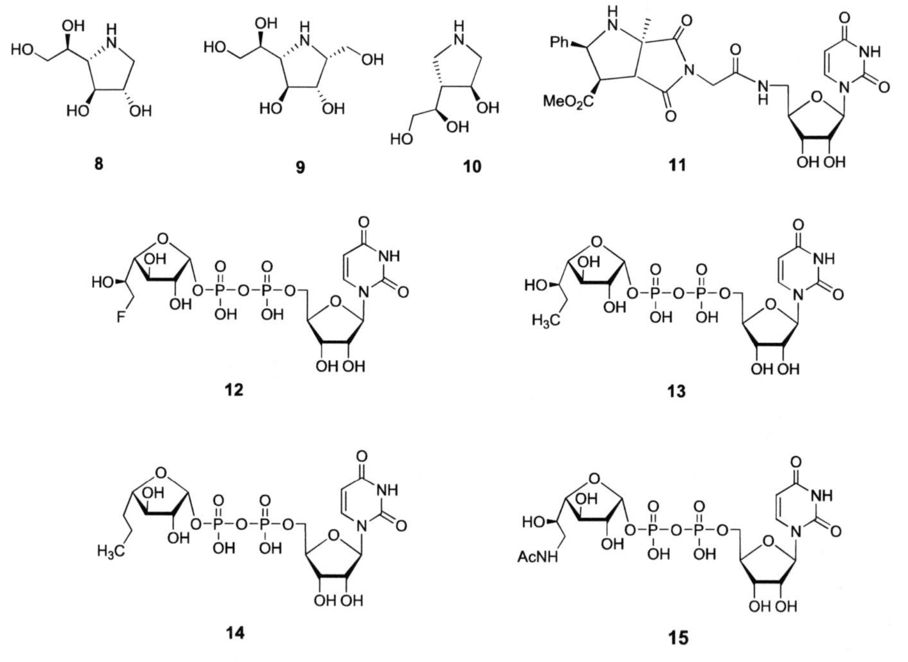

Figure 11.Synthetic compounds tested as inhibitors of UDP-Gal*f* transferases.

Conclusion and Perspective

Galactofuranose is an antigenic constituent of glycans in the surface of pathogenic bacteria, fungi and protozoa (Marino et al. 2012). Being xenobiotic in humans, the enzymes responsible for their assembly are promising targets for chemotherapy. Although the metabolism of β-D-galactofuranosides has been extensively studied, the α-D-Gal*f* biosynthetic machinery still remains unclear. The unique UDP-Gal*p* mutase (UGM) has been studied by several laboratories and the mechanism of action as well as its role in virulence was established. The UGM gen has been lately identified in the nematode *C. elegans* (Novelli et al. 2009, Wesener et al. 2013), a valuable model organism; their glycoconjugates, containing Gal*f* have not been identified and is an interesting topic for future studies.

Some β-D-Galactofuranosyltransferases, mainly from *Mycobacteria*, have been studied, and crystal structures have been only described for GlfT2, free and bound to UDP. The knowledge of the crystalline structures is essential for the design of high affinity inhibitors with clinical potential. The recent description of an efficient chemoenzymatic method for the preparation of the donor UDP-Gal*f* is an important step for further studies on Gal*f*-transferases (Poulin and Lowary 2010).

Nucleotides must be transported through a membrane of a cellular compartment prior to incorporation into the glycan. Only in *Aspergillus* spp a protein transporter for UDP-Gal*f* was described (Engel et al. 2009, Afroz et al. 2011).

The description of the enzymes involved in the introduction of α-D-Gal*f* residues in glycoconjugates found in several pathogenic microorganisms including bacteria, such as *Escherichia coli* and Streptococcus *pneumoniae*, and fungi, such as *Paracoccidioides brasiliensis*, the causative agent of paracoccidioidomycosis, is also a matter for future research.

ACKNOWLEDGMENTS

The authors are indebted to the University of Buenos Aires (UBA) and the National Research Council of Argentina (CONICET). C. Marino and R.M. de Lederkremer are research members of CONICET.

REFERENCES

Afroz S., El-Ganiny A. M., Sanders D. A. R., Kaminsky S. G. W. *Fungal Genet. Biol.* 48, 896-903 (2011).

Alderwick L. J., Dover L. G., Veerapen N., Gurcha S. S., Kremer L., Roper D. L., Pathak A. K., Reynolds R. C., Besra G. S., *Protein Expression Purif.* 58, 332-341 (2008).

Allard S. T. M., Giraud M. F., Naismith J. H. *Cell. Mol. Life Sci.* 58, 1650-1665 (2001).

Bakker H., Kleczka B., Gerardy-Schahn R., Routier F. H. *Biol. Chem.*386, 657-661 (2005).

Beis K., Srikannathasan V., Liu H., Fullerton S. W. B., Bamford V. A., Sanders D. A. R., Whitfield C., McNeil M. R., Naismith J. H. *J. Mol. Biol.* 348, 971-982 (2005).

Beláňová M., Dianišková P., Brennan P. J., Completo G. C., Rose N. L., Lowary T. L., Mikušová K., *J. Bacteriol.* 190, 1141-1145 (2008).

Beverley S. M., Owens K. L., Showalter M., Griffith C. L., Doering T. L., Jones V. C., McNeil, M. R. *Eukaryot .Cell* 4, 1147-1154 (2005).

Boechi L., de Oliveira C. A., Da Fonseca I., Kizjakina K., Sobrado P., Tanner J. J., McCammon J. A. *Protein Sci.* 22, 1490-501 (2013).

Borrelli S., Zandberg W. F., Mohan S., Ko M., Martinez-Gutierrez F., Partha S. K., Sanders D. A. R., Av-Gay Y., Pinto B. M. *Int. J. Antimicrob. Agents* 36, 364-368 (2010).

Brockhausen I. *Drug News and Perspectives* 19, 401-409 (2006).

Caravano A., Dohi H., Sinay P., Vincent S. P. *Chem.-Eur. J.* 12, 3114-3123 (2006).

Chad J. M., Sarathy K. P., Gruber T. D., Addala E., Kiessling L. L., Sanders, D. A. R. *Biochemistry* 46, 6723-6732 (2007).

Chlubnova I., L. Legentil, R. Dureau, A. Pennec, M. Almendros, R. Daniellou, C. Nugier-Chauvin, Ferrières V. *Carbohydr. Res.* 356, 44-61 (2012).

Cren S., Gurcha S. S., Blake A. J., Besra G. S., Thomas N. R. *Org. Biomol. Chem.* 2, 2418-2420 (2004).

Da Fonseca I., Kizjakina K., Sobrado P. *Arch. Biochem. Biophys.* 538,103-110 (2013).

Damveld R. A., Franken A., Arentshorst M., Punt P. J., Klis F. M., van den Hondel C. A. M. J. J., Ram, A. F. J. *Genetics* 178, 873-881(2008).

Dhatwalia R., Singh H., Oppenheimer M., Karr D. B., Nix J. C., Sobrado P., Tanner J. J. *J. Biol. Chem.* 287, 9041-9051 (2012a).

Dhatwalia R., Singh H., Oppenheimer M., Sobrado P., Tanner J. J. *Biochemistry* 51, 4968-4979 (2012b).

Dhatwalia R., Singh H., Solano L. M., Oppenheimer M., Robinson R. M., Ellerbrock J. F., Sobrado P., Tanner J. J., *J. Am. Chem. Soc.* 134, 18132-18138 (2012c).

Dureau R., Robert-Gangneux F., Gangneux J.-P. Nugier-Chauvin C., Legentil L., Daniellou R., Ferrières V. *Carbohydr. Res.* 345, 1299-1305 (2010).

Dykhuizen E. C., May J. F., Tongpenyai A., Kiessling L. L. *J. Am. Chem. Soc.* 130, 6706-6707 (2008).

El-Ganiny A. M., Sanders D. A., Kaminskyj S. G. *Fungal Genet. Biol.* 45, 1533-1542 (2008).

El-Sayed et al. *Science* 309, 409-415 (2005).

Engel J., Schmalhorst P. S., Dörk-Bousset T., Ferrières V., Routier F. H. *J. Biol. Chem.* 284, 33859-33868 (2009).

Errey, J. C., Mukhopadhyay, B., Kartha, K. P. R., Field R. A. *Chem. Commun.* 2706-2707 (2004).

Fontaine T., Delangle A., Simenel C., Coddeville B., van Vliet S. J., van Kooyk, Y., et al. *PLoS Pathog* 7, e1002372 (2011).

Fullerton S. W. B., Daff S., Sanders D. A. R., Ingledew W. J., Whitfield C., Chapman S. K., Naismith, J. H. *Biochemistry* 42, 2104-2109 (2003).

Gerardy-Schahn R., Oelmann S., Bakker H. *Biochimie* 83, 775-782 (2001).

Ghavami A., Chen J. J. W., Pinto B. M. *Carbohydr. Res.* 339, 401-407 (2004).

Gruber T. D.,Westler W. M., Kiessling L. L., Forest K. T. *Biochemistry* 48, 9171-9173 (2009).

Gruber T. D., Borrok M. J., Westler W. M., Forest, K. T., Kiessling L. L. *J. Mol. Biol.* 391, 327-340 (2009).

Guan, S., Clarke, A. J., Whitfield, C. *J. Bacteriol.* 183, 3318-3327 (2001).

Hirschberg C. B. *Annu. Rev. Biochem.* 67, 49-69 (1998).

Holden, H. M., Rayment, I., Thoden, J. B. *J. Biol. Chem.* 278, 43885-43888 (2003).

Huang W., Gauld J.W. *J. Phys. Chem. B* 116, 14040-14050 (2012).

Imamura A., Lowary T. *Trends Glycosci. Glyc.* 23, 134-152 (2011).

Itoh K., Huang Z., Liu H. *Org. Lett.* 9, 879-882 (2007).

Jin C. *Int. J. Microbiol.* 2012, 654251 (2012).

Kleczka B., Lamerz A. C., Van Zandbergen G., Wiese, M. *J. Biol. Chem.* 282, 10498-10505 (2007).

Komachi Y., Hatakeyama S., Motomatsu H., Futagami T., Kizjakina K., Sobrado P., Ekino K., Takegawa K., Goto M., Nomura Y., Oka T. *Mol. Microbiol.* 90,1054-1073 (2013).

Köplin R., Brisson J. R., Whitfield C. *J. Biol. Chem.* 272, 4121-4128 (1997).

Kremer L., Dover L. G., Morehouse C., Hitchin P., Everett M., Morris H. R., Dell A., Brennan P. J., McNeil M. R., Flaherty C., Duncan K., Besra G. S. *J. Biol. Chem.* 276, 26430-26440 (2001).

Latgé J. *Cell Microbiol.* 12, 863-872 (2010).

Latgé J. P. *Med. Mycol.* 47, Supp. 1, 104-109 (2009).

Lederkremer R. M., Nahmad V., Varela O. *J. Org. Chem.* 59, 690-692 (1994).

Lederkremer R. M., Colli W. *Glycobiology* 5, 547-552 (1995).

Lee M. J., Gravelat F. N., Cerone1 R. P., Baptista S. D., Campoli P. V. Choe S.-I., Kravtsov I., Vinogradov E., Creuzenet C., Liu H., Berghuis A. M., Latgé J.-P., Filler S. G., Fontaine T., Sheppard D. C. *J. Biol. Chem.* 289, 1243-1256 (2014).

Lee R. E., Smith M. D., Pickering L., Fleet G. W. J. *Tetrahedron Lett.* 40, 8689-8692 (1999).

Lee R. E., Smith M. D., Nash R. J., Griffiths R. C., McNeil M. R., Grewal R. K.,Yan W., Besra G. S., Brennan P., Fleet G. W. J. *Tetrahedron Lett.* 38, 6733-6736 (1997).

Liautard V., Christina A. E., Desvergnes V., Martin O. R. *J. Org. Chem.* 71, 7337-7345 (2006).

Lillelund V. H., Jensen H. H., Liang X., Bols M. *Chem. Rev.* 102, 515-53 (2002).

MacRae J. I., Obado S. O., Turnock D. C., Roper J. R., Kierans M., Kelly J. M., Ferguson M. A. J. *Mol. Biochem. Parasitol.* 147, 126-136. (2006).

Madeira da Silva, L., Owens, K. L., Murta, S. M., Beverley, S. M. *Proc. Natl. Acad. Sci. USA* 106, 7583-7588 (2009).

Marino C., Baldoni L. *ChemBiochem.* 15, 188-204 (2014).

Marino C., Gallo-Rodriguez C., Lederkremer R. M. in *Glycans: Biochemistry, Characterization and Applications* (Ed.: H. M. Mora-Montes), Nova Science Publishers, pp. 207-268 (2012).

Mariño K., Marino C., Lima C., Baldoni L., Lederkremer R. M. *Eur. J. Org. Chem.* 2958-2964 (2005).

Marlow, A. L, Kiessling, L. L. *Org. Lett* 3, 2517-2519 (2001).

May J. F., Levengood M. R., Splain R. A., Brown C. D., Kiessling L. L. *Biochemistry* 51, 1148-1159 (2012).

N'Go I., Golten S., Ardá A., Cañada J., Jimenez-Barbero J., LinclauB.,Vincent S. *Chem. Eur. J.* 20,106-112 (2014).

Nassau, P.M., Martin, S.L., Brown, R.E.,Weston, A., Monsey, D., McNeil, M.R., Duncan, K. *J. Bacteriol.* 178, 1047-1052 (1996).

Nikaido, H., Sarvas, M. *J. Bacteriol.* 105, 1063-1072 (1971).

Novelli J. F., Chaudhary K., Canovas J., Benner J. S., Madinger C. L., Kelly P., Hodgkin, J., Carlow, C. K. *Dev. Biol.* 335, 340-355 (2009).

Oppenheimer M., Poulin M. B., Lowary T. L., Helm R. F., Sobrado, P., *Arch. Biochem. Biophys.* 502, 31-38 (2010).

Oppenheimer M., Valenciano A. L., Kizjakina K., Qi J., Sobrado P. *PLoS ONE* 7, e32918 (2012).

Oppenheimer M., Valenciano A. L., Sobrado P. *Enzyme Res*: 415976. doi: 10.4061/2011/415976(2011a).

Oppenheimer M., Valenciano A.L., Sobrado, P. *Biochem. Biophys. Res. Commun.*407, 552-556 (2011b).

Pan F., Jackson M. Ma Y., McNeil M. R. *J. Bacteriol.* 183, 3991-3998 (2001).

Partha S. K, van Straaten K. E, Sanders D. A. R. *J. Mol. Biol.* 18, 394, 864-77 (2009).

Peltier P., Beláňová M., Dianisková P., Zhou R., Zheng R. B., Pearcey J. A., Joe M., Brennan J. C., Nugier-Chauvin, Ferriéres V., Lowary, T. L., Daniellou R., Mikusova K. *Chem. Biol.* 17, 1356-1366 (2010).

Peltier P., Euzen R., Daniellou R., Nugier-Chauvin C., Ferrières V. *Carbohydr. Res.*, 343, 1897-1923 (2008).

Poulin M. B., Zhou R., Lowary T. L. *Org. Biomol. Chem.* 10, 4074-4087 (2012).

Poulin, M. B., Lowary, T. L. *Methods Enzymol.* 478, 389-411 (2010).

Ram B. P., Munjal D. D. *CRC Crit. Rev. Biochem.* 17, 257-311 (1985).

Richards, M. R., Lowary, T. L. *ChemBioChem.* 10, 1920-1938 (2009).

Rose M. N. L., Completo G. C., Lin S. J., McNeil M., Palcic M. M., Lowary T. L. *J. Am. Chem. Soc.* 128, 6721-6729 (2006).

Sanders D. A. R., Staines A. G., McMahon S. A., McNeil M. R., Whitfield C., Naismith J. H. *Nat. Struct. Biol.* 8, 858-863 (2001).

Scherman M. S., Winans K. A., Stern R. J., Jones V., Bertozzi C. R., McNeil M. R. *Antimicrob. Agents Chemother.* 47, 378-382 (2003).

Schmalhorst P., Krappmann S., Vervecken W., Rohde, M., Müller M., Braus G. H., Contreras R., Braun, A., Bakker, H., Routier, F. H. *Eukaryotic Cell* 7, 1268-1277 (2008).

Snitynsky R. B., Lowary T. L., *Org. Lett.* 16, 212-215 (2014).

Soltero-Higgin M, Carlson E. E., Gruber T. D., Kiessling L. *Nat. Struct. Mol. Biol.* 11, 539-543 (2004).

Spath G. F., Epstein L., Leader B., Singer S. M., Avila H. A., Turco S. J., Beverley S. M. *PNAS* 97, 9258-9263 (2000).

Spath G. F., Garraway L. A.,Turco S. J., Beverley S. M. *PNAS*100, 9536-9541 (2003).

Stevenson G., Neal B., Liu D., Hobbs M., Packer N. H., Batley M. Redmond J.W., Lindquist L, Reeves P. *J. Bacteriol.* 176, 4144-4156 (1994).

Stoco P. H., Aresi C., Lückemeyer D. D., Sperandio M. M., Marques Sincero T. C., Steindel M., Miletti L. C., Grisard E. C. *Exp. Parasitol.* 130, 246-262 (2012).

Sun H.G., Ruszczycky M.W., Chang W.C., Thibodeaux C. J., Liu H.W., *J. Biol. Chem.* 287, 4602-4608 (2012).

Suzuki E., Tanaka A. K., Toledo M. S., Levery S. B., Straus A. H., Takahashi H. K. *Biochim. Biophys. Acta* 1780, 362-369 (2008).

Szczepina M. G., Zheng R. B., Completo G. C., Lowary T. L., Pinto B. M. *ChemBioChem* 10, 2052-2059 (2009).

Taha H. A., Richards M. R., Lowary T. L., *Chem. Rev.* 113, 1851-1876 (2012).

Tanner J. J., Boechi L., McCammonb, J. A. Sobrado P. *Arch. Biochem. Biophys.* doi: 10.1016/j.abb.2013.09.017 (2013).

Taylor M. E., DrickamerK. *Introduction to Glycobiology,* Oxford; New York; Oxford University Press, 3th Ed. (2003).

Tefsen B., Ram A.F., van Die I., Routier F. H. *Glycobiology* 22, 456-469 (2012).

Thibodeaux C. J., Melançon C. E. III, Liu, H.-w. *Angew. Chem. Int. Ed.*47, 9814-9859 (2008).

Trunkfield A. E., Gurcha S. S., Besra G. S., Bugg T. D. H., *Bioorg. Med. Chem.* 18, 2651-2663 (2010).

Tsvetkov Y. E., Nikolaev A. V. *J. Chem. Soc., Perkin Trans. 1* 889-8912 (2000).

van Straaten K. E., Routier F. H. Sanders, D. A. *Acta Crystallogr.* (F) 68, 455-459 (2012a).

van Straaten K. E., Routier F. H., Sanders D. A. R. *J. Biol Chem.* 287, 10780-10790 (2012b).

Veerapen N., Yuan Y., Sanders D. A. R., Pinto B. M. *Carbohydr. Res.* 339, 2205-2217 (2004).

Wesener D. A., May J. F., Huffman E. M., Kiessling L. L. *Biochemistry* 52, 4391-4398 (2013).

Weston A., Stern R. J., Lee R. E., Nassau P. M., Monsey D., Martin, S. L., Scherman, M. S. Besra, G. S., Duncan, K., McNeil M. R. *Tuber. Lung. Dis.* 78, 123-131 (1998).

Wheatley R. W., Zheng R. B., Lowary T. L., Ng K. K. S. *J. Biol.Chem.* 287, 28132-28143 (2012).

Wing C., Errey J. C., Mukhopadhyay B., Blanchard J.S., Field R. A. *Org. Biomol. Chem.* 4, 3945-3950 (2006).

Yao X., Bleile D. W., Yuan Y., Chao J., Sarathy K. P., Sanders D. A, Pinto B. M., O'Neill M. A. *Proteins* 74, 972-979 (2009).

Yuan Y., Bleile D.W., Wen X., Sanders D. A., Itoh K., Liu H.W., Pinto B. M. *J. Am. Chem. Soc.* 130, 3157-3168 (2008).

Yuan Y., Wen X., Sanders D. A. R., Pinto B. M. *Biochemistry* 44, 14080-14089 (2005).

Zhang K., Barron T., Turco S.J., Beverley S. M. *Mol. Biochem. Parasitol.* 136, 11-23 (2004).

Zhang Q., Liu H.-w. *J. Am. Chem. Soc.* 122, 9065-9070 (2000).

In: Galactose
Editor: Vitor Hugo Pomin

ISBN: 978-1-63117-928-0

Chapter 6

REGULATION OF THE GALACTOSE OPERON IN *E. COLI*

Dale E. A. Lewis* and Amlanjyoti Dhar
Laboratory of Molecular Biology, National Cancer Institute,
National Institutes of Health, Bethesda, MD, US

ABSTRACT

The galactose (*gal*) operon of *Eschericha coli* consists of four structural genes, E, T, K, and M, that respectively code for Epimerase, Transferase, Kinase and Mutarotase enzymes, needed for D-galactose metabolism. In addition to galactose being an energy source, galactose metabolites are anabolic substrates. The absence of either the *gal*E or *gal*T gene results in the accumulation of galactose intermediates, leading to multiple metabolic disorders. The *gal* genes are transcribed from two overlapping promoters, *P1* and *P2,* that have transcription start points (*tsp*) 5-bp apart. Both promoters are typically regulated by the repressor (GalR) and cyclic adenosine 3':5'-monophosphate (cAMP) receptor protein (CRP). GalR binds at two operators, O_E (external operator) located at position -60.5, and O_I (internal operator) located at +53.5 with respect to the *tsp* of *P1*. The binding of GalR to O_E alone represses *P1* and stimulates *P2*, while binding to O_I blocks transcription from both *P1* and *P2*. The cAMP and CRP acting as a complex (CCC) activates *P1* and

* Corresponding author: Dale E. A. Lewis. 37 Convent Drive, Room 5138, Bethesda, MD 20892-4255. Tel: (301) 496-9129, Fax: (301) 496-2212, E-mail: Lewisdal@mail.nih.gov.

represses *P2*. A histone-like protein, HU, binds to position +6.5, is also a key player in *gal* regulation by GalR. In this chapter, we will describe the key components of the regulation of the *gal* operon at the level of transcription.

INTRODUCTION

The Leloir Pathway

The metabolism of D-galactose is summarized in the Leloir pathway (Figure 1) [1, 2]. Two different pairs of sugars are used as substrates for enzymes. Melibiose and phenyl-α-D-galactose are converted by α-D-galactosidase into an α-D-galactose for further metabolism into energy source. Alternatively, in a two-step process, lactose and phenyl-β-D-galactose are converted by a β-D-galactosidase to β-D-galactose, after which, the *gal*M gene product, mutarotase, converts β-D-galactose to α-D-galactose for further degradation [3]. Galactokinase (kinase, 40 kDa), the *gal*K gene product, converts α-D-galactose to galactose-1-phosphate [4, 5]. The *gal*T gene product, galactose-1-phosphate uridyltransferase (transfera-se, 82 kDa), converts galactose-1-phosphate to uridine diphosphospho (UDP) galactose [6]. The *gal*E gene product, UDP galactose-4-epimerase (epimerase, 79 kDa), then converts UDP galactose to UDP glucose [7]. Finally, UDP glucose is converted to glucose-1-phosphate by glucose-1-phosphateuridylyl transferase (transferase, 33 kDa), the *gal*U gene product (mapped at 28 min) [8]. The *gal*U gene is genetically unlinked to the *gal* operon and is regulated in respond to the *gal* operon. A mutation in *gal*E, *gal*T, *gal*K or *gal*U gene results in the accumulation of D-galactose or its metabolic intermediates. The accumulation of galactose-1-phoshpate or UDP galactose in a *gal*E, *gal*T or *gal*U mutants after D-galactose addition to the cell is toxic, resulting in bacteriostasis (failure of cell to grow in galactose) or bacteriolysis (cell lysis) [9-13].

D-galactose and its non-metabolizable analogue, D-fucose, are inducers of the structural genes of the *gal* operon. The binding of D-galactose to the repressor, GalR, inactivates GalR permitting RNA polymerase to transcribe the structural genes. The structural genes are induced 10- to 15-fold by D-galactose and D-fucose [14-17]. As indicated earlier, D-galactose is composed of α- and β-galactose anomers. *In vitro* transcription assays show anomers of D-galactose induce the *P1* promoter equally efficiently [18].

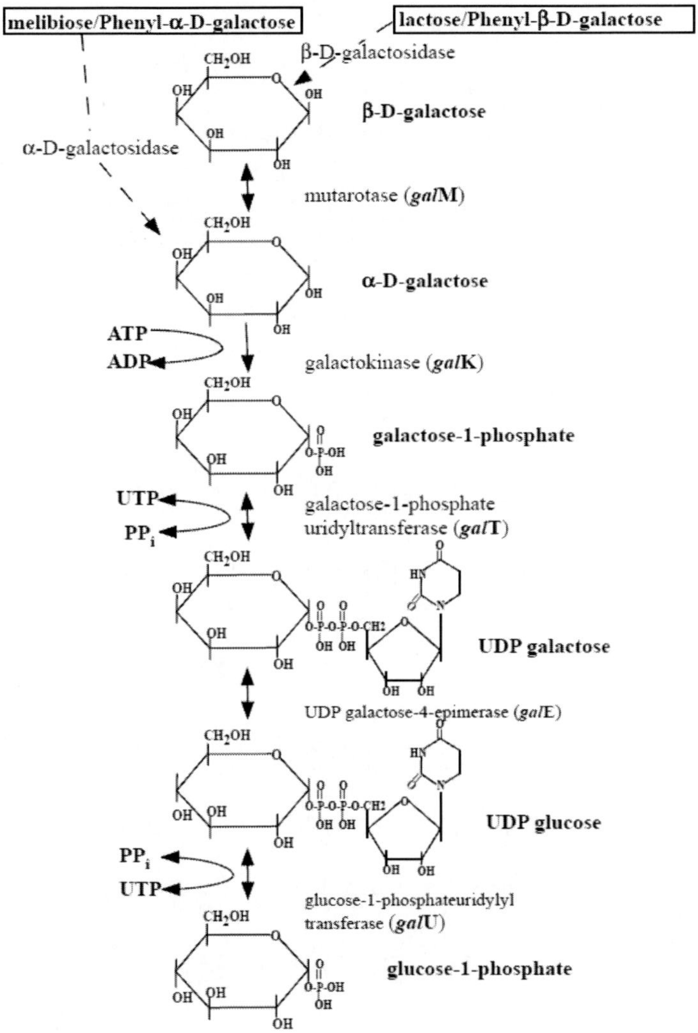

Figure 1. The Leloir pathway of D-galactose metabolism in *E. coli*. The names of the enzymes are abbreviated in the rest of the text.

Transport of galactose into the cells is mediated primarily by three permeases, galactopermease (*gal*P, mapped at 64 min), induced by D-galactose, methyl-β-D-galactopyranoside permease (*mgl*C, mapped at 48.17 min) induced by D-fucose, and methyl-β-D-thiogalactoside permease (*lac*Y, mapped at 7.78 min) induced by thiogalactosides [14, 19-22].

THE *GAL* OPERON

The galactose (*gal*) operon, located at 17 min of the chromosome in *E. coli* comprises regulatory elements and structural genes that control the metabolism of D-galactose (Figures 1-3). The regulatory DNA elements include the operators (O_E and O_I), the promoters (*P1* and *P2*), and the activating site (AS). Regulatory proteins, such as GalR, GalS, CRP and HU, bind to the regulatory elements of *P1* and *P2*. The structural genes, *gal*E, *gal*T, *gal*K and *gal*M, code for the enzymes epimerase, transferase, kinase, and mutarotase, respectively, are involved in the metabolism of D-galactose [3, 23-26].

THE *GAL* OPERON PROMOTERS

Transcription from the *gal* structural genes are driven by two overlapping promoters, *P1* and *P2*, which have start points that are separated by 5-bp, a half-helical turn (Figures 2 and 3) [27-29]. Expression of *gal* polypeptides from *P1* and *P2* is dissimilar.

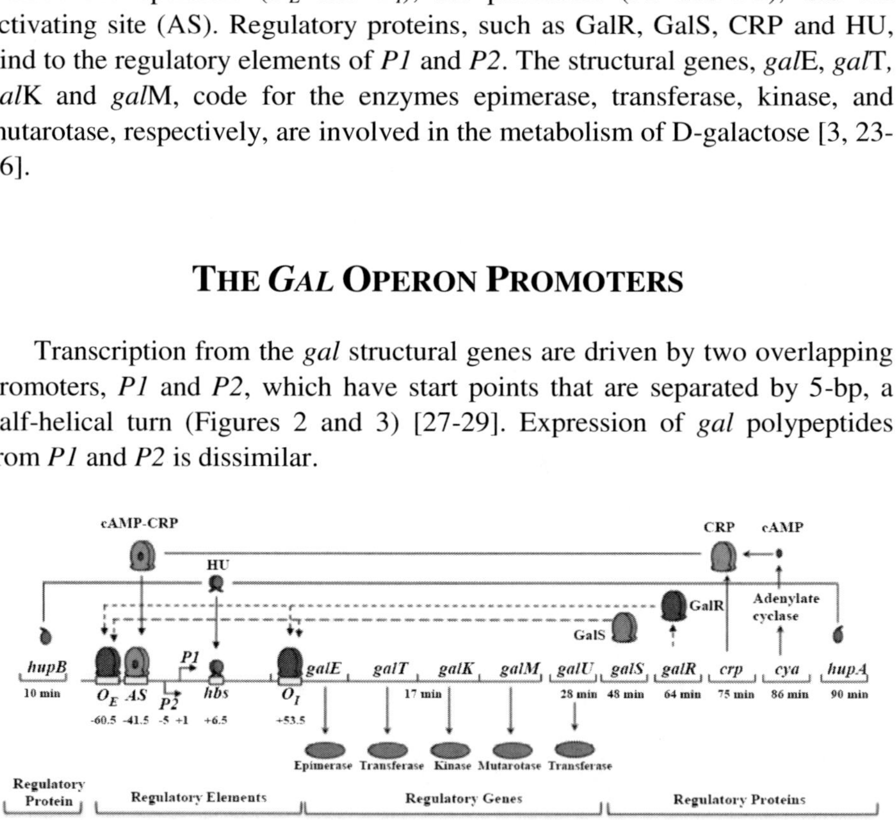

Figure 2. The *gal* regulon. The *gal* structural genes (*gal*ETKM) mapped at 17 min on the *E. coli* chromosome. The *gal*ETKM gene products: Epimerase, Transferase, Kinase and Mutarotase, respectively. The transcription start point (*tsp*) of *P1* is +1 and that of *P2* is -5 in the *gal* operon. The numbering system is relative to +1, with numbers downstream of +1 as positive (+) and those upstream as negative (-). Operators (O_E and O_I), hbs: HU binding site, AS: activating site. The *gal*U gene codes for transferase mapped at 28 min, *gal*S at 48 min codes for GalS (orange), *gal*R at 64 min codes for GalR (red), *crp* at 75 min codes for CRP (green), *cya* at 86 min codes for adenylate cyclase, which makes cAMP (red), *hup*A at 90 min and *hup*A at 10 min codes for HUαβ (blue). GalR binds to O_E and O_I, but in the absence of GalR, GalS binds to O_E and O_I. The map is not drawn to scale.

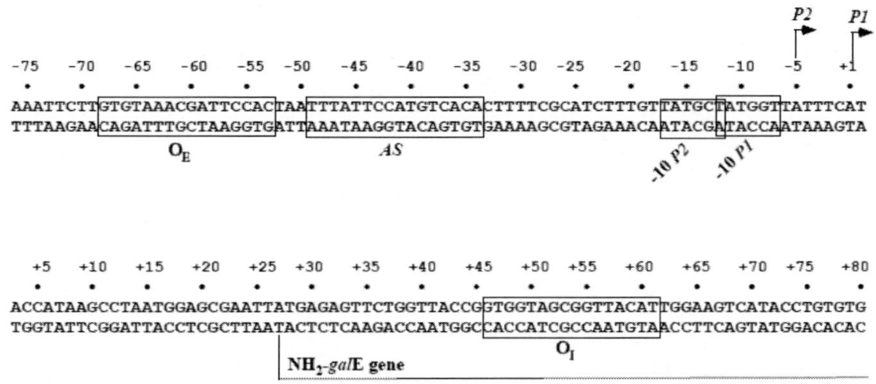

Figure 3. The DNA sequence of the *gal* operon from -76 to +80. The *tsp* of *P1* (+1) and *P2* (-5), -10 element of *P1* (-10 *P1*) (box), -10 element of *P2* (-10 *P2*) (box), O_E and O_I (box). AS: activating site (box). The N-terminal of *gal*E start at +27.

Equimolar amounts of *gal* polypepetides (*galE*TKM) are made from *P1*; however, *P2* exhibits polarity of transcription as distal polypeptide is expressed at lower levels than the proximal one [30, 31]. The *tsp* of *P1* is +1 and that of *P2* in the *P1* numbering system is -5 (Figure 3) Nucleotides located upstream of *P1* (+1) are represented as negative values (-) and those located downstream of *P1* are expressed as positive values (+). *P1* contains a -10 element ($^{-12}$TATGGT^{-7}), an extended -10 element ($^{-15}$TG^{-14}), and a extremely weak -35 element ($^{-35}$CACTTT^{-30}), with a 17-bp spacer between the -10 and -35 segments [32]. Similarly, *P2* contains a -10 element ($^{-17}$TATGCT^{-12}), an extended -10 element ($^{-20}$TG^{-19}), and a very weak -35 element ($^{-35}$ATGTCA^{-30}) [32]. The *ex-10* element provides additional contacts for RNAP to recognize a promoter without a -35 element as in *P1* and *P2* [33, 34]. Mutations in the -10 regions of *P1* that inactivate one or both promoters have been identified. Substitutions of the conserved bases -12T, -11A, and -7T inactivate *P1*. Base substitutions of -12T, the 1st base of the -10 element of *P1* and the 6th base of the -10 element of *P2* inactivate both *P1* and *P2*. The -11A is suggested to play a "master" role in DNA melting [35]. Only a purine with no side chain in position C2 at -11 is sufficient for DNA melting and favors transcription [36]. Structurally, the -11A and -7T bases flip out of the stacked bases and insert into a hydrophobic pocket of σ^{70} RNA polymerase [35, 37, 38]. Mutation of the extended -10 element of *P1* ($^{-15}$TG^{-14}) or *P2* ($^{-20}$TG^{-19}) inactivates *P1* or *P2*, respectively [33, 34, 39-44]. A purine in the nontemplate strand is the preferred base for efficient *tsp* of *P1* and *P2* [45]. Normally, the *tsp* is the 12th base counting downstream from position -11 for *P1* or *P2* [45]. However, a single base pair deletion between -11A and +1A shifts the *tsp* to the next available purine, which is located at +3 in *P1*. Any base pair deletion within -24 to -12 positions did not change the *tsp* [45].

cAMP-CRP Effect

The cyclic adenosine 3,:5-monophosphate (cyclic AMP) and cyclic AMP receptor protein (CRP) complex (CCC) binds to the activating site (AS) also known as "*cat*" with midpoint at -41.5 ($^{-49}$TTTATTCC.ATGTCACA^{-34}) and no symmetry [46] (Figures 2 and 3). DNase I protection shows that cAMP-CRP complex (CCC) protects -52 to -30 [47]. Mutation of -35C:G base pair to -35G:C or -37C:G to -37T:A inhibits action of CCC [48, 49]. This complex activates *P1* and represses *P2* as shown by *in vitro* transcription assays using supercoiled DNA and purified CRP [27, 29, 46, 47] (Figure 4). The *galP1* is classified as a Class II CCC dependent promoter since it AS is located at -41.5 as compared to Class I CCC dependent promoter of *lac* where the AS is located at -61 [50, 51]. The CCC at AS is located on the same face of the DNA as RNAP at the *P1* promoter, but on the opposite face of the *P2* promoter. Amino acid residues in CRP that are involved in the interaction between CCC and RNAP are localized to three activating regions (AR1, AR2 and AR3) of CRP [50-56]. The alpha carboxyl-terminal domain (αCTD) of RNAP interacts with CRP at AR1, the alpha amino-terminal domain (αNTD) of RNAP interacts with AR2 and the sigma (σ) subunit of RNAP interacts with AR3. The crystal structures of CRP (also known as catabolic activator protein, CAP), and the αCTD have been solved [56]. The structure is consistent with the genetic and biochemical data in the predicted models of CCC action. Three domains (AR1, AR2 and AR3) of the CCC make specific contacts with RNAP to activate *P1* in *gal* [50-56]. CCC bends the *gal* promoter region 94°C [57]. CCC induces bending of approximately 90°C at *P1* promoter [58].

The *crp* gene (mapped at 75 min), codes for CRP, a basic allosteric dimeric protein of 209 amino acids (22.5 kDa/monomer) [59, 60]. The intra-cellular concentration of CRP in log and stationary phases of growing cells is 1,050 and 1,300 molecules, respectively (Ishihama et al. submitted for publication). The *cya*A gene, located at 86 min on the *E. coli* chromosome map, codes for adenylate cyclase (98 kDa, 15 molecule per cell) [61] (Figure 2).

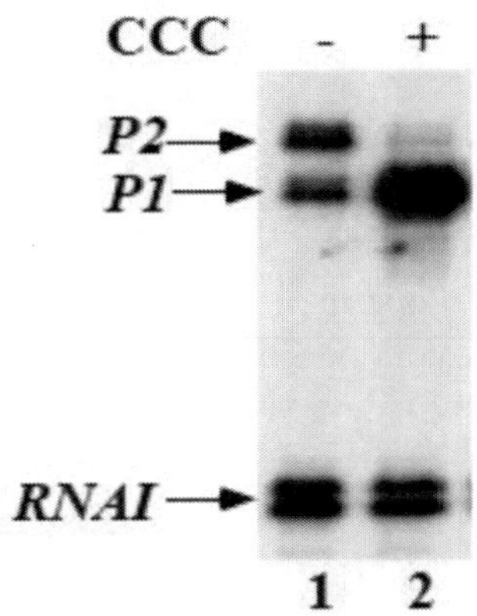

Permission from Elsevier, [109].

Figure 4. Regulation of *P1* and *P2* by CCC. mRNAs made from *P1* and *P2*. RNAI transcripts are from a control promoter.

Adenylate cyclase catalyzes the hydrolysis of ATP to cAMP [62]. One molecule of cAMP binds to each monomer of CRP with an associa-tion constant, $K_{a,}$ of about 10^{-5} M [59, 63]. The cAMP molecule binds to the N-terminal of CRP and induces an allosteric transition that changes the binding property of the carboxyl domain [63-66].Transcription from *P1* or *P2* is dependent on the level of CCC in the cell, where cAMP levels are approximately 10^{-6} M in *E. coli* [67].

How does CCC regulate *P1* and *P2* in opposite direction? At *P1*, CCC enhances the formation of the closed complex (rate-limiting step) by RNAP binding to the promoter region and increases the isomerization step from closed to open complex. At *P2*, CCC prevents closed complex formation by preventing RNAP access to the promoters. In the presence of CCC there is a 5-fold greater level of stimulation of *P1* [68].

CRP mutants (*crp**) that function independent of cAMP have been isolated [63, 66]. The mutations are located in the D-helix of CRP (G141S, R142H and A144T) and C-helix (E72A). CRP* contains bulkier side groups than wild type CRP and elicit a conformational changes similar to that of CCC allowing its helix-turn-helix (H-T-H) to bind in the major grooves of the DNA. Compared to CRP, CRP* and CCC are sensitive to chymotrypsin cleavage, indicating a conformation change in the protein exposing the protease cleavage site. Suppressor mutations of *crp** 141 (T127A) and of *crp** 144 (R169C and E171G) are located to a second site with bulkier side groups [69]. These suppressor mutations regain the dependency on cAMP for promoter function.

GalR

The product of the unlinked *gal*R gene, GalR (343 amino acids), mapped to 64 min on the *E. coli* chromosome [14, 16, 70]. Immunoblot assay reveals that wild type cells contain approximately 25 molecules of dimer per cell [71]. The *gal* operon includes two operators, O_E (located centrally at -60.5) and O_I (located at +53.5). O_E is located external to the *gal*E gene while O_I is located internal of the *gal*E gene [29] (Figures 2 and 3). Purified GalR, a dimer of 74 kDa, binds specifically to O_E and O_I to generate DNaseI footprinting protection for O_E (-73 to -51) and O_I (+45 to +67) [72, 73]. The half-maximal concentrations of GalR for binding to O_E and O_I are 1.3 nM and 2.9 nM, respectively [74]. The half- maximal concentrations of D-fucose and D-galactose for the release of GalR repression are 1 mM and 0.5 mM, respective-ly [75]. This value is close to the concentration of D-galactose *in vivo* of 0.1 to 0.2 mM. GalR induces DNA bending of 97° for O_E and 112° for O_I [57]. Mutations in O_E and O_I prevent GalR binding [72].

Mechanisms of GalR Regulation: Contact Inhibition, Contact Activation, and Repressosome Inhibition

GalR binding to O_E alone represses *P1* and activates *P2* (Figures 5a, 5b, and 5d). The repression of *P1* is described as "contact inhibition" because the carboxyl-terminal domain (αCTD) of RNAP contacts GalR, preventing RNAP from escaping, and inhibiting transcription from *P1* (Figures 5a and 5d, lanes 1-2). Deletion of the αCTD domain, [α-256 (lacking amino acids 256-329) or α-235 (lacking 235-329)], releases the inhibition of RNAP, resulting in transcription from *P1* [76, 77]. The activation of *P2* is a result of presumably the same contact between αCTD of RNAP and GalR (Figures 5b and 5d, lanes 1-2) [78]. Mutations in the αCTD (R265W, R265A, R265K, N209W, C269W, L270W) domain have dual effects on *P1* and *P2*, preventing the inhibition of *P1* and the activation of *P2* (Table 1) [78].

Repression of *P2* requires DNA looping, which is achieved through protein-protein interactions between GalR bound at O_E (GalR-O_E) and GalR bound at O_I (GalR-O_I) in the presence of the histone-like protein, HU (Figure 5c). The weak interactions between GalR-O_E and GalR-O_I are stabilized by the binding of HU, which binds to the apex of the DNA. The formation of this higher-order structure prevents open complex formation by RNAP, resulting in strong repression of both *P1* and *P2* [79]. This higher-order structure is referred to as "repressosome" (Figures 5c and 5d, lanes 1 and 3). The details of DNA looping are discussed below.

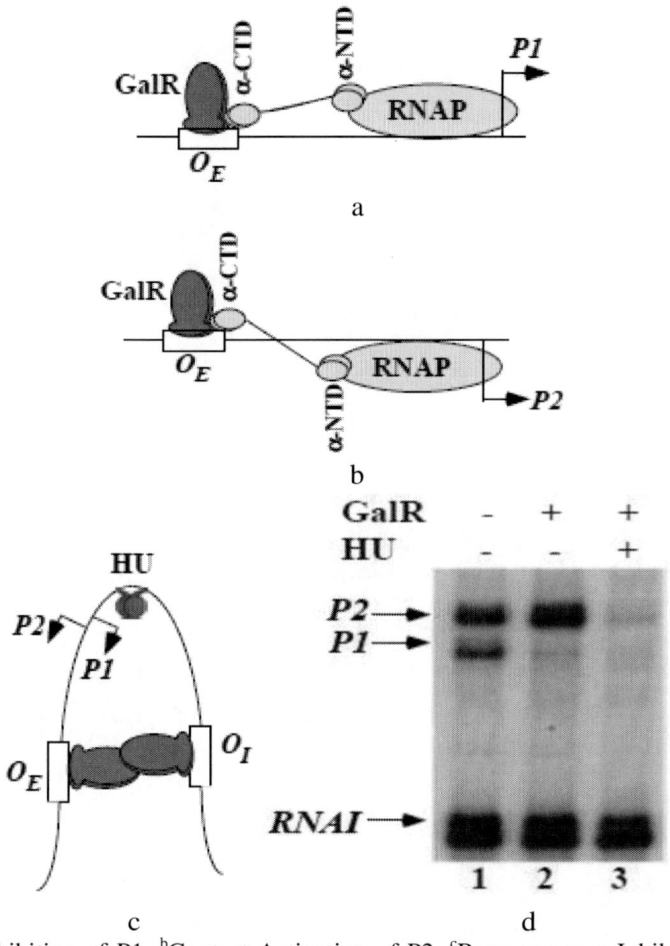

[a]Contact Inhibition of P1. [b]Contact Activation of P2. [c]Repressosome Inhibition of P1 and P2.

Permission from Elsevier, [109].

Figure 5. Regulation by GalR and HU. a) Contact inhibition of *P1*: GalR (red) at O_E is interacting with the α-CTD of RNAP (green). b) Contact activation of *P2*. c) Repressosome formation by GalR-O_E and GalR-O_I interactions, HU (blue) binds to the cognate DNA site. d) mRNAs made from *P1* and *P2* in the absence and presence of GalR (80 nM) and HU (40 nM).

Table 1. Effect of α-CTD mutations on *P1* repression and *P2* activation using reconstituted RNAP

αCTD amino acid	*P1* repression	*P2* repression
WT	++++	++++
L262W	++++	++++
T263W	++++	++++
R265W	-	-
R265a	-	-
R265K	-	-
N268W	-	-
C269W	-	-
L270W	-	-

Amount of transcrips of wild-type reconstituted RNAP relative to mutant reconstituted RNAP is expressed as 80-100% (++++) and less than 20% is indicated by (-) Permission from Elsevier, [75].

During transcription elongation from *gal* promoters by RNAP, GalR-O_I does not block or impede RNAP progress [80]. However, insertion of a 5 bp (GATCT) sequence upstream of the O_I sequence (GAGA<u>GATCT</u>GTTCTGG-TTACCG[O_I]) results in blockage of more than 60% of RNAP elongation as a result of RNAP pausing at the strong DNA-RNA hybrid immediately upstream of the 5 bp insertion. When the strong DNA-RNA hybrid is weake-ned by mutating GAGA to TATA (<u>T</u>A<u>T</u>A<u>GATCT</u>GTTCTGGTTAC-CG[O_I]), no blockage of RNAP is observed, suggesting that the strength of the DNA-RNA hybrid immediately upstream of O_I affects RNAP elongation.

THE *GAL* OPERATORS

GalR binds to O_E and O_I to control transcription. The constitutive operator mutations, (O^C and O^a) identified O_E as the 16 bp palindromic sequence ($^{-68}$GTGTAAAC.GATTCCAC^{-53}) [12, 27, 75, 81, 82]. A similar 16 bp palindromic sequence defined O_I ($^{+46}$GTGGTAGC.GGTTACAT^{+61}), which is the first example of an operator element located within a structural protein-coding region. As expected, mutation of O_I results in constitutive expression of the *gal* genes.

DNA LOOPING

Irani et al. (1983) first proposed DNA looping to explain the observations in the *gal* operon of two complexes of GalR-O_E and GalR-O_I located 113 bp apart on the DNA [81]. Genetic, microscopic and biochemical evidences of DNA looping are listed below.

Genetic evidence: The *gal* operators O_E and O_I are separated by 113 bp or 11 DNA helical turns, assuming 10.4 bp/turn. *In vivo*, a set of operators ($O_E^G - O_I^G$, $O_E^G - O_I^L$, $O_E^L - O_I^G$, $O_E^L - O_I^L$) is constructed by converting *gal* operators ($O_E^G - O_I^G$) to *lac* operators ($O_E^L - O_I^L$) [83]. Protein-protein interactions between spatially separated operators are investigated by monitoring galactokinase activity, a product of the *gal* operon in the presence of GalR and LacI. Table 2 shows that in the presence of GalR, galactokinase activity is repressed (R) only on the $O_E^G - O_I^G$ template. In the presence of LacI, galactokinase activity is repressed (R) only on the $O_E^L - O_I^L$ template. On heterologous operators ($O_E^G - O_I^L$ and $O_E^L - O_I^G$), galactokinase activity is derepressed (D). These results imply that protein-protein interactions occur between GalR and GalR or LacI and LacI bound to their respective operator sites forming a DNA loop [83]. The occupation of both heterologous operators by respective repressors is not sufficient for repression.

Electron Microscopy

Electron microscopy studies provide direct evidence for a 113 bp DNA loop on the $O_E^L - O_I^L$ DNA fragment by LacI but not by $LacI^{adi}$, a mutant of LacI that cannot tetramerize because of the absence of an anti-parallel four-helix bundle [84-88] (Figure 6). $LacI^{adi}$ can form dimers and bind to *lac* operators on the $O_E^L - O_I^L$, but it cannot form a loop. Thus, mere occupation of the sites is not sufficient for DNA looping. The $LacI^{adi}$ occupation of both *lac* operators does not promote repression [76].

In Vitro Transcription Assay

In vitro transcription assays demonstrate the repression of *P1* and the activation of *P2* on the $O_E^G - O_I^G$ template in the presence of GalR in the absence of DNA looping (Figure 7a) [76, 77]. Both repression of *P1* and the activation of *P2* are due solely to contact-inhibition and -activation by GalR-O_E. In contrast, both *P1* and *P2* are repressed on the $O_E^L - O_I^L$ template in the presence of LacI (Figure 7b), but not $LacI^{adi}$ (Figure 7c). DNA loop is formed with the tetrametric LacI that bind to two spatially separated operators but not with dimeric GalR or $LacI^{adi}$, which can bind to the operators without forming tetramers due to the absence of protein-protein interactions between dimers (Figures 7b and 7c) [89].

Table 2. *In Vivo* analysis of GalR and LacI effect on *gal* repression with the conversion of *gal* to *lac* operators

Operator genotype	Protein present in cells			
	LacI & GalR	GalR	LacI	None
$O_E^G - O_I^G$	R	R	D	D
$O_E^G - O_I^L$	D	D	D	D
$O_E^L - O_I^G$	D	D	D	D
$O_E^L - O_I^L$	R	D	R	D

D: derepression and R: repression.
Adapted from Haber and Adhya 1988.

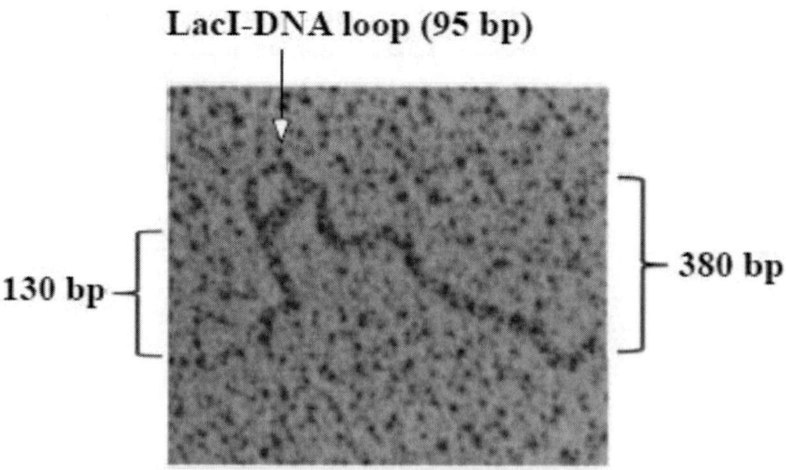

Permission from Cold Spring Harbor Laboratory Press, [85].

Figure 6. Electron micrograph of LacI-DNA loop. The arrow points to the DNA loop of 95 bp containing LacI-$O_E^L - O_I^L$ DNA. One end of the DNA is 130 bp from the loop and the other end is 380 bp.

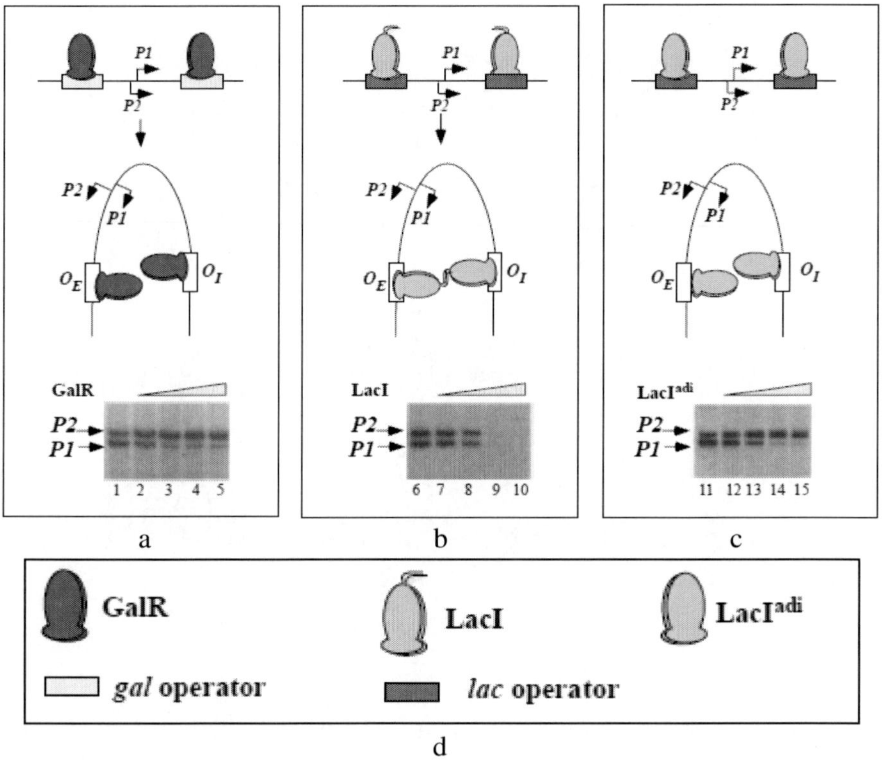

[a]GalR-*gal*O_E-O_I. [b]LacI-*lac*O_E-O_I. [c]LacI^{adi}-*lac*O_E-O^I.

A) and C) are reproduced with permission from John Wiley and Sons Ltd [76] and B) with permission from the National Academy of Sciences, US, [77].

Figure 7. RNAs made from *P1* and *P2*. a) Increasing concentration of GalR (red) binding to $O_E^G - O_I^G$ to form an unstable loop. b) Increasing concentration of LacI (green) binding to $O_E^L - O_I^L$ to form stable loop. c) Increasing concentration of LacI^{adi} (green) binding to $O_E^L - O_I^L$ to form an unstable loop.

Co-Factor of DNA Looping (HU)

In vitro evidence: In vivo studies show that GalR binding to O_E and O_I repress *P1* and *P2* by forming a DNA loop [83]. However, *in vitro* studies show that GalR binding to O_E and O_I fails to repress *P2* [89]. These data suggest that a factor (looping factor) present in cell aids DNA looping and is lacking *in vitro*. The factor is purified from cell extract (Figure 8a).

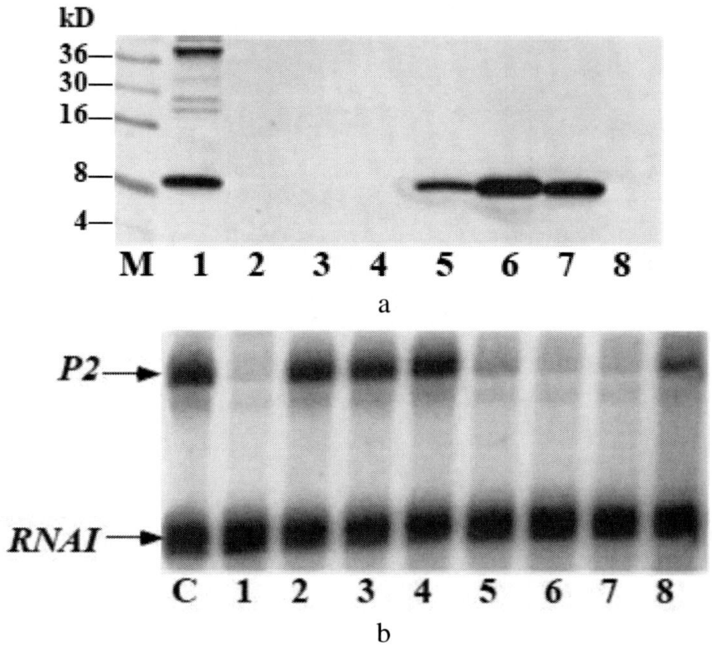

Permission from John Wiley and Sons Ltd, [90].

Figure 8. Isolation of a looping factor (HU). a) SDS-page of protein purification of the looping factor. b) RNAs made from *P2* in the presence of GalR and fractions (1-8) from *E. coli* cell extract.

When fractions of crude cell extract (figure 8a) is added to *gal P2* DNA in the presence of GalR in the *in vitro* system, *P2* is completely repressed presumably by a looping factor present in the fractions (Figure 8b, lanes 1 and 5-7) [90]. The purified factor is identified as HU, which binds to a DNA site called *hbs* (HU binding site) and mapped to +6.5 on the *gal* DNA [79]. HU binds to this region in the apex of a transient loop between weakly interacting GalR-O_E and GalR-O_I, thus stabilizing the higher-order structure. This higher-order structure results in repression not by preventing RNAP binding to the promoters, but by preventing a post-binding site [79]. In figure 5, both *P2* and *P1* are repressed as expected when GalR and HU are added to supercoiled DNA containing both promoters (Figure 5, lane 3).

Physiological studies: The histone-like protein, HU, is a heterodimer of HUα (~10 kDa) and HUβ (~10 kDa) [91-93]. The *hup*A gene, which codes for HUα mapped to 90 min and the *hup*B gene, which codes for HUβ, is located to 10 min on the *E. coli* chromosome (Figure 2) [94].

During the logarithmic growth phase, there are approximately 30,000 HU dimers per cell [91, 95, 96]. Physiological studies also provide evidence of a role for HU in the repression of *P2*.

In the absence of HUα or HUβ, the repression of *P2* is still observed with homodimer HUα or HUβ (Figure 9A) [97]. In the absence of HUαβ, the repression of *P2* is lifted as indicated by the high level β-glucuronidase activity of *P2* (Figure 9a). The expression of *P2* is derepressed by the presence of inducer, D-galac-tose, which inactivates GalR (Figure 9b).

HELICAL REQUIREMENT OF DNA LOOPING

As mentioned above, O_E and O_I are separated by 113 bp and form a DNA loop in the presence of GalR and HU. The operators are separated by 11 DNA helical turns, which means that GalR-O_E and GalR-O_I are located on the same face of the DNA to facilitate looping. The relative angular orientation of the operators on DNA and thus repression is tested by sequentially deleting 12 bp or inserting 21 bp to change the helical arrangement between GalR-O_E and GalR-O_I [98].

As expected, the repression of the *P2* promoter in the presence of GalR and HU depends on the proper helical phasing of the two operators. *P2* is completely repressed when the two operators (O_E and O_I) are separated by integral DNA helical turns, 10 turns (103 bp), 11 turns (113 bp), 12 turns (123 bp) and 13 turn (134 bp) (Figure 10).

The presence of non-integral turns, 10.5 turns (108 bp), 11.5 turns (118 bp) and 12.5 turns (128 bp) between the operators, weakens repression of *P2* in periodic fashion demonstrating that the feasibility of DNA looping depends on relative angular orientation of the operators.

In addition, insertion of a series of 3 additional turns (31 bp), 4 turns (42 bp), 5 turns (52 bp), 6 turns (63 bp), 7 turns (73 bp), 8 turns (84 bp), 9 turns (94 bp) and 10 turns (105 bp) between O_E and O_I to increase the loop size from 113 bp to 218 bp [99].

Repression of *P2* by DNA looping is observed by the addition of up to 8 turns, making a total of 19 helical turns. Repression of *P2* decreases above 19 helical turns.

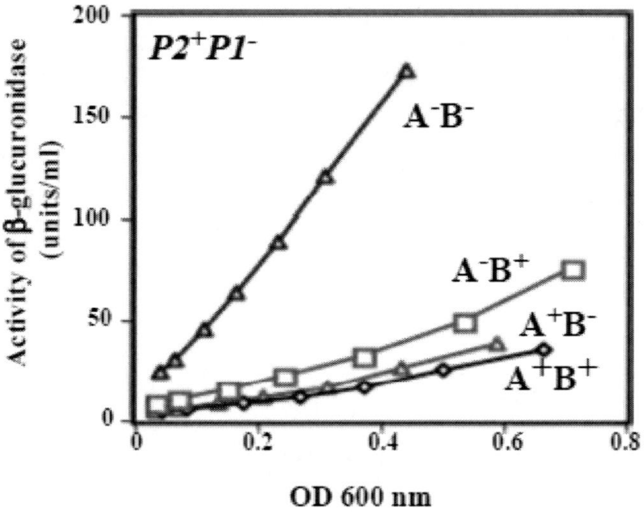

a

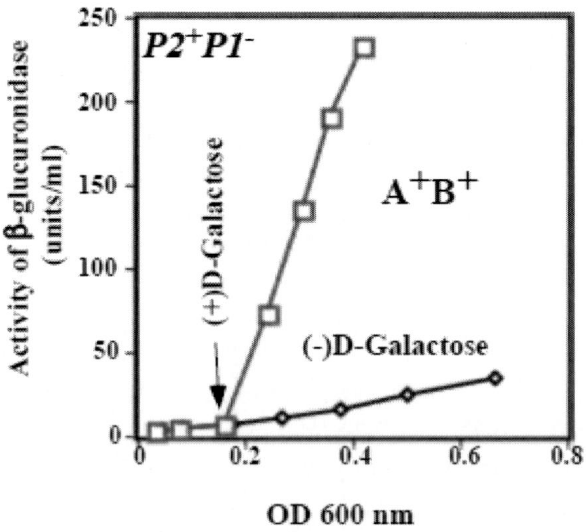

b

Permission from John Wiley and Sons Ltd, [97].

Figure 9. Effect of HU and D-galactose on *P2 in vivo*. a) β-glucuronidase activity as a reporter of the *gal* open on WT (*hup*$A^{+}B^{+}$) and mutants (*hup*$A^{+}B^{-}$, *hup*$A^{-}B^{+}$ and *hup*$A^{-}B^{-}$) strains. b) β-glucuronidase activity on WT (*hup*$A^{+}B^{+}$) in the absence and presence of D-galactose. In each panel, the x-axis shows cell OD.

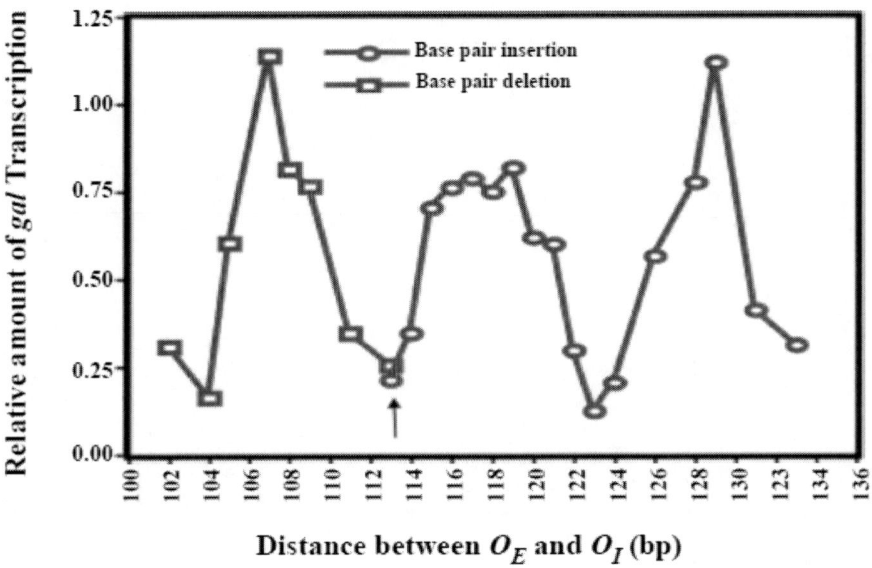

Adapted from [98].

Figure 10. Looping repression of *gal* transcript is dependent on the helical distance between operators. Relative amount of transcription vs distance between two operators in bp. Deleted base pairs (12 bp) are in red and inserted base pairs (21 bp) are in green.

REQUIREMENT OF SUPERCOILED DNA

Any requirement of supercoiled DNA on looping is tested by the addition of coumermycin, an antibiotic drug that inhibits DNA gyrase and reduces or removes DNA supercoiling in the cell [100-102]. The *P2* activity is assayed by a reporter gene expression in cells growing in the absence and presence of coumermycin. In the absence of coumermycin, *P2* is repressed; however, in the presence of coumermycin, *P2* repression is lifted (Figure 11) [97]. This result shows that DNA looping is not form *in vivo* when DNA super-coiling is removed or reduced. When D-galactose and coumermycin are added, *P2* is derepressed, which is similar to that of D-galactose alone, suggesting that the promoter strength of *P2* is not affected by the presence of coumermy-cin. On the other hand, *P1* is repressed in the presence of coumermycin, indicating that GalR is still bound to O_E although DNA supercoiling is reduced or removed [97].

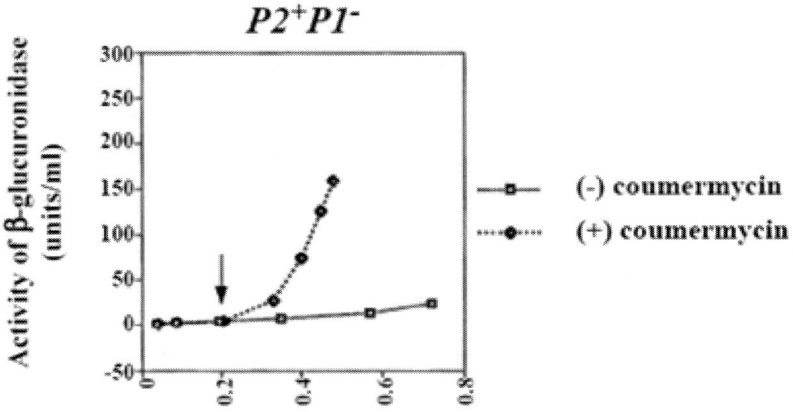

a

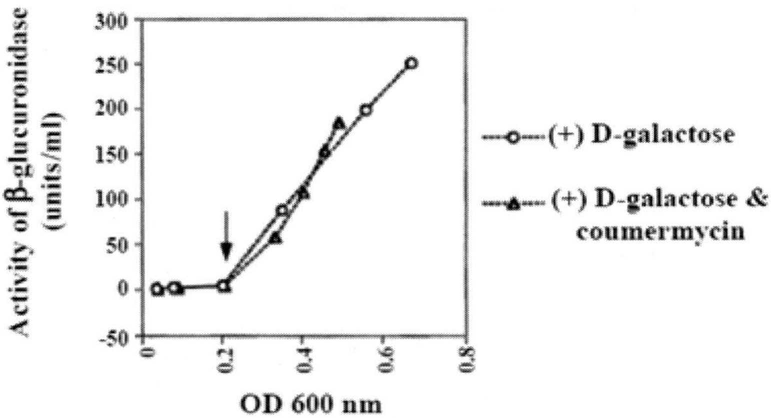

b

Permission from John Wiley and Sons Ltd, [97].

Figure 11. Effect of supercoiling DNA on the expression of *P2*. a) β-glucuronidase activity on *P2*$^{+}$*P1*$^{-}$ ~gusA template in the presence and absence of coumermycin, and b) in the presence of D-galactose and coumermycin.

Use of Atomic Force Microscope (AFM)

Atomic force microscopy (AFM) is used to visualize the DNA loop with GalR, HU and about 688-bp supercoiled DNA containing the *gal* operators. AFM reveals a figure-eight loop structure of a small loop (113-bp) and a large loop (575-bp) of a small circular DNA of 688-bp, a ratio of 1:5 [103]. The small size of the loop makes the geometry of the loop difficult to trace. A 84-

bp fragment (42-bp between O_E and promoter, and 42-bp between promoter and O_I) is inserted between O_E and O_I to increase the loop size to 197-bp to obtain a size ratio of 1:2 for small and large loops in a 599-bp DNA circle showed that in the absence of protein, only DNA circle of 599-bp is visualized (Figure 12a) [99]. When GalR and HU are added, a figure-eight structure containing two DNA loops is observed (Figure 12b). When the *gal* operators are replaced by the *lac* operators, a DNA loop structure is observed in the presence of LacI, giving a similar size ratio of 1:2 as in the case of GalR-HU loop (Figure 12c). Both GalR-HU-DNA and LacI-DNA form loops as indicated by AFM.

Antiparallel vs. Parallel DNA Looping

Two mechanisms (antiparallel and parallel loop) are adduced to explain the formation of the loop structure observed in the AFM studies. In the antiparallel mechanism, GalR-O_E and GalR-O_I bend the DNA permitting only a transient protein-protein interaction with HU stabilizing the DNA loop (Figures 12d and 12e). In an "antiparallel loop" the 3′-end of the O_E DNA is in the opposite direction of the 3′ end of the O_I DNA (head-to-head, A1) (Figure 13a) or the 5′-ends of both DNAs are in the opposite direction (tail-to-tail, A2) (Figure 13b). In a "parallel loop", the DNA between GalR-O_E and GalR-O_I twists or loops around to aid the GalR-GalR interactions in either of two arrangements (P1 or P2) (Figures 12f, 13c and 13d). In the P1 arrangement, the 3'-end of the O_E DNA is oriented in the same direction as the 5'-end of O_I DNA (tail-to-head) (Figure 13c). In the P2 arrangement, the 5′-end of O_I is in the same direction as the 5'-end of O_E (head-to-tail) (Figures 13d). The AFM image demonstrates an eight-shaped structure with two loops in a ratio of 2:1, as expected for a minicircle of 588-bp with a loop size of 197 bp between GalR-O_E and GalR-O_I. The AFM image corresponds with an antiparallel loop (Figures 12d and 12f). No parallel loop was observed [99].

Biochemically, four DNA templates are designed to investigate whether GalR prefers parallel (A1 or A2) or antiparallel (P1 or P2) arrangement [104]. The strategy involves designing mutant GalR with different affinity for each half-site of O_E (GTGTAAAC.GATACCAC) and O_I (GTGTAAAC.GATAC-CAT) operators. The mutant GalR^{V15T} contains a change from valine to

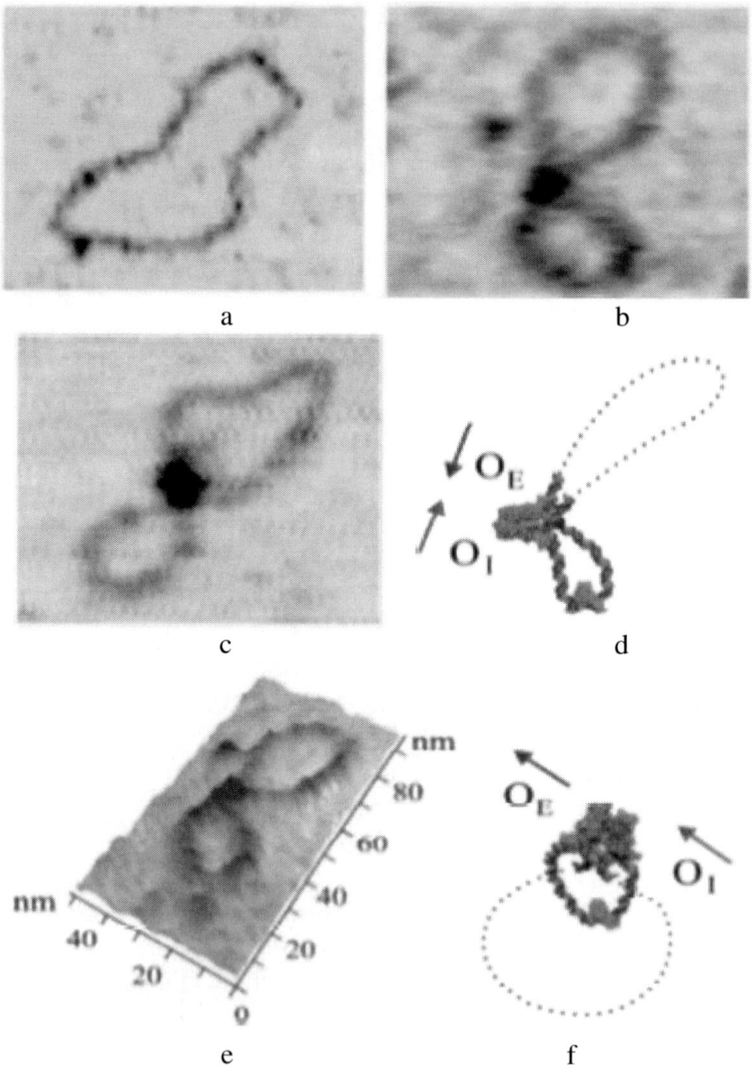

[a]DNA. [b]GalR, UH and *gal* operators. [c]LacI and *lac* operators. [d]antiparallel Loop. [e]AFM of antiparallel Loop. [f]Parallel Loop.

Permission from Elsevier, [99].

Figure 12. Atomic force microscopy of GalR-HU DNA and LacI DNA loops. a) Relaxed DNA of 599 bp. b) Loop of GalR, HU and $O_E^G{-}O_I^G$. c) Loop of LacI and $O_E^L{-}O_I^L$ DNA. d) Model of antiparallel loop. e) AFM of antiparallel loop as in (b). f) Model of parallel loop.

threonine at position 15 of the recognition helix of GalR, while mutant GalR^{A16T} contains a change from alanine to threonine at position 16. GalR^{V15T} binds only to the left half-site (refer here as "A") while GalR^{A15T} binds only to the right half-site (refer here as "B"). Hence, four different templates are designed to allow the tetramerization interfaces to form DNA loop only in one of the four configurations. For parallel AI and A2 configurations, the O_E and O_I operators are arranged as AB--AB and BA--BA, respectively (Figures 13a and b).

For antiparallel P1 and P2, the operators are arranged as AB--BA and BA--AB, respectively (Figures 13. c and d). Therefore, a heterodimer GalR$^{V15T/A16T}$ binds to each operator in a specific arrangement as shown in figure 13. The repression of *P2* by GalR$^{V15T/A16T}$ is observed only for the A1 form (Figure 13a) and not for A2, P1and P2 forms (Figures 13b-d). The result supports the AFM result above describing the *gal* DNA loop as antiparallel loop in the A1 configuration.

INACTIVATION OF THE REPRESSOSOME

D-fucose and D-galactose induce the *gal* operon 10-15 fold by binding to GalR and preventing it from binding to either O_E or O_I [14-17]. The repressosome involves GalR-O_E, GalR-O_I, GalR-GalR or GalR-HU to bring about the repression of *P1* and *P2* by DNA looping. To determine how the loop dissemble during the induction process of the operon by D-galactose, electrophoresis mobility shift assays (EMSA) are performed on O_E or O_I template by first forming the complex of GalR-O_E or GalR-O_I before titrating it with D-galactose to investigate GalR dissociate pro-perties from each operator (Figure 14) [105]. The EMSA experiment shows that GalR is released earlier from GalR-O_I than from GalR-O_E by the reduction in the GalR operator complex band and the restoration of free DNA of O_E or O_I. This suggests that GalR-O_E is more stable than GalR-O_I. The result also suggests that the last step in the dissociation of the repressosome involves the release of GalR from GalR-O_E. In summary, GalR-GalR interaction is first disrupted by D-galactose, resulting in the release of HU from *hbs* and GalR from O_I (Figures 15a and 15b), followed by the dissociation of GalR from O_E (Figure 15c).

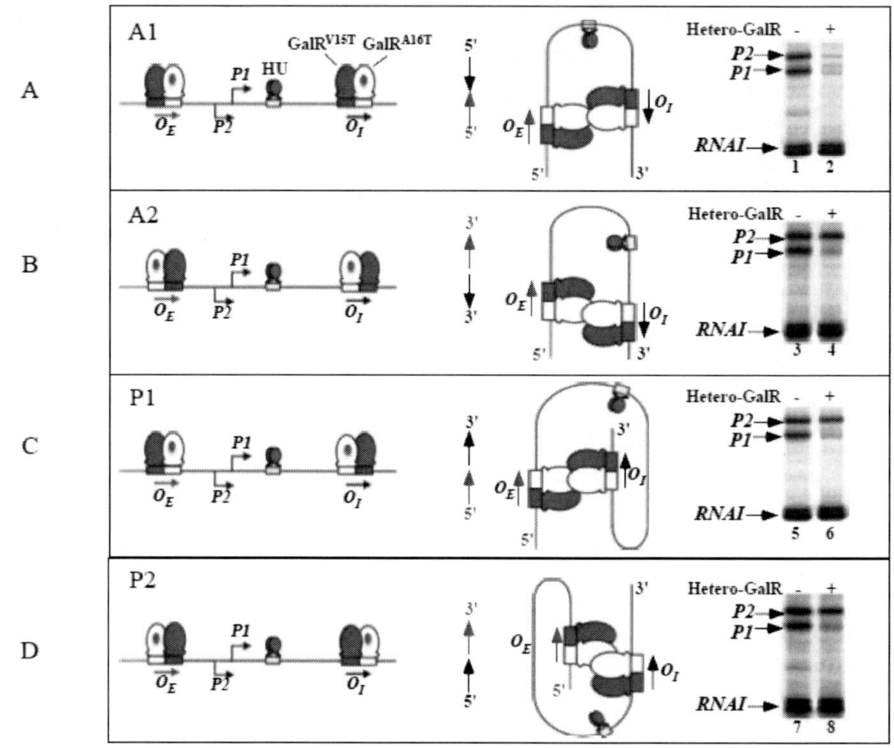

Permission from Cold Spring Harbor Laboratory Press, [104].

Figure 13. Antiparallel vs parallel models of GalR-DNA loops. a) The $GalR^{V15T}$ (red) binds to one half-site (red) of O_E and O_I while $GalR^{A16T}$ (white) binds to one half-site (white) of O_E and O_I. The green circle represents the interacting interface for tetramerization. The arrows (red) and (black) represents the direction of O_E and O_I. The loop configuration represents the antiparallel A1. The mRNAs made from gal *P1* and *P2* promoters in the absence and presence of the heterodimer $GalR^{V15T/A16T}$. *RNAI* is a control mRNA. Similarly, b) represents antiparallel A2 and (c-d) represents parallel P1 and P2 configurations.

Transcription Initiation

The rate of base pairs opening during transcription initiation by the binding of RNAP to the *galP1* promoter region is monitored by the fluorescence of 2-amino purine (2-AP) (analog of purine). In dsDNA, the fluore-scence of 2-AP is quenched, but in ssDNA, the fluorescence is enhanced. Therefore, the amount of fluorescence is an indica-tion of DNA melting or opening. Thus, adenine (A) is replaced by 2-AP at different positions from -12 to +3 to measure the fluorescence during isomerization or promoter melting (Figure 16) [106]. The 2-AP base pairs with thymine (T) in the opposite strand. The result shows two kinds of base pairs opening based on the rate of the fluorescence increase at each position. The first group shows a fast opening of the base pairs at positions -12, -10, -4, -2 +1 and +3, while the second group shows a slow opening of the base pairs at positions at -7, -5 and +2 (Figure 16a). There is no fluorescence activity at position -11A. It is known that any base pair substitution for -11A inactivates the *P1* promoter activity as shown for p8-3, p211 or p11 (-11AT to TA) mutations [32, 47, 48, 107].

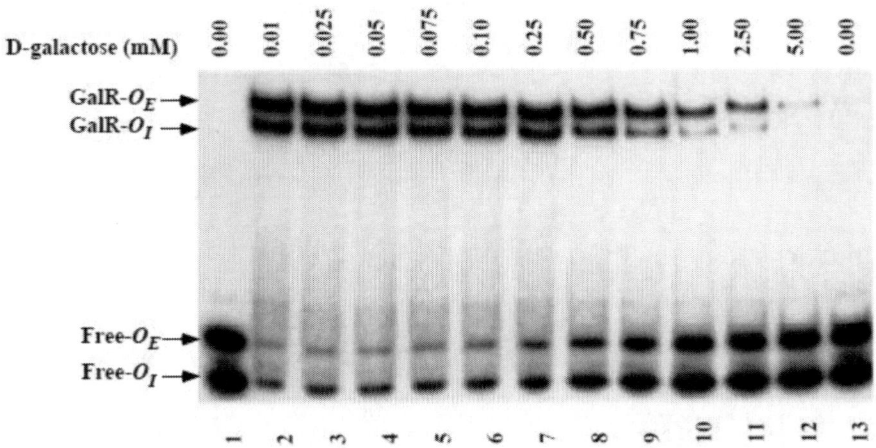

Permission from Elsevier, [105].

Figure 14. Inactivation of GalR by D-galactose. Radiolabeled DNA of O_E and O_I were bound by GalR prior to D-galactose addition at increasing concentrations.

CCC activates *P1* and it is important to determine whether CCC affects the fast or slow base pair opening step during this process. CCC has no effect on the fast opening of base pairs at positions +1 and +3, but has a stronger effect on the slow opening of base pairs at positions -7, -5 and +2 (Figure 16b), showing that CCC enhances the isomerization by helping the slow base pairs opening step.

SINGLE DNA MOLECULE STUDIES

In the presence of supercoiled DNA template and HU, the interaction of GalR-O_E and GalR-O_I form a DNA loop. Single DNA molecule techniques is used to investigate not only the DNA loop, but also to obtain additional information about conformational transition between loop and unloop states in the DNA, as well as the time spend in both states. The forces need to form the loop are also determined. Magnetic tweezers are used to twist and apply force to the tethered DNA molecule of *gal* DNA containing O_E and O_I separated by 113 bp, which is attached to a magnetic bead (Figure 17a) [108]. The unlooped DNA has a persistence length (L) and the change in the length due to DNA looping has a new length (L-1) (Figure 17a).

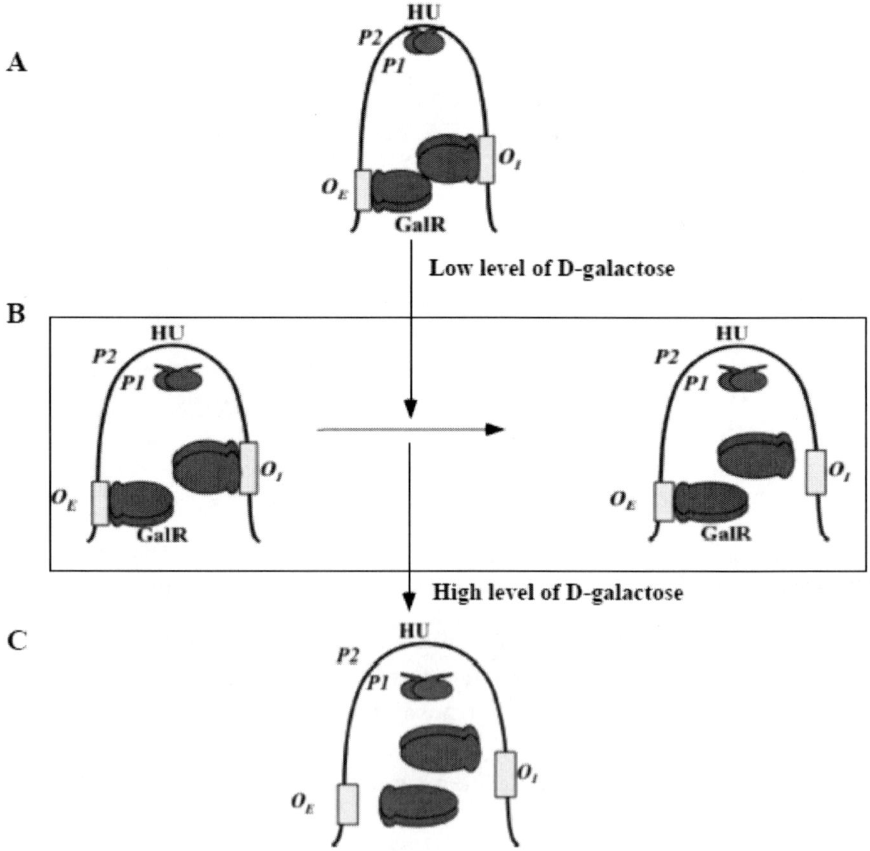

Adapted from [105].

Figure 15. Models of repressosome disassembly. a) Repressosome structure, b) Dissociation of HU, GalR-GalR and GalR-O_I, c) Dissociation of GalR from O_E).

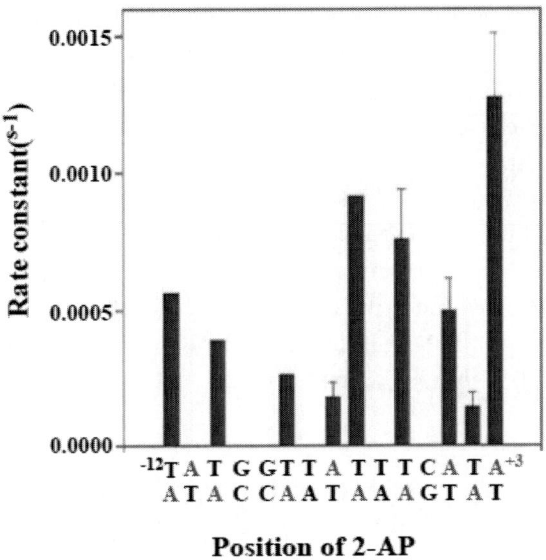

a

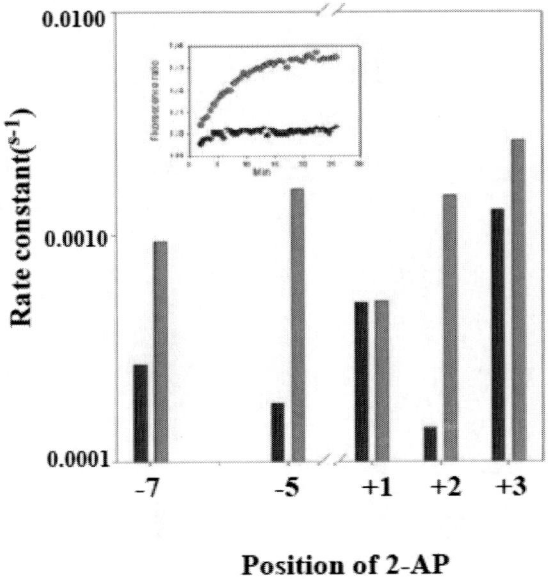

b

Permission from John Wiley and Sons, Ltd [106].

Figure 16. Effect of base pair opening after RNA polymerase addition by 2,AP. a) Positions -12, -11, -10, -7, -5, -4, -2, +1, +2, and +3 were replaces by 2, AP. b) Effect of CCC on base pair opening at -7, -5, +1, +2 and +3 by 2, AP.

A force (F) of 0.88 pN is applied to negative supercoiled DNA (σ = -0.03) in the presence of GalR (25 nM) and HU (50 nM), resulting in DNA loop (Figures 17a and 17b, trace 2) [108]. The loop is specific to GalR-GalR interactions because loop is not observed in the presence of D-galactose, the inducer of GalR (trace 5). The occurrence of loop decreases with increased force of 1.05 (trace 3) and 1.32 (trace 4). The lifetime of the unlooped to loop state is 0.1 ms and 21 sec, respectively [108]. DNA looping is not observed in relaxed (σ = 0), positive supercoiled (σ = +0.03) or small negative supercoiled templates (σ = -0.015), but only with negative supercoiled (σ = -0.03 and -0.06) (Figure 17c) [108]. Therefore, DNA looping is dependent on the super-helical density of the DNA.

GalR-HU-CRP Actions

The regulation of *gal* promoters, *P1* and *P2,* is dependent on the concentration of GalR, HU and CCC in the cell under different physiological conditions. The relationship among these proteins is investigated by monitoring the activation and repression levels of *P1* and *P2* by *in vitro* transcription assays [109].

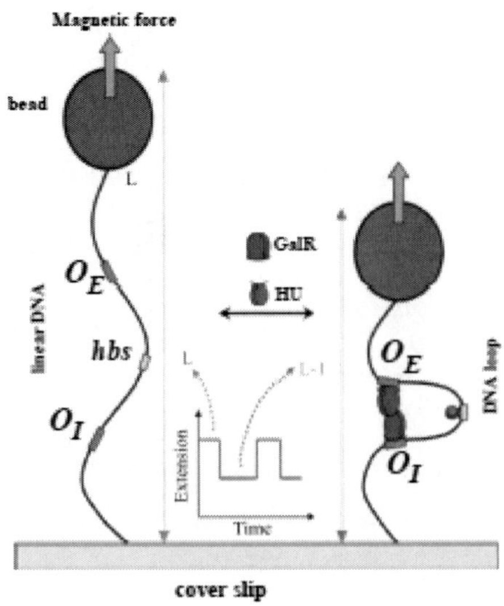

a

Figure 17. (Continued).

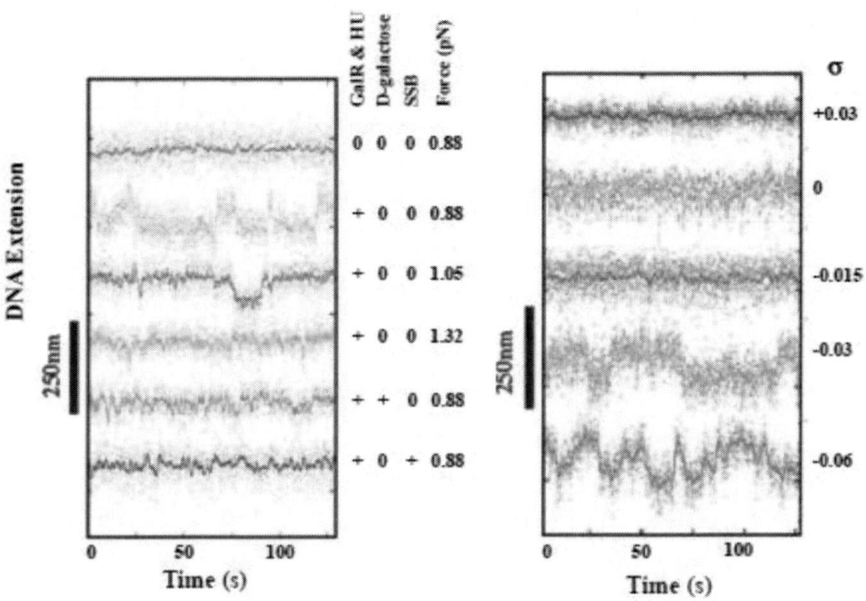

b c

[a]Single DNA molecule. [b]DNA looping by GalR and HU. [c]Looping vs Supercoiling. Permission from the National Academy of Sciences, US, [108].

Figure 17. Single DNA molecule analysis of DNA looping. a) The *gal* DNA is attached to a cover slip and being pulled by a magnetic force. DNA loop cause the length to change from L to L-1 upon the addition of GalR and HU. b) DNA looping of GalR and HU in the presence of D-galactose, single stranded binding protein (SSB) and different force. c) Effect of supercoiling DNA on loop formation.

P1 is repressed by GalR-O_E (contact inhibition) complex alone and *P2* is stimulated by GalR-O_E (contact activation) (Figure 18, lanes 1-2). When GalR and HU are present, both *P1* and *P2* are repressed by GalR-O_E and GalR-O_I, with HU stabilizing a DNA loop also called repressosome (lane 3). In the presence of CCC, *P1* is stimulated strongly while *P2* is repressed (lane 4); CCC enhances both closed and open complex at *P1* while represses that at *P2*. However, when both GalR and CCC are present, GalR prevents the stimulatory action of CCC on *P1* by preventing RNAP from open complex formation (lane 5). In the presence of GalR-HU and CCC, both *P1* and *P2* are repressed (lane 6). When CCC is added first, it prevents the inhibitory effect of GalR on *gal* transcription, since open complexes are formed before GalR is added. The addition of GalR and RNAP prior to CCC prevents *P1* transcription transcription, while the addition of CCC and RNAP prior to GalR is resistant to GalR effect on *P1* [110].

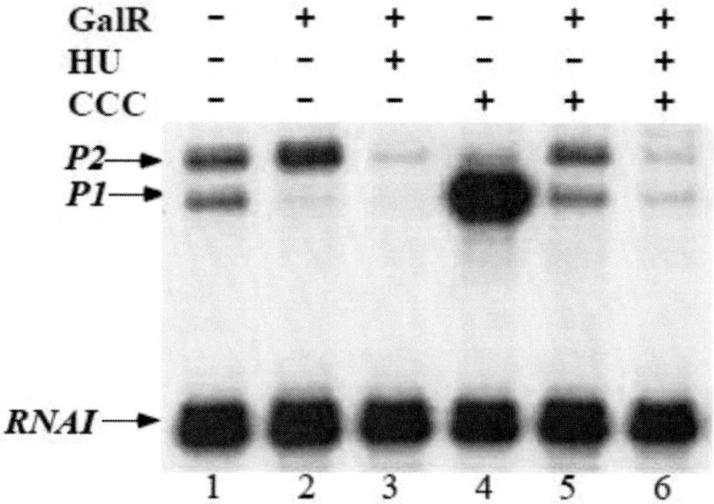

Permission from Elsevier, [109].

Figure 18. Simultaneous effect of GalR, HU and CCC on *gal* promoters. mRNAs made from *P1* and *P2* in the absence (-) and presence (+) of GalR, HU and CCC.

GALS, AN ULTRAINDUCTION FACTOR

GalS is an isorepressor of GalR, 346 aa, 37 kDa [111]. GalR and GalS are members of the GalR-LacI family [111]. GalR and GalS are 53% identical and 69% similar by amino acid sequences. The gene *gal*S is located at 46 min on the *E. coli* chromosome [112]. GalS is discovered following the observation that the *gal* operon is induced by another 2-3 fold by D-fucose and D-galactose in a Δ*galR* strain [71]. Normally, the *gal* operon is induced by 10- to 15-fold by D-galactose *in vivo*. In a Δ*galR* strain, the operon is de-repressed 10-fold in the absence of any inducer. However, when D-fucose or D-galactose is added, the operon is further induced as mentioned [113]. The term "ultrainduction " is used to describe such an observation where the *gal* operon is further induced in the absence of GalR. However, in a mutant with a defective *gal*S gene, a higher level of expression is observed which is not further inducible by D-Fucose or D-Galactose addition [112]. GalS also binds to O_E and O_I, however, GalS does not form DNA loops by GalS-O_E and GalS-O_I interactions.

Conclusion

The galactose regulon of *E. coli* plays an important role in cellular metabolism by both catabolic and anabolic pathways. In the catabolic pathway, D-galactose is broken down to glucose-1-phosphate, carbon and energy. In the anabolic pathway, glycolytic intermediates substrates such as UDP galactose and UDPglucose are synthesized. In this chapter, we presented an overview of the regulation of the galactose operon of *E. coli*. What is our current understanding of the galactose system? The *gal* operon consists of four structural genes (*gal*ETKM), which codes for enzymes for the metabolism of galactose. These genes are transcribed from two *gal* promoters, *P1* and *P2*, which are located 5-bp apart. Why does *gal* has two promoters? The promoters are regulated differentially under different cellular conditions. In the presence of GalR, which binds to the operators, O_E and O_I, *P1* is repressed while *P2* is activated by GalR contacts with α-CTD of RNAP. Mutations in the α-CTD release the repression of *P1* and the activation of *P2*. Another important protein in the regulation of the promoters is a looping factor identified as HU, a histone like protein. Prior to the discovery of HU and its role in DNA loop formation or higher order structure "repressosome" with GalR, DNA looping mediated repression *in vitro* and *in vivo* was not in agreement due to opposite result. Now, both *in vitro* and *in vivo* studies are in agreement on the regulation of the promoters by DNA looping. The DNA loop can display four different conformations (antiparallel loop of A1 or A2, Parallel loop of P1 or P2). DNA looping in *gal* prefers the antiparallel configuration. This was clearly demonstrated by microscopy and biochemical studies described above. The *gal* promoters are also regulated differentially by cAMP-CRP complex (CCC), which activates *P1* and represses *P2*. CCC activates *P1* by enhancing the sow base pair opening of the promoter region. Because of the importance of the galactose systems in cellular metabolism, it seems as if one of the promoter is always on to transcribes the structural *gal* genes except when both promoters are repressed by DNA looping. The intermediate products of the *gal* metabolism are used as building blocks for cell wall synthesis, carbon source and energy source. Thus, the necessity of a multivalent controls system.

Significance: The study of galactose metabolism regulation in *E. coli* as a model system is important since mutations in the pathway of *gal* metabolism lead to accumulation of galactose intermediates, which are toxic to the cell. In human, those who lack *gal*E or *gal*T enzyme accumulate UDP-galac-tose or galactose-1-phosphate, respectively, resulting in galactosemia, an inborn metabolic disease. In these cases, newborn children cannot digest milk (lactose and galatose).

FUNDING

This work was supported by the Intramural Research Program of the National Institutes of Health, the National Cancer Institute, and the Center for Cancer Research.

ACKNOWLEDGMENTS

We thank Sankar Adhya and Kara Lewis for critical reading of the manuscript. We thank Akira Ishihama for proving us the intracellular concentration of CRP.

REFERENCES

[1] H. M. Kalckar, Uridinediphospho galactose; metabolism, enzymology, and biology, *Advances in enzymology and related subjects of biochemistry*, 20 (1958) 111-134.
[2] R. Caputto, L. R. Leloir, et al., The enzymatic transformation of galactose into glucose derivatives, *J. Biol. Chem.*, 179 (1949) 497.
[3] G. G. Bouffard, K. E. Rudd, S. L. Adhya, Dependence of lactose metabolism upon mutarotase encoded in the gal operon in Escherichia coli, *J. Mol. Biol.*, 244 (1994) 269-278.
[4] D. B. Wilson, D. S. Hogness, The enzymes of the galactose operon in Escherichia coli. 3. The size and composition of galactokinase, *J. Biol. Chem.*, 244 (1969) 2137-2142.
[5] J. R. Sherman, J. Adler, Galactokinse from Escherichia coli, *J. Biol. Chem.,* 238 (1963) 873-878.

[6] R. Raychowdhury, D. H. Schlesinger, D. B. Wilson, E. coli galactose-1-phosphate uridyl transferase: N-terminal and C-terminal sequences, *Molecular and cellular biochemistry*, 23 (1979) 167-175.
[7] D. B. Wilson, D. S. Hogness, The Enzymes of the Galactose Operon in Escherichia Coli. I. Purification and Characterization of Uridine Diphosphogalactose 4-Epimerase, *J. Biol. Chem.*, 239 (1964) 2469-2481.
[8] J. A. Shapiro, Chromosomal location of the gene determining uridine diphoglucose formation in Escherichia coli K-12, *J. Bacteriol.*, 92 (1966) 518-520.
[9] H. C. Wu, H. M. Kalckar, Endogenous induction of the galactose operon in Escherichia coli K12, *Proc. Natl. Acad. Sci. US*, 55 (1966) 622-629.
[10] T. A. Sundararajan, A. M. Rapin, H. M. Kalckar, Biochemical observations on E. coli mutants defective in uridine diphosphoglucose, *Proc. Natl. Acad. Sci. US,* 48 (1962) 2187-2193.
[11] T. A. Sundararajan, Interference with Glycerokinase Induction in Mutants of E. Coli Accumulating Gal-1-P, *Proc. Natl. Acad. Sci. US*, 50 (1963) 463-469.
[12] G. Buttin, [Regulatory Mechanisms in the Biosynthesis of the Enzymes of Galactose Metabolism in Escherichia Coli K 12. I. The Induced Biosynthesis of Galactokinase and the Simultaneous Induction of the Enzymatic Sequence], *J. Mol. Biol.*, 7 (1963) 164-182.
[13] H. Nikaido, Galactose-sensitive mutants of Salmonella. I. Metabolism of galactose, *Biochimica et biophysica acta*, 48 (1961) 460-469.
[14] S. Adhya, H. Echols, Glucose effect and the galactose enzymes of Escherichia coli: correlation between glucose inhibition of induction and inducer transport, *J. Bacteriol.*, 92 (1966) 601-608.
[15] H. M. Kalckar, K. Kurahashi, E. Jordan, Hereditary Defects in Galactose Metabolism in Escherichia Coli Mutants, I. Determination of Enzyme Activities, *Proc. Natl. Acad. Sci. US*, 45 (1959) 1776-1786.
[16] G. Buttin, [Regulatory Mechanisms in the Biosynthesis of the Enzymes of Galactose Metabolism in Escherichia Coli K 12. Ii. The Genetic Determinism of the Regulation], *J. Mol. Biol.*, 7 (1963) 183-205.
[17] G. Buttin, [Regulatory Mechanisms in the Biosynthesis of Galactose Metabolism Enzymes in Escherichia Coli K12. Iii. Effect of "Derepression" Induced by the Development of Phage Lambda], *J. Mol. Biol.,* 7 (1963) 610-631.
[18] S. J. Lee, D. E. Lewis, S. Adhya, Induction of the galactose enzymes in Escherichia coli is independent of the C-1-hydroxyl optical configuration of the inducer D-galactose, *J. Bacteriol.*, 190 (2008) 7932-7938.

[19] B. L. Horecker, J. Thomas, J. Monod, Galactose transport in Escherichia coli. II. Characteristics of the exit process, *J. Biol. Chem.*, 235 (1960) 1586-1590.

[20] B. Rotman, A. K. Ganesan, R. Guzman, Transport systems for galactose and galactosides in Escherichia coli. II. Substrate and inducer specificities, *J. Mol. Biol.*, 36 (1968) 247-260.

[21] A. R. Robbins, R. Guzman, B. Rotman, Roles of individual mgl gene products in the beta-methylgalactoside transport system of Escherichia coli K12, *J. Biol. Chem.*, 251 (1976) 3112-3116.

[22] S. Harayama, J. Bollinger, T. Iino, G. L. Hazelbauer, Characterization of the mgl operon of Escherichia coli by transposon mutagenesis and molecular cloning, *J. Bacteriol.*, 153 (1983) 408-415.

[23] J. A. Shapiro, S. L. Adhya, The galactose operon of E. coli K-12. II. A deletion analysis of operon structure and polarity, *Genetics*, 62 (1969) 249-264.

[24] G. Buttin, [On the structure of the galactose operon in Escherichia coli K12], *C R Hebd. Seances Acad. Sci.*, 255 (1962) 1233-1235.

[25] E. Jordan, M. B. Yarmolinsky, H. M. Kalckar, Control of inducibility of enzymes of the galactose sequence in Escherichia coli, *Proc. Natl. Acad. Sci. US*, 48 (1962) 32-40.

[26] H. Echols, J. Reznichek, S. Adhya, Complementation, Recombination, and Suppression in Galactose Negative Mutants of E. Coli, *Proc. Natl. Acad. Sci. US*, 50 (1963) 286-293.

[27] S. Adhya, W. Miller, Modulation of the two promoters of the galactose operon of Escherichia coli, *Nature*, 279 (1979) 492-494.

[28] H. Aiba, S. Adhya, B. de Crombrugghe, Evidence for two functional gal promoters in intact Escherichia coli cells, *J. Biol. Chem.*, 256 (1981) 11905-11910.

[29] R. E. Musso, R. Di Lauro, S. Adhya, B. de Crombrugghe, Dual control for transcription of the galactose operon by cyclic AMP and its receptor protein at two interspersed promoters, *Cell*, 12 (1977) 847-854.

[30] A. Ullmann, E. Joseph, A. Danchin, Cyclic AMP as a modulator of polarity in polycistronic transcriptional units, *Proc. Natl. Acad. Sci. US*, 76 (1979) 3194-3197.

[31] H. J. Lee, H. J. Jeon, S. C. Ji, S. H. Yun, H. M. Lim, Establishment of an mRNA gradient depends on the promoter: an investigation of polarity in gene expression, *J. Mol. Biol.*, 378 (2008) 318-327.

[32] M. Irani, R. Musso, S. Adhya, Cyclic-AMP-dependent switch in initiation of transcription from the two promoters of the Escherichia coli gal

operon: identification and assay of 5'-triphosphate ends of mRNA by GTP:RNA guanyltransferase, *J. Bacteriol.*, 171 (1989) 1623-1630.
[33] T. Burr, J. Mitchell, A. Kolb, S. Minchin, S. Busby, DNA sequence elements located immediately upstream of the -10 hexamer in Escherichia coli promoters: a systematic study, *Nucleic Acids Res.*, 28 (2000) 1864-1870.
[34] K. A. Barne, J. A. Bown, S. J. Busby, S. D. Minchin, Region 2.5 of the Escherichia coli RNA polymerase sigma70 subunit is responsible for the recognition of the 'extended-10' motif at promoters, *Embo J.*, 16 (1997) 4034-4040.
[35] H. M. Lim, H. J. Lee, S. Roy, S. Adhya, A "master" in base unpairing during isomerization of a promoter upon RNA polymerase binding, *Proc. Natl. Acad. Sci. US*, 98 (2001) 14849-14852.
[36] H. J. Lee, H. M. Lim, S. Adhya, An unsubstituted C2 hydrogen of adenine is critical and sufficient at the -11 position of a promoter to signal base pair deformation, *J. Biol. Chem.*, 279 (2004) 16899-16902.
[37] A. Feklistov, S. A. Darst, Structural basis for promoter-10 element recognition by the bacterial RNA polymerase sigma subunit, *Cell*, 147 (2011) 1257-1269.
[38] Y. Zhang, Y. Feng, S. Chatterjee, S. Tuske, M. X. Ho, E. Arnold, R. H. Ebright, Structural basis of transcription initiation, *Science*, 338 (2013) 1076-1080.
[39] S. Busby, N. Truelle, A. Spassky, M. Dreyfus, H. Buc, The selection and characterisation of two novel mutations in the overlapping promoters of the Escherichia coli galactose operon, *Gene*, 28 (1984) 201-209.
[40] A. H. Bingham, S. Ponnambalam, B. Chan, S. Busby, Mutations that reduce expression from the P2 promoter of the Escherichia coli galactose operon, *Gene*, 41 (1986) 67-74.
[41] S. Busby, A. Spassky, B. Chan, RNA polymerase makes important contacts upstream from base pair - 49 at the Escherichia coli galactose operon P1 promoter, *Gene*, 53 (1987) 145-152.
[42] G. Kuhnke, A. Krause, C. Heibach, U. Gieske, H. J. Fritz, R. Ehring, The upstream operator of the Escherichia coli galactose operon is sufficient for repression of transcription initiated at the cyclic AMP-stimulated promoter, *Embo J.*, 5 (1986) 167-173.
[43] F. Johnston, S. Ponnambalam, S. Busby, Binding of Escherichia coli RNA polymerase to a promoter carrying mutations that stop transcription initiation, *J. Mol. Biol.*, 195 (1987) 745-748.

[44] J. E. Mitchell, D. Zheng, S. J. Busby, S. D. Minchin, Identification and analysis of 'extended -10' promoters in Escherichia coli, *Nucleic Acids Res.,* 31 (2003) 4689-4695.
[45] D. E. Lewis, S. Adhya, Axiom of determining transcription start points by RNA polymerase in Escherichia coli, *Mol. Microbiol.*, 54 (2004) 692-701.
[46] T. Taniguchi, M. O'Neill, B. de Crombrugghe, Interaction site of Escherichia coli cyclic AMP receptor protein on DNA of galactose operon promoters, *Proc. Natl. Acad. Sci. US*, 76 (1979) 5090-5094.
[47] S. Busby, H. Aiba, B. de Crombrugghe, Mutations in the Escherichia coli operon that define two promoters and the binding site of the cyclic AMP receptor protein, *J. Mol. Biol.*, 154 (1982) 211-227.
[48] S. Busby, M. Irani, B. Crombrugghe, Isolation of mutant promoters in the Escherichia coli galactose operon using local mutagenesis on cloned DNA fragments, *J. Mol. Biol.*, 154 (1982) 197-209.
[49] S. Busby, M. Irani, S. Adhya, B. de Crombrugghe, Systems for generating and detecting mutations in the galactose operon promoter region, *Annales de microbiologie*, 133 (1982) 219-224.
[50] R. H. Ebright, Transcription activation at Class I CAP-dependent promoters, *Mol. Microbiol.*, 8 (1993) 797-802.
[51] S. Busby, R. H. Ebright, Transcription activation at class II CAP-dependent promoters, *Mol. Microbiol.*, 23 (1997) 853-859.
[52] S. Busby, R. H. Ebright, Transcription activation by catabolite activator protein (CAP), *J. Mol. Biol.*, 293 (1999) 199-213.
[53] W. Niu, Y. Kim, G. Tau, T. Heyduk, R. H. Ebright, Transcription activation at class II CAP-dependent promoters: two interactions between CAP and RNA polymerase, *Cell*, 87 (1996) 1123-1134.
[54] N. J. Savery, G. S. Lloyd, M. Kainz, T. Gaal, W. Ross, R. H. Ebright, R. L. Gourse, S. J. Busby, Transcription activation at Class II CRP-dependent promoters: identification of determinants in the C-terminal domain of the RNA polymerase alpha subunit, *Embo J.*, 17 (1998) 3439-3447.
[55] Y. Zhou, X. Zhang, R. H. Ebright, Identification of the activating region of catabolite gene activator protein (CAP): isolation and characterization of mutants of CAP specifically defective in transcription activation, *Proc. Natl. Acad. Sci. US*, 90 (1993) 6081-6085.
[56] B. Benoff, H. Yang, C. L. Lawson, G. Parkinson, J. Liu, E. Blatter, Y. W. Ebright, H. M. Berman, R. H. Ebright, Structural basis of transcrip-

tion activation: the CAP-alpha CTD-DNA complex, *Science*, 297 (2002) 1562-1566.

[57] J. Kim, C. Zwieb, C. Wu, S. Adhya, Bending of DNA by gene-regulatory proteins: construction and use of a DNA bending vector, *Gene*, 85 (1989) 15-23.

[58] S. C. Schultz, G. C. Shields, T. A. Steitz, Crystal-Structure of a Cap-DNA Complex - the DNA Is Bent by 90-Degrees, *Science*, 253 (1991) 1001-1007.

[59] M. Takahashi, B. Blazy, A. Baudras, An equilibrium study of the cooperative binding of adenosine cyclic 3',5'-monophosphate and guanosine cyclic 3',5'-monophosphate to the adenosine cyclic 3',5'-monophosphate receptor protein from Escherichia coli, *Biochemistry*, 19 (1980) 5124-5130.

[60] W. B. Anderson, E. R. Stadtman, Purification and functional roles of the P I and P II components of Escherichia coli glutamine synthetase deadenylylation system, *Arch. Biochem. Biophys.*, 143 (1971) 428-443.

[61] J. K. Yang, W. Epstein, Purification and characterization of adenylate cyclase from Escherichia coli K12, *J. Biol. Chem.*, 258 (1983) 3750-3758.

[62] R. L. Perlman, I. Pastan, Pleiotropic deficiency of carbohydrate utilization in an adenyl cyclase deficient mutant of Escherichia coli, *Biochem. Biophys. Res. Commun.*, 37 (1969) 151-157.

[63] S. Adhya, S. Garges, How cyclic AMP and its receptor protein act in Escherichia coli, *Cell*, 29 (1982) 287-289.

[64] J. Kim, S. Adhya, S. Garges, Allosteric changes in the cAMP receptor protein of Escherichia coli: hinge reorientation, *Proc. Natl. Acad. Sci. US,* 89 (1992) 9700-9704.

[65] S. Ryu, J. Kim, S. Adhya, S. Garges, Pivotal role of amino acid at position 138 in the allosteric hinge reorientation of cAMP receptor protein, *Proc. Natl. Acad. Sci. US*, 90 (1993) 75-79.

[66] S. Garges, S. Adhya, Sites of allosteric shift in the structure of the cyclic AMP receptor protein, *Cell*, 41 (1985) 745-751.

[67] I. Pastan, S. Adhya, Cyclic adenosine 5'-monophosphate in Escherichia coli, *Bacteriological reviews*, 40 (1976) 527-551.

[68] M. Herbert, A. Kolb, H. Buc, Overlapping promoters and their control in Escherichia coli: the gal case, *Proc. Natl. Acad. Sci. US*, 83 (1986) 2807-2811.

[69] S. Garges, S. Adhya, Cyclic AMP-induced conformational change of cyclic AMP receptor protein (CRP): intragenic suppressors of cyclic AMP-independent CRP mutations, *J. Bacteriol.*, 170 (1988) 1417-1422.

[70] B. von Wilcken-Bergmann, B. Muller-Hill, Sequence of galR gene indicates a common evolutionary origin of lac and gal repressor in Escherichia coli, *Proc. Natl. Acad. Sci. US*, 79 (1982) 2427-2431.

[71] J. P. Tokeson, Ultrainduction of the Escherichia coli galactose operon, *Doctoral Dissertation*, (1989).

[72] A. Majumdar, S. Adhya, Probing the structure of gal operator-repressor complexes. Conformation change in DNA, *J. Biol. Chem.*, 262 (1987) 13258-13262.

[73] A. Majumdar, S. Adhya, Demonstration of two operator elements in gal: in vitro repressor binding studies, *Proc. Natl. Acad. Sci. US*, 81 (1984) 6100-6104.

[74] M. Geanacopoulos, S. Adhya, Functional characterization of roles of GalR and GalS as regulators of the gal regulon, *J. Bacteriol.*, 179 (1997) 228-234.

[75] S. Nakanishi, S. Adhya, M. E. Gottesman, I. Pastan, In vitro repression of the transcription of gas operon by purified gal repressor, *Proc. Natl. Acad. Sci. US,* 70 (1973) 334-338.

[76] H. E. Choy, S. W. Park, T. Aki, P. Parrack, N. Fujita, A. Ishihama, S. Adhya, Repression and activation of transcription by Gal and Lac repressors: involvement of alpha subunit of RNA polymerase, *Embo J.*, 14 (1995) 4523-4529.

[77] H. E. Choy, S. W. Park, P. Parrack, S. Adhya, Transcription regulation by inflexibility of promoter DNA in a looped complex, *Proc.Natl. Acad. Sci. US*, 92 (1995) 7327-7331.

[78] H. E. Choy, R. R. Hanger, T. Aki, M. Mahoney, K. Murakami, A. Ishihama, S. Adhya, Repression and activation of promoter-bound RNA polymerase activity by Gal repressor, *J. Mol. Biol.*, 272 (1997) 293-300.

[79] T. Aki, S. Adhya, Repressor induced site-specific binding of HU for transcriptional regulation, *Embo J.,* 16 (1997) 3666-3674.

[80] D. E. Lewis, N. Komissarova, P. Le, M. Kashlev, S. Adhya, DNA sequences in gal operon override transcription elongation blocks, *J. Mol. Biol.,* 382 (2008) 843-858.

[81] M. H. Irani, L. Orosz, S. Adhya, A control element within a structural gene: the gal operon of Escherichia coli, *Cell*, 32 (1983) 783-788.

[82] M. Irani, L. Orosz, S. Busby, T. Taniguchi, S. Adhya, Cyclic AMP-dependent constitutive expression of gal operon: use of repressor titra-

tion to isolate operator mutations, *Proc. Natl. Acad. Sci. US*, 80 (1983) 4775-4779.

[83] R. Haber, S. Adhya, Interaction of spatially separated protein-DNA complexes for control of gene expression: operator conversions, *Proc. Natl. Acad. Sci. US*, 85 (1988) 9683-9687.

[84] A. M. Friedman, T. O. Fischmann, T. A. Steitz, Crystal structure of lac repressor core tetramer and its implications for DNA looping, *Science*, 268 (1995) 1721-1727.

[85] N. Mandal, W. Su, R. Haber, S. Adhya, H. Echols, DNA looping in cellular repression of transcription of the galactose operon, *Genes Dev.,* 4 (1990) 410-418.

[86] S. Alberti, S. Oehler, B. von Wilcken-Bergmann, H. Kramer, B. Muller-Hill, Dimer-to-tetramer assembly of Lac repressor involves a leucine heptad repeat, *New Biol.*, 3 (1991) 57-62.

[87] S. Alberti, S. Oehler, B. von Wilcken-Bergmann, B. Muller-Hill, Genetic analysis of the leucine heptad repeats of Lac repressor: evidence for a 4-helical bundle, *EMBO J.,* 12 (1993) 3227-3236.

[88] M. Lewis, G. Chang, N. C. Horton, M. A. Kercher, H. C. Pace, M. A. Schumacher, R. G. Brennan, P. Lu, Crystal structure of the lactose operon repressor and its complexes with DNA and inducer, *Science*, 271 (1996) 1247-1254.

[89] H. E. Choy, S. Adhya, Control of gal transcription through DNA looping: inhibition of the initial transcribing complex, *Proc. Natl. Acad. Sci. US*, 89 (1992) 11264-11268.

[90] T. Aki, H. E. Choy, S. Adhya, Histone-like protein HU as a specific transcriptional regulator: co-factor role in repression of gal transcription by GAL repressor, *Genes Cells*, 1 (1996) 179-188.

[91] K. Drlica, J. Rouviere-Yaniv, Histonelike proteins of bacteria, *Microbiol. Rev.*, 51 (1987) 301-319.

[92] J. Rouviere-Yaniv, F. Gros, Characterization of a novel, low-molecular-weight DNA-binding protein from Escherichia coli, *Proc. Natl. Acad. Sci. US*, 72 (1975) 3428-3432.

[93] J. Rouviere-Yaniv, N. O. Kjeldgaard, Native Escherichia coli HU protein is a heterotypic dimer, *FEBS Lett.*, 106 (1979) 297-300.

[94] Y. Kano, K. Osato, M. Wada, F. Imamoto, Cloning and sequencing of the HU-2 gene of Escherichia coli, *Mol. Gen. Genet.*, 209 (1987) 408-410.

[95] N. E. Dixon, A. Kornberg, Protein HU in the enzymatic replication of the chromosomal origin of Escherichia coli, *Proc. Natl. Acad. Sci. US*, 81 (1984) 424-428.

[96] K. Geider, H. Hoffmann-Berling, Proteins controlling the helical structure of DNA, *Annu. Rev. Biochem.*, 50 (1981) 233-260.

[97] D. E. Lewis, M. Geanacopoulos, S. Adhya, Role of HU and DNA supercoiling in transcription repression: specialized nucleoprotein repression complex at gal promoters in Escherichia coli, *Mol. Microbiol.*, 31 (1999) 451-461.

[98] D. E. Lewis, S. Adhya, In vitro repression of the gal promoters by GalR and HU depends on the proper helical phasing of the two operators, *J. Biol. Chem.*, 277 (2002) 2498-2504.

[99] K. Virnik, Y. L. Lyubchenko, M. A. Karymov, P. Dahlgren, M. Y. Tolstorukov, S. Semsey, V.B. Zhurkin, S. Adhya, "Antiparallel" DNA loop in gal repressosome visualized by atomic force microscopy, *J. Mol. Biol.*, 334 (2003) 53-63.

[100] K. Drlica, M. Snyder, Superhelical Escherichia-Coli DNA - Relaxation by Coumermycin, *Journal of Molecular Biology*, 120 (1978) 145-154.

[101] M. Gellert, M. H. Odea, T. Itoh, J. Tomizawa, Novobiocin and Coumermycin Inhibit DNA Supercoiling Catalyzed by DNA Gyrase, *P. Natl. Acad. Sci. US,* 73 (1976) 4474-4478.

[102] M. Gellert, K. Mizuuchi, M. H. Odea, H. A. Nash, DNA Gyrase - Enzyme That Introduces Superhelical Turns into DNA, *P. Natl. Acad. Sci. US,* 73 (1976) 3872-3876.

[103] Y. L. Lyubchenko, L. S. Shlyakhtenko, T. Aki, S. Adhya, Atomic force microscopic demonstration of DNA looping by GalR and HU, *Nucleic Acids Res.*, 25 (1997) 873-876.

[104] S. Semsey, M. Y. Tolstorukov, K. Virnik, V. B. Zhurkin, S. Adhya, DNA trajectory in the Gal repressosome, *Genes Dev.*, 18 (2004) 1898-1907.

[105] S. Semsey, K. Virnik, S. Adhya, Three-stage regulation of the amphibolic gal operon: from repressosome to GalR-free DNA, *J. Mol. Biol.*, 358 (2006) 355-363.

[106] S. Roy, H. M. Lim, M. Liu, S. Adhya, Asynchronous basepair openings in transcription initiation: CRP enhances the rate-limiting step, *Embo J.,* 23 (2004) 869-875.

[107] H. E. Choy, S. Adhya, RNA polymerase idling and clearance in gal promoters: use of supercoiled minicircle DNA template made in vivo, *Proc. Natl. Acad. Sci. US*, 90 (1993) 472-476.

[108] G. Lia, D. Bensimon, V. Croquette, J. F. Allemand, D. Dunlap, D. E. Lewis, S. Adhya, L. Finzi, Supercoiling and denaturation in Gal repressor/heat unstable nucleoid protein (HU)-mediated DNA looping, *Proc. Natl. Acad. Sci. US*, 100 (2003) 11373-11377.
[109] D. E. Lewis, Identification of promoters of Escherichia coli and phage in transcription section plasmid pSA850, *Methods Enzymol.*, 370 (2003) 618-645.
[110] S. Nakanishi, S. Adhya, M. Gottesman, I. Pastan, Studies on the mechanism of action of the gal repressor, *J. Biol. Chem.*, 248 (1973) 5937-5942.
[111] M. J. Weickert, S. Adhya, Isorepressor of the gal regulon in Escherichia coli, *J. Mol. Biol.*, 226 (1992) 69-83.
[112] A. Golding, M. J. Weickert, J. P. Tokeson, S. Garges, S. Adhya, A mutation defining ultrainduction of the Escherichia coli gal operon, *J. Bacteriol.*, 173 (1991) 6294-6296.
[113] J. P. Tokeson, S. Garges, S. Adhya, Further inducibility of a constitutive system: ultrainduction of the gal operon, *J. Bacteriol.*, 173 (1991) 2319-2327.

Editor Contact Information

Dr. Vitor Hugo Pomin
Hospital Universitário Clementino Fraga Filho
Laboratório de Coagulação e Trombose
Instituto de Bioquímica Médica, Programa de Glicobiologia
Universidade Federal do Rio de Janeiro
Ilha do Fundão, Rio de Janeiro
RJ, 21941-590, Brasil
Tel: +55-(21)-2562-2939
vhpomin@gmail.com

INDEX

A

F

G

H

I

J

K

L

O

P

Q

R

S

T

U

V

W

X

Y

Z